Dangerous Masculinity

CRITICAL ISSUES IN CRIME AND SOCIETY

Raymond J. Michalowski, Series Editor

Critical Issues in Crime and Society is oriented toward critical analysis of contemporary problems in crime and justice. The series is open to a broad range of topics including specific types of crime, wrongful behavior by economically or politically powerful actors, controversies over justice system practices, and issues related to the intersection of identity, crime, and justice. It is committed to offering thoughtful works that will be accessible to scholars and professional criminologists, general readers, and students.

For a list of titles in the series, see the last page of the book.

Dangerous Masculinity

FATHERHOOD, RACE,
AND SECURITY INSIDE
AMERICA'S PRISONS

ANNA CURTIS

RUTGERS UNIVERSITY PRESS
New Brunswick, Camden, and Newark, New Jersey, and London

Library of Congress Cataloging-in-Publication Data

Names: Curtis, Anna, author.
Title: Dangerous masculinity : fatherhood, race, and security inside
America's prisons / Anna Curtis.
Description: New Brunswick, N.J. : Rutgers University Press, [2019] | Series: Critical
issues in crime and society | Includes bibliographical references and index.
Identifiers: LCCN 2018058705 | ISBN 9780813598345 (pbk. : alk. paper)
Subjects: LCSH: Prisoners—Family relationships—United States. |
Fatherhood—United States. | Masculinity—United States.
Classification: LCC HV8886.U5 C87 2019 | DDC 365/.608110973—dc23
LC record available at https://lccn.loc.gov/2018058705

A British Cataloging-in-Publication record for this
book is available from the British Library.

www.rutgersuniversitypress.org

Manufactured in the United States of America

CONTENTS

Dangerous Masculinity

Introduction

MASCULINITY, FATHERHOOD, AND RACE INSIDE AMERICA'S PRISONS

G WAS A BLACK man with short salt-and-pepper hair. A member of one of the prison fatherhood groups I observed, he was forty-eight years old at the time of his interview. G stated that his primary motivation for joining the program was to be a better father for his youngest child than he had been for his four older children. During one group meeting, the group facilitator Alice directed the conversation toward ways to reduce the stress of visits for both themselves and their families. "Think about the things you want to know ahead of time," she advised. G raised his hand and said setting expectations can be stressful: "You might not get to say everything you want and then at the end, you need to prepare to get emotionally distant." He continued, referencing a visit when he and his son had connected, remarking that "it was the worst day, watching him walk away. I had tears. I had to . . ." He sucked in his belly and pinched his face into a flat expression. "I'm a man; I don't want to be weak." Several other men nodded in agreement. Alice tried to persuade G that crying "doesn't make you weak," but it was difficult to do so. A central tenet of masculinity plays out in most institutional contexts for men: "To display weakness is unmanly."[1] This is true for both corrections officers (COs) and prisoners.[2] Emotional connections to children can open up vulnerabilities that place men at risk within the confines of prison. At the same time, remaining connected to children offers men opportunities for more positive growth while incarcerated, makes it more likely that they will be involved in their children's lives once they are released, and increases their chances of desisting from further criminal activities.[3]

Fatherhood offers a valuable lens for examining how prisoners and COs manage life in prison. The often unquestioned, commonsense understanding of what kind of men prisoners are—as a category of people—impacts both security protocols and incarcerated fathers' access to their children. The organization of a prison reduces the space men have to be parents, and individual prisoners must manage their identities as both men and fathers. This tension is not limited to men in prison; indeed, balancing expectations around fathering with the practices of masculinity is challenging for most men with children.

For those in the workplace, being masculine and being a "good worker" intertwine to both support and undermine men's fathering practices. For example, being a good provider is closely linked with being a good worker, and for many men, this is the central obligation they must meet as fathers. At the same time, many men express a desire to spend more time nurturing their children. While men today do spend more time with their children as compared to forty years ago, men are still more likely to play with their offspring rather than to deal with the nitty-gritty and more nurturing-oriented details of caring, such as changing diapers and managing doctor appointments.[4]

For incarcerated fathers, on the other hand, it is prison rather than work that mediates men's access to their families. Prison rules and staff circumscribe phone privileges, access to writing materials, and visits.[5] Perhaps even more important, however, are the ways in which the penal system shapes men's gender performances. Incarcerated men must negotiate how they will enact violence and aggression in terms of both the expectations placed upon prisoners by the prison system and staff as well as their own and other prisoners' responses to these expectations. Additionally, men undergo changes in their relationships with the mothers of their children during incarceration, particularly since women now serve as "gatekeepers" who control when and how men are in contact with their children. "Gatekeeping" is an active process in which mothers deny or encourage access to children. This takes on a particular shape in prison, since women have no expectation of either financial or nurturing care from those imprisoned. As a result, imprisoned men's access to children often hinges on being able to meet the emotional expectations of their children's mothers.[6] As the power dynamics between the parents shift, men may find that previously acceptable masculine behaviors are no longer effective. As a result, relationships between men and the mothers of their children often devolve, become hostile, and fall apart. This directly limits how involved men can be in their children's lives both during incarceration and after they return home.

I focus on a set of questions about how people within the prison system negotiate their expectations about "real" men and "good" fathers. In what ways did the fatherhood programs I observed help men be better fathers? How do prisoners negotiate their relationships with their families, coparents, and children? In what ways do these negotiations reflect their understandings of masculinity? How do race, gender, and age inform and create the solutions both prisoners and COs develop to manage relationships with the outside world? How does fatherhood support and challenge the rules of the facility? What can the negotiations around masculinity and fatherhood inside prison tell us about gender inequality, racism, and the ideological underpinnings of security practices?

The Fatherhood Programs at NCI and SY

Between 2007 and 2009, I attended fatherhood groups at two prison facilities—one for adults (over eighteen) and one for youth offenders (ages fourteen to twenty-one)—in a northeastern state. I accessed these programs through a social work–oriented nonprofit agency, Healthy Connections, which ran a number of programs for prisoners and their families all over the state. The adult facility, North Correctional Institution (NCI), and the youth facility, Southeast Youth Correctional Institution (SY), were both high security (level four out of five).[7] There are two main sources of data for this ethnography: participant observation and life history interviews. I conducted 118 interviews with forty-nine men (147 interview hours total) who participated in one of the two fatherhood programs I observed. I interviewed fathers between two and four times, with the average complete interview lasting three hours. I recorded and transcribed most of these interviews.[8] Fourteen of the forty-nine fathers were incarcerated at the youth facility. Roughly 40 percent (n = 21) of my interviewees self-identified as black, 30 percent (n = 16) as Latino or Hispanic, 16 percent (n = 8) as white, and the remaining 8 percent (n = 4) provided racial or ethnic identifications that I coded as "multiracial." All the fathers at SY were eighteen or nineteen. The average age of the fathers at NCI was thirty-three and ranged from twenty-one to fifty.

I also engaged in 280 hours of participant observation, including the fatherhood group meetings, informal interactions with COs and staff as I entered and exited prison, and the "special visits" that served as the reward for successfully completing the Healthy Connections programs. Each fatherhood group meeting lasted between thirty and ninety minutes, depending on how long it took the group facilitator to get through security and whether the COs completed the afternoon or evening count in a timely fashion. A total of eighty-two fathers participated in the group during my observation. Most of the men in the group were willing to let me interview them. However, I only ended up being able to interview 60 percent of the men I met in group because I didn't receive approval to proceed with interviewing until eight months after I began attending fatherhood groups. By then, some of the men who were willing to talk to me had been moved to another facility without warning. In the end, only six men actively refused my request for an interview.

I also observed the men interacting with their children during the special visits, which were roughly two hours long. During the visits, men were allowed an unusually high amount of physical contact with their children. In normal visits, prisoners and visitors were allowed to hug briefly at the start of the visit, then were expected to stay on opposite sides of a table with no physical contact. During the special visits, men could hold their children throughout, sit next to them, hug them at will, and play games that were unavailable during normal visits. The promise of these visits motivated many men to take part in the program. As a participant, I helped set up games and decorations and then spent most of my time walking around, listening, watching, and helping fetch items (such as markers or stickers) for the fathers and their families.

While I did not formally interview COs, entering and exiting a prison takes time. Both the COs and I filled that time with informal interactions that had a powerful impact on my understanding of prison life. In the two and a half years I spent conducting fieldwork, I chatted with more than 130 COs as I signed in, waited in the lobby, waited in traps (a space between two doors as one enters and exits), and as they escorted me down hallways. It was the COs, not the prisoners, who sought to teach me the official rules of the facility. I learned these rules through abrupt and impatient orders, teasing and humorous interactions as I tried to get through the metal detector, and casual conversations as I waited to enter the facility, as well as when COs pointed out things I did that made their jobs more difficult and expressed concerns for my safety. I also had extensive time to observe how COs processed and interacted with visitors in the lobby and in the visiting room and to note the differences between how they responded to a volunteer and to someone visiting a prisoner.

The structure of the fatherhood programs at both facilities was very similar. Both programs placed an emphasis on the importance of communication, were small group settings with roughly four to ten men at a given time, and created opportunities for prisoners to have high-contact visits with their children. The fatherhood groups at both facilities had two potentially positive outcomes for the incarcerated fathers who participated. First, the groups offered men support for their attempts to remain engaged as fathers. Though the two groups had different focuses in terms of content, both aimed to encourage men to believe that they had something to offer their children. Without a doubt, this message was positively received, though many men continued to express doubt about their ability to provide anything of value to their children. The groups also attempted to provide men with advice about how to approach their coparents in new ways that might improve their ability to be fathers to their children. Second, the facilitators of both groups organized special visits that had a much higher level of physical contact between fathers and children than regular visits. The special visits were highly anticipated events, especially at the adult facility. Of course, a combination of problems such as transfers to other facilities and familial tensions made organizing and receiving the special visits difficult.

There were a couple of key differences between the two groups. The same man ran the group at SY the entire time I was there: Jasper, an older black man in his fifties. He'd grown up in the South and had a child at a young age.

Jasper's experiences as a young father were an important aspect of his work with the men in the fatherhood group. He used his own success in maintaining a relationship with his child despite numerous challenges (including geographic distance) as fodder for inspirational speeches about the value of commitment for fathers. While an administrator at the prison had to approve a man's addition to the group, Jasper had a great deal of control over who was allowed to join. In his own way, Jasper served as a gatekeeper to the resources the group could offer young fathers, and he only wanted men who were "serious" about becoming better fathers. For Jasper, being a "better" father meant being a "better" man. This link between manhood and fatherhood was overt and consistent. Jasper didn't rely on a particular set of documents for his group; he brought in whatever appealed to him. This meant that it was his perspective that dominated the messaging in the group rather than any particular curriculum. Additionally, the group at SY was ongoing, and as a result, Jasper had relationships with some of the young men that spanned years.

In comparison, a changing roster of women ran the twelve-week fatherhood groups at NCI (which were called "cycles" by the staff at Healthy Connections). A woman named Alice ran two of the five cycles I observed. When she left Healthy Connections for another job, I observed a cycle where a supervisor trained a new employee, Katelyn, to run the group. Katelyn ran the fourth cycle alone and then she also left for another position. A woman named Star ran the fifth cycle. The group facilitators relied on curricular materials provided by Healthy Connections, and while there was variety in what each cycle covered specifically, there was nonetheless a strong central message that focused on maintaining communication with children. Group facilitators had no control over who joined the group; the volunteer coordinator of the adult prison facility, Baxter, decided who would be in a particular group. Finally, the twelve-week time frame for the group meant that the facilitators often had to rush to get through the material. In theory, the fatherhood program at NCI also included six support group meetings that were supposed to occur after the special visit and help men put into practice the things they learned. These meetings, however, occurred haphazardly, none of the five cycles received all six support group meetings, and there were no specific curricular materials associated with them.

THE PRISON SETTING

I would like to take a moment to present a metaphor of the organization of prison to clarify what I am—and am not—discussing about prison facilities. Imagine a prison as a hard-boiled egg. While reality is messier than a hard-boiled egg, this metaphor allows us to consider the prison as a layered institution. The shell separates the egg from the rest of the world; this is the barbed concertina wire, walls, cameras, and wide-open spaces that literally separate a prison from the community in which it is located. The inside of prison, the yolk, has its own set of rules and social norms, and the interactions that occur there do so out of the public eye. Some scholars call this "prison culture," though I am leery of such a term as it obfuscates the links between the prison and the outside world. In the yolk of a prison facility—the cellblocks, the segregation units, the exercise yard—the ties between race and masculinity play out in particular ways. For example, male prisoners still belong to gangs based on racial identity,[9] and white prisoners are more likely to commit suicide than black or Hispanic prisoners.[10] Racial identity also affects COs' work experiences.[11] I can only allude to these patterns of interactions that emerge out of the sight of outsiders.

Instead, this is a project that focuses on the egg white of prison. These are the portions of the facility where outsiders and insiders meet and mesh. The egg white of the prison is the lobby, the visiting room, and the hallways where volunteers move from the outside to the places where classes occur. These are the places where COs must ratchet up their security protocols to manage people who may be entirely oblivious to the rules that govern life inside the yolk of prison. These are the places where prisoners connect with the world outside of the eggshell and where they sometimes have the opportunity to remind themselves that they are not just prisoners. Visitors, social workers, COs, and prisoners all move through the different layers of the prison, though only COs and other staff can travel through all three at will. The research project presented in this book took place entirely within the egg white.

I would also like to provide a description of the facilities, as many people have only ever seen a prison on television or from a distance. The scale of certain parts of both prisons was enormous. The security fences, twenty feet high with barbed concertina wire, were set within two hundred feet of the main building. The prison buildings were wide rather than tall, and behind the fences, the grounds and structures sprawled for several hundred yards in each direction. NCI housed just over two thousand prisoners and the facility sat in the center of a one-hundred-forty-acre property. SY housed six hundred prisoners and was placed in the center of a seventy-acre property. Both facilities were hard to see from the road, and NCI, in particular, was hidden behind trees and set quite far back from the road. Inside the buildings, the scale of the areas visitors and outsiders could access was similarly large. The waiting room and visiting room were large rectangular rooms designed to fit fifty to sixty people spaced evenly apart. The hallways farther inside the facility, where group sessions took place, had high ceilings and were about twenty feet wide.

The interior-decorating scheme at both facilities was industrial drab, which emphasized monotony and suggested that when it came to prison construction, cheap was always better. The cinderblock walls and concrete floors of the interiors of the buildings were done in gray, salmon-orange, browns that drew from the feces family of colors, white, and light blue. Furniture—the tables and chairs in the visiting rooms and places where the fatherhood groups took place—was plastic or stainless steel and often bolted to the floor or to other furniture. When combined with the overhead fluorescent lighting, the spaces inside the prisons often felt washed out and lifeless. The uniforms also contributed to the feeling of monotony: prisoners wore tan, COs wore navy blue, and people in street clothes stuck out like sore thumbs.

As one might expect, it was quite difficult to move from one point in the prison to another. The inability to move easily contributed to a feeling of claustrophobia despite the high ceilings and wide hallways. Entering the facility involved moving through "traps"—small hallways that had two or three locked doors. Each door could only open if all the other doors were locked and a CO inside a security station operated the doors. Similarly, the long hallways had gates every twenty feet or so that COs could close in order to limit movement. At SY, if the COs weren't paying attention or were doing something else, it was possible to end up cooling your heels in the trap for upward of ten minutes. At NCI, volunteers often ended up waiting in the trap as a CO made his way down the hallway to provide us with an escort. Though approved social workers could technically walk down the main hallway inside the facility by themselves, the COs at NCI ignored that particular rule. At SY, the group facilitator and I were more frequently allowed to move around the main hallway unescorted.

Accentuating the feeling of claustrophobia was the fact that one was almost always observed in prison. This, too, was hardly surprising. And yet the cameras, security stations, patrolling COs, signs declaring that your belongings and car were subject to search at any time, and body alarms volunteers wore while inside the main prison facility all contributed to a feeling of being hemmed in. Observation also created a specific kind of security. I was never entirely alone with a prisoner or a CO, and there were times I was grateful that this was the case. However, the knowledge of being observed changes the way people interact with one another. I always had to be mindful of what I was saying or doing and had to assume that other people were doing the same. I was always aware that someone was watching and judging whatever I did (a condition I shared with the COs and the prisoners). It was only during interviews, which occurred in small rooms off the main visiting rooms, that I had any semblance of unobserved interactions with prisoners. I did, however, record most of my interviews. There were no cameras in the interview rooms, as this was where prisoners met with their lawyers. For the same legal reasons, there weren't any COs in the interview rooms. Instead, the COs were positioned outside the room. At SY, the officers' desk was across the room and at least thirty feet from the interview room. At NCI, the officers' desk was just outside the interview room. The doors of the interview rooms at both facilities had long, narrow windows in the doorways.

Despite the intense dedication to routine, life in prison was also unpredictable. Sometimes the prisoners and staff seemed on edge, glaring at one another, and the sounds of the prison seemed louder and more staccato. This was often related to a particular incident within the prison (a fight or a lockdown), the weather (extreme heat or cold), or some other disruption in the routine of the prison. For example, once, the water heater at NCI went out; there was no hot water available for close to a week, and everyone was crabby and on edge. Other times, there was no discernable reason, to an outsider at least, for the intensely hostile feel of the facility.

Access to the prisons was also unpredictable. The facilities would sometimes be closed or on lockdown with minimal (and sometimes no) prior warning. I could call ahead to check, though this seemed to annoy the COs and did not always mean the facility would still be open by the time I arrived. The kind of paperwork COs needed me to produce in order for me to conduct interviews was unpredictable as well. Some COs were satisfied with the paperwork provided by the Department of Corrections (DOC) volunteer coordinator. Others were much more suspicious, particularly about my computer and the unusually long time the DOC administration granted me to conduct each interview. They wanted additional paperwork and would sometimes call the volunteer coordinator to ensure that I was actually allowed to bring my computer into the interview room. This unpredictability also applied to the paperwork I had to provide to the prisoners, with some correctional officers instructing me to give the prisoners nothing even though the prison administration required me to provide prisoners with a copy of the informed consent form.

The setting of the prison facility—simultaneously enormous and claustrophobic, highly routinized but also unpredictable—created a specific institutional context that shaped the behavior of prisoners, COs, visitors, social workers, and myself. Initially, I responded to this context by trying to ignore it and focusing on the people I wanted to study. By the time I finished my research project, I had learned to recognize the powerful impact that the prison setting played in shaping what kind of behavior made sense in any given situation. While that realization is not front and center in the analysis of this book, the influence of the institutional setting undergirds the conclusions of my analysis.

HISTORICAL CONTEXT FOR MASS INCARCERATION IN THE TWENTY-FIRST CENTURY

There are some important historical events and intellectual developments that a reader should know about in order to add nuance to the book that follows. While these historical contexts are not directly linked to fatherhood in prison, they are responsible for establishing the context in which fathers in prison are forced to operate. Mass incarceration developed as a solution to a series of problems and the rise of a particular economic school of thought, and in order to understand the current experience of fathers in prison, we must be cognizant of three distinct aspects of this history. First, I discuss the economic restructuring that occurred in the United States in the 1970s and 1980s, a shift colloquially referred to as deindustrialization. Second, I discuss the rise of neoliberal governance in the last decades of the twentieth century as part of the solutions to economic restructuring and its far-reaching impact on American society, including the criminal justice system. Finally, I discuss the unfolding of the War on Drugs and its impact on the structure of the American legal system.

Deindustrialization

In 1979, 20 percent of the American workforce held a manufacturing job. By 2006, this number had dropped to 11 percent.[12] Put another way, the American economy shed five million manufacturing jobs between 1979 and 2006, nearly all of which were low-skilled jobs that nonetheless paid relatively well and often came with benefits. Technological changes in production and growing international interconnectedness meant that corporations needed fewer workers to produce the same or more goods, could more easily move factories to places with lower wages and weaker or nonexistent unions, and faced stiffer international competition. Losses in steel and automobile manufacturing were particularly devastating to the American low-skilled manufacturing employment base.[13]

This did not mean that all manufacturing work vanished in the United States. It did, however, mean that manufacturing work decreased and changed location. Companies shed domestic workers by simultaneously investing in more efficient equipment that needed fewer employees to run and by outsourcing production work to places with lower wages. Though some of this shift was domestic, with some factories moving from the American Midwest to the Southwest, many corporations moved factories to international locations in Southeast Asia and Mexico. Corporate headquarters often remained in major American cities, and this pushed a spurt of growth in high-skilled manufacturing jobs.[14] Additionally, some of the low-skilled job loss among manufacturing work was offset by an expansion of low-skilled service industry work (e.g., food service workers or home health aides).[15] Women were more likely to step into service industry work as men lost manufacturing and other industrial work.

This is a brief and necessarily incomplete description of the economic changes of the 1970s and 1980s. It is important, however, to have a basic grasp of this profound and far-reaching shift in the American workforce for two reasons. First, this economic restructuring (along with a number of other events) created a feeling of uncertainty and fear about the future in the 1970s. Neoliberal economic thought, decades in the making, offered simple, ready-made solutions that didn't require a major redistribution of wealth from the top to the bottom. Second, this economic restructuring created a surplus labor force that needed managing. The War on Drugs and an expansion of the prison system offered a set of solutions for doing so.

Neoliberalism

While neoliberalism draws on older philosophical concepts, it began to form as a school of intellectual thought in the late 1940s and did not gain traction in terms of influencing actual policies and laws until the 1970s.[16] The original founders of this school of thought, Milton Friedman and Friedrich Hayek, began from the position that a strong welfare state was dangerous, particularly to those running businesses. Putting this ideology into practice has been a rough road, but the current approach to neoliberal policies emphasizes creating a "good business environment" and dismantling social welfare programs such as social security and Medicare. Creating a good business environment, from a neoliberal perspective, means maintaining flexible labor markets (often at the expense of unionized labor), state-supported infrastructure (that is, the government takes on or eases some of the costs of business with things like tax breaks or road maintenance), and easy access to political decision-making structures for those running businesses. Perhaps most importantly, in the event of a conflict between financial institutions and individuals, laws and rules should protect the institutions at the expense of the individuals. Some potent catchphrases of the last decade such as "borrower beware" or "too big to fail" encapsulate a neoliberal understanding of the relationship among business, individual taxpayers, and the government.

The expansion of neoliberal thought in the 1970s had an enormous impact on the employment landscape in the United States. Keynesian economics, the school of thought that dominated the first half of the twentieth century in the United States, focused on a low unemployment rate as the most important sign of economic health. This focus made things like the work programs put in place during the 1930s to employ people make sense, even though the government (and therefore taxpayers) had to foot the bill. Neoliberal theory, on the other hand, privileges the GDP (along with low rates of inflation) as the central and most important measure of national success. As a result, the emphasis of neoliberal government policies focuses on maximizing economic growth whether or not such growth decreases unemployment. A number of neoliberal policies actually intensified the process of deindustrialization with their emphasis on decentralization and deregulation of government services, particularly those services that emphasized alleviating poverty.[17] Neoliberal economic thought urged businesses to become "lean and mean" in the new globalized capitalist system and suggested that by doing so everyone, including workers, would benefit.[18] That these benefits have not materialized for most low-skilled workers does not appear to matter. While neoliberalism was initially most effective at infiltrating economic policies, its particular approach to solving problems quickly bled over into other areas of life.

Despite the commitment of neoliberal policymakers to protecting the institution over the individual, a major tenet of neoliberal theory is the importance of "individual responsibility." Indeed, it is personal responsibility that provides the logic for decreasing governmental interference in the free market. The ideal neoliberal subject is one who governs him or herself in ways that most effectively serve the state with little direct coercion from state actors or agencies. A deserving citizen under a neoliberal regime is one who does not rely on the state unless absolutely necessary, who is individually responsible for their success or failure, and who ultimately understands and supports the importance of the free market. Thus the strategies for dealing with "undeserving" members of society hinge on teaching, demanding, and coercing individual responsibility.[19] The combination of the "free market" and "individual responsibility" has had a profound impact on the social welfare net and the criminal justice system, including laws that increasingly link the social welfare apparatus with the criminal justice system and laws that criminalize debt.[20]

In his book *The Culture of Control*, sociologist David Garland outlines the "sudden and startling reversal" of policies and practices in the criminal justice system.[21] The dominant approach to crime control in the United States between the 1890s and 1960s was one that reflected a strong belief by the public and state actors that individuals can and should be rehabilitated as well as an assumption that the state could diminish or even eliminate crime with the right set of policies. This entire approach, which Garland refers to as "penal-welfarism," was thrown out the window in less than a decade. In its place arose an ethos that not only abandoned rehabilitation as an ideal but also emphasized deterrence as the central focus of the law. A proliferation of mandatory-minimum and zero-tolerance laws were the result. At the same time, state actors and the public developed a profound lack of faith in the ability of the government to do anything to address the underlying causes of criminal behavior.

This is not to say that without the rise of neoliberal economic thought, America would not have engaged in a project of mass incarceration. On the contrary, part of what makes neoliberal thought appealing in the United States is the way it neatly fits with long-standing patterns of American political thought. In particular, the neoliberal economic perspective merged easily with the uniquely American approach, grounded in its puritanical Christian roots, to managing intoxication, as well as the long-standing hostile race relations between the majority white population and the minority black population that predate the creation of the nation.[22] Importing neoliberal approaches into the political arena and the criminal justice system provided politicians with clear answers to big problems: drugs, not deindustrialization, were responsible for violence and crime; the solution to crime was to focus on deterrence rather than fruitlessly trying to rehabilitate criminals; and it was not racism that prompted the corralling of black bodies into prison but rather their individual criminal tendencies. This neoliberal shift in the criminal justice system co-occurred with, and helped justify, the creation of the War on Drugs.

The War on Drugs and Getting Tough on Crime

There is no way to talk meaningfully about incarceration in America without addressing the conglomeration of laws and policies dubbed "the War on Drugs." The drug war in the United States emerged to legitimate the seismic shifts in the America legal system, including mandatory minimums and three-strike laws, which extended the length of prison sentences, and "truth-in-sentencing" laws, which made it harder to get parole.[23] These legal changes directly produced the prison boom, and while the laws were beginning to change before the federal government declared the War on Drugs, the link to narcotics tapped into a long-standing pattern in the United States—moral outrage about mind-altering substances in America has legitimated widespread, punitive legal changes multiple times in our short history.[24] Despite the overwhelming evidence of racial disparities in the creation and enforcement of drug laws, community policing, sentencing, and the racial differences in postprison experiences and civil punishments, the War on Drugs remains the powerful and central focus of the criminal justice system.[25]

In the 1960s, a number of criminologists and other academics believed prisons were going the way of the dinosaur.[26] And yet in the decades that followed, the incarceration rate in the United States rocketed upward. By the end of the 1970s, the landscape of social life in the United States had changed drastically. Massive deindustrialization, rising unemployment in urban areas, white flight to the suburbs, the rise of neoliberal solutions in response to the global economic slump of the 1970s, a spike in the crime rate, and a backlash against the civil rights movements of the 1960s helped reshape the American criminal justice system. The new political and economic landscape demanded cost-effective measures for "protecting the public" from "unruly youth, dangerous predators, and incorrigible career criminals" that were (and still are) imagined to be both male and black.[27] In a kind of self-fulfilling prophecy, increasingly punitive laws and enforcement meant that minority men were (and continue to be) incarcerated at much higher rates than their white counterparts.

As Jim Crow laws crumbled, many people—both consciously and subconsciously—sought new ways to control the "threat" of minorities.[28] "Tough on crime" became the rallying cry for reworking the criminal justice system to keep order. Initially, Republicans led the charge toward a more punitive criminal justice system, though it didn't take long for Democrats to jump on the bandwagon. Being "tough" on crime became a requirement for political success and drove the expansion of punitive policies such as three-strike laws that incarcerate people who commit three felonies for twenty-five years to life. The Comprehensive Crime Control Act of 1984 ushered in the U.S. Sentencing Commission and the creation of mandatory-minimum sentencing. In theory, the goal of mandatory minimums was to diminish bias in sentencing on the part of judges. In practice, however, changes in sentencing shifted power from judges and public courtrooms to prosecutors and private offices. For example, the plea bargain rate rose sharply after the creation of this new sentencing structure, and, in 2013, 96.9 percent of cases ended in plea bargains.[29] Mandatory minimums also punished the possession of some drugs far more harshly than others, including treating different preparations of cocaine (i.e., powder vs. crack) as distinct substances. This political and legal shift disproportionately targeted the poor, many of whom were minorities; it also resulted in a massive expansion of the U.S. prison population.

Initially, police departments were hesitant to engage the War on Drugs, but federal programs offered grants and other financial incentives, including training programs and access to high-grade military weaponry, to direct their attention to drugs. An added incentive was the expansion of civil forfeiture laws; by this legal policy, police departments keep a substantial portion of the assets they seize in the course of waging the War on Drugs, and the burden of proof lies with the accused, not with the government. For example, if a local police department seizes a car because officers state that it is "affiliated" with a drug crime, it is up to the owner to prove that the car is "innocent." Because it is an object, instead of a person, owner has no guarantee of counsel and must foot the bill. Unsurprisingly, most civil forfeiture cases go uncontested.[30]

This new political and legal regime produced profound changes in American prisons. In 2010, the total number of people incarcerated in city and county jails, state prisons, and federal penitentiaries was just over 2.3 million.[31] The U.S. incarceration rate is the highest in the world at approximately 744 per 100,000 people.[32] Furthermore, the number of incarcerated persons has increased nearly every year of the past four decades.[33] These numbers are so enormous that it is difficult to grasp how deeply the penal system reaches into our larger society, yet the raw number of people locked up at a particular moment in time actually underestimates the expanse of the criminal justice system. In 2009, more than 7.2 million people were under some form of criminal justice supervision, such as parole or probation.[34] In 2010, an estimated 12.9 million people moved through county and city jail facilities.[35] While not all the people moving in and out of jails will be convicted of the crime they are accused of committing, the number remains staggering. And none of these statistics include the family members or communities that are also affected by the sheer magnitude of the criminal justice system.

The legitimacy of the War on Drugs is deeply embedded in a long history of tying nonwhite masculinity to deviant and criminal behavior. This has most notably been true of the connections between criminality and black men, but such ties have easily extended to include men who are members of other racial or ethnic minorities.[36] The United States disproportionately locks up a particular group of people: poor, primarily black or brown men without high school diplomas.[37] In the mid-1960s, the prison population was approximately 65 percent white and the total number of people incarcerated was about two hundred thousand.[38] Even though the incarceration rate was racially disproportionate in the 1960s, the majority of prisoners were white. As the number of persons in the penal system increased, so too did the racial disproportionality. By the end of 2005, 60 percent of the national state and federal prison populations were black or brown.[39] No other country in the world incarcerates so many of its citizens, nor along such clearly racialized lines.

After race, it is a lack of education that most increases someone's chances of being locked up. In 1997, 81 percent of the total incarcerated population had not received a high school diploma.[40] White men in prison are racially privileged, but these men possess low levels of education and have, in comparison to their more highly educated white counterparts, fewer employment possibilities. Regardless of race, high school dropouts are five times more likely to go to prison than high school graduates.[41] One out of eight white men without high school diplomas between the ages of twenty and thirty-four are behind bars. This is a far smaller ratio than black men in the same educational category (one in three) but higher than that of similarly aged Hispanic men (one in fourteen).[42] The white men incarcerated in America's prisons are not representative of American white men in general. Rather, the white men in America's prisons are likely to be a part of the "surplus labor" in need of inflexible regulation in the post-1970s neoliberal economic world.

Mass incarceration re-creates and reinforces a racial caste system that defines the meaning of blackness in America: black people, especially men, are criminals.[43] Sociologists Aliya Saperstein and Andrew Penner have found that once incarcerated, "individuals who were not seen as black before [going to prison] are more likely to be seen as such, and inmates who previously identified as white may strip themselves, or can be stripped by others, of their racial privilege."[44] That is, their data indicates that a prison record primed interviewers collecting data for the 1979 National Longitudinal Survey of Youth to perceive someone who had been convicted of a crime as black even when the participant had been coded as white before incarceration. Similarly, individuals who had been incarcerated were also more likely to self-identify as not white even when they had identified as white previously. The ties between the perception of race and criminal behavior are important, particularly as the changing laws of the past thirty years have rapidly increased the number of incarcerated persons in the United States. The prison system plays an important role in shaping both individual racial identity and the race-based social hierarchy in the United States by strengthening the association between criminality and minority status.

Masculinity, Fatherhood, and Race inside America's Prisons

There is an expectation that men and boys in the United States will be rowdy, aggressive, and always up for (heterosexual) sex, a set of behaviors captured in the phrase "boys will be boys."[45] It is tempting to treat characteristics such as strength or aggression as attributes rather than practices, but there is nothing natural or innate about gender.[46] People learn how to enact gender in ways that reflect their positions in the class and racial hierarchies of their societies. Men can exhibit these behaviors in a variety of ways, only some of which are considered normal or acceptable. Put another way, sexual aggression and violence are fundamental aspects of masculine gender performance for all men.[47] Yet most people expect that these behaviors won't spiral out of control, expressing shock and surprise when such behaviors show clear links to school shootings and high-profile cases of sexual assault.[48]

Additionally, masculinity and violence are linked in ways that are highly racialized. Media and public conversations often portray minority men as uncontrollable sexual predators, and there is a long history of the cultural representations of black sexuality being used to legitimate and support racist practices, policies, and institutions.[49] Such stereotypes extend to include Latino men who, rather than predatory, are assumed to be unduly "macho" and domineering.[50] These representations also profoundly affect the contours of the American criminal justice system. For men in prison, there is no valued or "normal" way to exhibit aggression; all behavior reinforces the divisions between "dangerous" prisoners and "normal" men. This is not to say that men in prison don't resist the assumption that they are little better than animals. Indeed, relationships with their children and family on the outside offer prisoners a way to push back against their stigmatized masculinity. The fatherhood programs offered by Healthy Connections offered such an avenue, and men responded positively to having the space to think about creating and maintaining their connections with their children.

Incarcerated men bring their own sets of masculine practices into prison from the outside world, and these practices affect how prisoners interact with one another, with COs and other staff, and with their families. Because the United States incarcerates poor people at a rate that outstrips all other groups, there are clear ties between "the street" and prison.[51] "The street" usually refers to the rules of the illicit drug economy in the United States, which relies on high levels of interpersonal violence to regulate the market. As in the licit market, men dominate street-level illegal drug sales; being physically strong, aggressive, "bad" or crazy, and loyal are all masculinized qualities of a skilled drug dealer.[52] The social relations and kinds of violence that are part of street life are also a part of life in prison.

The prison staff, COs, and volunteers also have a particular understanding of "the prisoner"—informed by class, race, and gender—that I characterize as "dangerous masculinity." I develop this term further in chapter 3. To briefly summarize here, both staff and the larger public understand prisoners to be hyperviolent and hyperheterosexual. This understanding is rooted in a legal system that most effectively punishes crimes that result from individual deviance as opposed to large-scale white-collar criminal behavior, such as fraud or government malfeasance.[53] In short, politicians, policymakers, and the larger public have primarily used the U.S. legal system to make illegal those kinds of crimes that people with lower socioeconomic status are more likely to commit.[54] In the context of the U.S. legal regime, only criminals practice threatening "street" masculinity.

In response to the confinement of prison, many male prisoners protect masculine practices such as strength, heterosexuality, and whatever vestiges of independence they can muster. Not only does this help them survive inter-actions with COs, but these responses also seek to preemptively address the threat of physical or sexual assault. The *threat* of violent sexual assault is pervasive within the penal system regardless of the rate of assault at a particular facility or whether a particular prisoner has been victimized.[55] Prisoners must always be on guard against the potential of assault.[56] Prison does reduce the range of possibilities for masculine performance, particularly a man's ability to identify as a father, but the belief that incarcerated men are somehow fundamentally different from nonincarcerated men should not be taken at face value; rather, it serves the strategic purpose of simplifying and legitimating a particular set of security measures within the prison. From the institutional point of view, prisoners possess and enact a particularly dangerous version of masculinity, and correctional stuff must respond accordingly.

On the same day that G expressed concern about showing too much emotion when his son visited, a large African American CO escorted us into the prison facility. About six feet tall and broad across the chest, Officer Pace was in his early thirties or late twenties. He had escorted us before and was generally friendly. We stopped on our way to the cafeteria so that Alice could pick up her body alarm from an enclosed and manned security station. The alarm was roughly four inches long, narrow, and black. It had three settings; its most sensitive setting allowed it to go off if it sat horizontal for more than fifteen seconds. Alice preferred the least sensitive setting, which required her to purposefully hit the red button at one end to set off the alarm. A moment after she had collected the device, the intercom crackled. I didn't understand the words, but Office Pace nodded and told Alice to give the alarm back: "[The CO] wants to make sure it's working. We don't want someone to jump you. This is jail, not Yale."

Alice pursed her lips and then said, "Well, I don't know about those boys at Yale." Officer Pace, misunderstanding her, nodded seriously and said, "These guys [prisoners] are dangerous." Alice had recently had an unpleasant inter-action with a CO over the level of her body alarm. Demanding she set it at its most sensitive setting, the guard had informed her, "We're here for punishment," and then lectured her in a way that Alice described as "nasty and condescending." Though Officer Pace wasn't being either of these things, I could tell Alice was annoyed. Jumping in, I said, "I don't know. I wouldn't want to meet any of them in a dark alley." I paused and then added, "Not that I spend a lot of time in dark alleys." We all laughed, though it wasn't funny. As soon as Alice had the body alarm again, she checked to make sure it was at the level she wanted. Office Pace suggested she might want to set it at a more sensitive level, "just in case something is going down." Alice smiled politely and shook her head: "I move around a lot."

Though they go home at the end of their shifts, the workplace culture shapes (and is shaped by) COs. While the saying "This is jail, not Yale" was undoubtedly meant to be humorous, it also captured something real about who COs oversee daily. Young men at Yale are much less likely than the average inmate to carry a gun or deal drugs in open-air markets. College men do, however, get into fights, deal and do drugs, and commit sexual assault.[57] And the young men at elite schools are also going to be in positions to commit white-collar crimes at far higher rates than prisoners and street-level drug dealers. Indeed, the class and race assumptions built into "jail, not Yale" are so strong that Officer Pace didn't hear what Alice was really saying and the suggestion that a Yale student might assault me in a dark alley was treated as though it was funny.

What makes someone a "good" CO also reflects the gendered expectations that men are more capable of violence and that physical aggression is the main way to maintain control over a prison. While the percentage of women who work as COs is slowly increasing, three-quarters of COs are men.[58] Positions dealing directly with dangerous inmates—as opposed to the more feminine care work demanded in the lobby and visiting room— are understood as the better, more masculine work to do. For similar reasons, many COs prefer to work in male prisons rather than female prisons. In the masculinized workplace, the male prisoner, like the male CO, is the "generic" inmate. As a result, the male prisoner is understood to be more predictable in his behavior—violent for logical (i.e., masculine) reasons—and free of the bodily problems associated with women.[59] The prisoner, however, is a specific kind of male: a dangerous "other," both in terms of race and class, who must be controlled, managed, and dominated.

For COs and many people in the outside world, the prisoner always hovers on the edge of violence and sexual assault, and these tendencies reflect the prisoner's inherent flaws rather than the constraints of the prison system or systemic inequalities. The structure of prison and the institutional actors within the prison treat prisoners as if they share a uniform masculinity in order to reinforce the division between prisoners and "normal" men. Indeed, the shared understanding that all male prisoners are violent, hyperheterosexual, and have little to offer their families means that prison staff have little obligation to provide incarcerated men with access to their children and loved ones.

OVERVIEW OF CHAPTERS

I focus on the fatherhood programs themselves in chapter 1. At the adult facility, the materials and group facilitators focused on the importance of maintaining communication. As part of this emphasis, they offered men the chance to have a special visit that temporarily suspended some of the security protocols around in-person visits. The special visit, for many men, was their primary reason for participating in the fatherhood group. At the youth facility, the group facilitator, Jasper, focused on teaching the young fathers to be "men of honor." Indeed, for Jasper, being a man of honor and being a good father were the same thing. The strong personal connection between the young men and the group facilitator was, for many of the fathers, the main reason they stayed in the group, though Jasper also organized special visits as well as individual visits between fathers and their children.

The belief that men could have value to their children despite incarceration was the most powerful resource either program offered, and men responded positively to it. Men also valued the increased access to their children. That said, the programs focused on individual responsibility in part because that was the kind of programming the state was prepared to fund. In this, the program material echoed the larger cultural shifts that assume "undeserving" members of society must be taught, or coerced, to take responsibility for their lives no matter the structural circumstances. This meant that group facilitators, no matter their personal feelings, had little space in the program to address structural barriers such as the unpredictable but powerful limits of security practices in the prison or the likelihood that men would go home and face bleak employment prospects.

In chapter 2, I highlight the different parenting obligations men felt toward their sons and daughters. As the interviewees in this study discussed their obligations to their children, they also discussed the costs and rewards of being a "real" man in prison. For many of the fathers I interviewed, fatherhood served as an important connection to the outside world and provided a way for men to resist at least some of the negative assumptions about prisoners that serve as the bedrock for the organization of prison life. A responsible father raises his son to be a man—strong, emotionally distant, and heterosexual—at least in part because boys will be expected to fight and stand up for themselves. At the same time, many of the men in this study experienced anxiety that their daughters would be tricked into having sex or would be hurt by men who cared little about them. In short, many of the incarcerated fathers I spoke with felt they had to protect their daughters from the kind of men they were raising their sons to be.

Drawing on my ethnographic experiences moving in and out of the prison facilities, chapter 3 focuses on the prison as a gendered organization and examines the links between security practices and the expectation that all prisoners share a uniform masculinity. I outline my definition of "dangerous masculinity" and then examine how the correctional staff treat this hypersexual and hyperviolent view of prisoners as commonsense knowledge about criminals. These implicit and normalized assumptions about masculinity allow prison staff and administrators to legitimate security concerns, rules, and policies in ways that are explicitly colorblind but implicitly racialized. With regard to fatherhood, correctional staff and the public alike treat male prisoners as neither interested in nor of use to their families, often resulting in prison policies and rules that isolate men from their children and families.

Young men in prison are not exempt from the belief that criminals are intrinsically violent and hyperheterosexual. In the 1980s and 1990s, the belief that a new juvenile "superpredator" was emerging justified increasingly punitive laws for young offenders, including trying juveniles as adults at rising rates and applying the death penalty to cases involving youth offenders. These "superpredators" were implicitly racialized—young black boys who were simply born bad.[60] And yet the laws and actors within the U.S. juvenile penal system have historically been more open to the possibility of rehabilitation for young offenders than the those in the adult penal system. Correctional officers and other staff are often willing to believe that younger offenders can still be rehabilitated. Despite this belief, elements of dangerous masculinity are still a part of the organization of the youth facility. Furthermore, even though there are contradictory expectations on the part of prison staff regarding young offenders, a prisoner is still a prisoner: the masculinity of young male prisoners is understood as uniform and in need of inflexible regulation.

Male prisoners also contribute to and actively resist the expectations that they are hypersexual and hyperviolent. In chapter 4, I outline how the men in this study addressed the challenges they faced in trying to be dangerous enough to reduce their chances of victimhood, but not so dangerous that they would end up in fights, have negative interactions with COs, and lose what few privileges they had. In particular, I emphasize how men in prison understand when and where it is appropriate to be violent, both within the context of prison and on the outside. I show how a prisoner's navigation of the murky waters of dangerous masculinity *reinforces* the structural expectation that prisoners will erupt in violence and how the prisoners' enactments of violence further isolate them from their children.

The exploration of the ways in which violence imbues multiple aspects of social life is one of the most important facets of this project. Violence is an overt element of masculine performance for *all* men, and intragroup violence along race, class, and gender lines is embedded in our legal system.[61] Many people can avoid direct violence because they can rely on socially acceptable, well-organized groups—the police and the military—who are trained and prepared to manage violence with violence. Understanding the interaction among fatherhood, masculinity, and violence inside prisons allows us to ask questions about the overall purpose of the American penal system and, perhaps, consider some of the more unpalatable aspects of violent behavior in our society.

CHAPTER 1

Neoliberal Responsibility and "Being There" as a Father

IN 2007, MEN ACCOUNTED for 92.8 percent of incarcerated persons in the United States, and more than half of these men were fathers.[1] Even though the incarceration rate has slowed down over the past few years, the overall number of incarcerated persons has remained fairly steady. Roughly 1.5 million U.S. children (approximately 2.2 percent of those under the age of eighteen) have a father in prison.[2] Socioeconomic status has a significant impact on incarceration and, therefore, on children's likelihood of experiencing parental incarceration. Half of all children born in 1990 to high school dropouts had a father who had been imprisoned by the time they were fourteen.[3] Like other aspects of the criminal justice system, children of color disproportionately bear the brunt of parental incarceration. By the time they turned fourteen, one out of four black children born in 1990 had a parent incarcerated as compared to one out of twenty-five white children born in the same year.[4]

The penal institution is the primary mediator of prisoners' access to their families, as well as the major institution shaping how and when they can enact both masculinity and fatherhood. By isolating them from their families, the institution of prison severely limits prisoners' attempts to perform fatherhood either as an identity or as a set of practices.[5] Indeed, prison rules, and the staff members who enforce them, circumscribe prisoners' access to phone privileges, writing materials, and visits. Prisoners are often housed far from families, making visits costly, and the experience of visiting prison can be, for both children and adults, emotionally difficult. Arranging to touch base with family via the phone can be challenging because prisoners' schedules are dependent on COs and calls are expensive. In 2013, the Federal Communications Commission (FCC) issued a ruling that capped the costs of interstate phone calls for prisoners. Calls within states, however, remained untouched, and most state prisons use telephone services that charge exorbitant sums when prisoners call home.[6] Writing letters is less expensive, though stamps, pens, and paper cost more in prison than they do in the outside world. Many prison systems also mark letters with a stamp warning that the letter comes from a correctional facility. For some families, the stamp causes enough embarrassment that they do not want to receive letters.[7]

The loss of a father to incarceration is strongly correlated with negative outcomes for children, including an increase in family instability, financial hardship, compromised attachment between fathers and children, diminished psychological well-being, and an increase in social stigma. Despite these negative consequences for children, a father going to prison can also decrease violence and instability in the family unit.[8] For men who do not have a history of domestic violence, the research generally supports the assertion that keeping incarcerated men in contact with their children decreases the negative impact of parental incarceration on children. The best way to do that, however, remains a matter of debate, in no small part because fatherhood programs require financial resources and, if they are to be effective, a brief suspension of the normal routine of prison life.

Improving or maintaining parent–child ties also positively impacts incarcerated fathers. While access to housing and employment have an enormous impact of the likelihood of men recidivating, the maintenance of strong ties to children is also correlated with a decreased chance of returning to prison after release.[9] In order to maintain ties with children, incarcerated men must successfully navigate relationships with the mothers of their children, both during and after incarceration.[10] Doing so can be tricky since incarceration decreases trust between coparents, changes the power dynamic between them, and increases the chances that mothers will repartner. There must also be space in the prison facility for communication with family, including phone calls, letters, and physical visits.

According to a 2010 national survey of wardens from male and female prisons, most prison facilities offered some kind of parenting program.[11] Parenting classes that only involved the incarcerated parent were the most common kind of program, with 51 percent of male facilities offering such a program. Parenting programs that directly involved children were far less common, with only 10 percent of male facilities reporting this kind of parenting program. While research on the efficacy of parenting programs is still developing, what research there is suggests that programs that directly include the children are more effective at promoting the parent-child bond.[12] From this perspective, the high levels of contact during the special visits that were a part of the Healthy Connections fatherhood programs were rare and valuable.

BARRIERS TO FATHER-CHILD RELATIONSHIPS

The men at both facilities in this study experienced four distinct barriers to successful father-child relationships. First, many men struggled to believe that they had something of value to offer their children.[13] Several researchers have examined this issue, as this is an area in which policies in prison might be adjusted in order to create space for men to remain connected to their families.[14] Justin Dyer, a human development and family studies scholar, suggests that opportunities to learn new job skills might help incarcerated men feel like they are "providing" for their families or that programs that allow men to fulfill roles as playmates could make significant differences in how men see themselves. Such programs include allowing men to record themselves reading children's stories or encouraging men to keep journals that they send home.[15]

The fact that the performance of fatherhood and certain aspects of the performance of masculinity within prison undermine one another contributes to the difficulty that incarcerated men have viewing themselves as good fathers. Emotional connections with children and family introduce vulnerability and can undermine practices that communicate strength, independence, and masculinity within prison. For example, correctional staff treat prisoners' connections to the outside world as a privilege that can be rescinded or limited in order to encourage obedience to the rules. Using isolation as a motivation to encourage criminals to reform is one of the original organizing principles of the American prison system and remains a central method of control.[16] As such, there is a strong incentive among incarcerated men to cut ties with the outside world in an effort to ease their own pain as well as the pain of their families.[17] Incarceration does provide some men with the motivation to become or remain connected with their children, but time in prison can also diminish a man's belief that he is a good father and increase his feelings of helplessness.[18] Despite the prison system's emphasis on isolation, male prisoners who remain connected to their families may be less likely to recidivate, and most prisoners return to their communities upon release.[19]

Some prisoners are more successful at remaining committed fathers than others. Sociologist Brad Tripp found that despite the difficulties of remaining in contact, men who focused their fathering obligations on remaining in contact with their children, providing emotional support, and teaching children to be well behaved considered themselves to be better fathers than men who emphasized the importance of activities such as playing with children. Regardless of which orientation they took to fathering from prison—contact versus activities—all the men in Tripp's study emphasized the importance of providing financial support.[20] Both inside and outside prison, the ability to fulfill the breadwinner role remains a central component of successful fathering.

Not only is this something that is basically impossible to do from prison, but incarceration also has a devastating effect on future employment.[21] Whether incarcerated fathers identify as breadwinners, nurturers, or both, a prison sentence can undermine their ability to support and connect with their children. There are a limited number of programs aimed at keeping incarcerated men connected to their families.[22]

Second, men struggled to manage their relationships with the mothers of their children. These relationships had often been tumultuous before men arrived at the facility, and the stresses of incarceration increased that instability. Mothers could refuse to bring the children for visits or to let someone else (usually the prisoner's mother) do so, could refuse to pay for phone calls, and could prevent children from seeing or reading letters from their fathers.[23]

The fatherhood groups at both facilities primarily focused on what men could do to address these first two barriers. At the adult facility, the group facilitators advised fathers to be consistent in their communication with their children and spend time considering their coparents' perspectives, as these coparents controlled access to their children. At the youth facility, the group facilitator focused on becoming a good man, a man who could offer children a valuable role model, in order to be a good father.

The third barrier to men's successful relationships with their children was the cost of contact with families. Phone calls were cripplingly expensive, and writing materials, such as paper and stamps, were also quite costly (though much more reachable for many men). Family visits were inconvenient, time-consuming, and potentially emotionally difficult for children, coparents or other family, and the men.

The fourth barrier was the most difficult to overcome: the bureaucracy and security apparatus of these prisons made maintaining connections with the outside world difficult. Conflict with prison staff or other prisoners resulted in loss of contact privileges, time spent in solitary confinement, loss of jobs (and the minimal income that came with them), and changes in prisoners' security ratings.[24] Additionally, prisoners were moved from facility to facility with little warning, both in response to their security levels dropping and as part of the DOC's strategy to minimize the possibility for stable gang formation in prison.

The third and fourth barriers were beyond the scope of the mandate at Healthy Connections because the fatherhood programs at NCI and SY were individualized, neoliberal projects. That is, they sought to change the prisoners rather than the prison system, with an emphasis on individual responsibility. From the perspective of the staff at Healthy Connections, this was a more realistic approach. There was little state support for programs that aimed at reorganizing prison to make it easier for prisoners to access families, particularly in the adult facility. There was, however, money available to fund programs that focused on teaching prisoners to take responsibility for their actions. Sociologist Suzan Ilcan refers to this as a "responsibilizing ethos," which "supports the idea that certain individuals and groups can maximize their own social and economic advancement themselves and take hold of all possible opportunities that can improve their conditions of life, no matter how fair or unjust."[25] It is a cultural mentality that is essential for making sense of the larger neoliberal economic changes that swept across the United States in the late twentieth century. Bending to fit these neoliberal expectations is necessary for any nonprofit that intends to survive the repeated cuts to the social welfare net, and Healthy Connections was no exception.[26]

Men at the youth facility faced an additional barrier that the program had difficulty addressing: few job options exist for a young ex-convict. Most of the fathers at the youth facility were serving sentences of fewer than five years, whereas nearly all the men at the adult facility were serving sentences of more than ten years. Returning home and facing the challenges of reintegrating into the outside world were very real hurdles for the young men, and they experienced anxiety about how successful they were going to be when forced to face the job market. In particular, these men expressed doubt about their ability to get legitimate jobs. This doubt was based on previous experience that accessing work in the legal economy was difficult.

For many prisoners, fatherhood is primarily a set of aspirational goals. Even the most involved incarcerated fathers have very little contact with their children. Much of the research on incarcerated fathers focuses on what happens when men return home. For example, sociologist Anne Nurse argues that the inability of paroled juvenile fathers to keep the primarily financial but also relational promises they made to the mothers of their children while incarcerated increased distrust and hostility between the coparents once men returned home.[27] The disjuncture between promises and action often resulted in decreased contact with their children. Indeed, once men leave prison, they face significant difficulties reconnecting with their children, including limited work options, negative or nonfunctioning relationships with their children's mothers, and tensions between the demands of parenting the children they live with and their noncustodial children.[28] However, these issues often develop well before men return to their communities.[29] Incarceration places its own set of pressures on incarcerated men and their families. What happens to fathers as they transition back into the community is important, but their time in prison plays a key role in shaping incarcerated men's identities and practices as both men and fathers.

The demographic characteristics of incarcerated men look quite similar to those of nonresidential fathers in general, something that was reflected in the group of men I interviewed. The majority of participants in this study were minority men without high school degrees who occupied the lower socioeconomic rungs of American society and became fathers via nonmarital births. Only three of the forty-nine men that I spoke to were (or had been) married to the mothers of their children, and of those three, only two had fathered all their children within the context of marriage. Two of the three who had been married were white.

FOCUSING ON COMMUNICATION AT NCI

The staff at Healthy Choices focused on communication as a central component of fatherhood at the North Correctional Institution because it was practical. It was something all the men could potentially achieve, even if they weren't returning home in the near future. It didn't necessarily require that anyone bring his children to visit (though that would help facilitate communication). All communication required was for caregivers to refrain from blocking letters mailed home from the prison, something that many men could hope to achieve. Phone calls from prison were limited to fifteen minutes and were expensive, but even an occasional phone call could make a difference in the level of communication between a father and child.[30] The emphasis on communication was the most successful aspect of the fatherhood program, one that sought to help men see themselves as having something to offer their children and to provide the motivation to work through issues with their coparents.

Fifty-nine of the ninety-two (62 percent) handouts in the adult fatherhood programs included some kind of encouragement to think about how children are seeing or experiencing their father's incarceration.[31] Of those fifty-nine handouts, twenty-six (44.07 percent) exclusively addressed the child's perspective, thirty documents (50.85 percent) encouraged men to consider the children and coparents's point-of-view simultaneously, and the remaining three (5.08 percent) aimed at getting men to consider how they had been parented and in what ways that might influence, either positively or negatively, their own approach to parenting their children. In addition to the thirty documents combining mother/child perspectives, an additional five handouts encouraged men to think about the experiences and perspectives of their children's mothers (or whoever was functioning as the coparent) and how that might affect their ability to parent and connect to their children. Only six handouts (6.52 percent) focused primarily on how men thought about themselves as fathers.[32]

The men in the fatherhood groups at NCI enjoyed the groups and spoke positively of their experiences with the program. As we discussed being a father in their interviews, twenty-six of the thirty-five men (74.29 percent) listed specific reasons they valued the program. The most common thing men felt they gained from the program was knowledge about being a father (n = 10). G, for example, applied to participate in the program because he wanted to be a better father. He frequently participated in the group, often by trying to tell younger men about the "reality" of incarceration and the barriers to fatherhood. During one of the group meetings of G's cycle, the group facilitator, Alice, passed around a handout that discussed the challenges presented by distance. The sheet referenced both the physical and the emotional distance that incarceration creates between fathers and children. The loss of the parental role was listed as one of the issues that can intensify emotional distance. Alice asked the group how that loss affected their self-esteem. G was quick to say, "I'm not a father. I know I'm not a father." Alice, in an effort to encourage him, replied, "You can still be a father [in prison]; you just have to work harder." She continued, suggesting that with "some kids, it's going to be a lot of work. Is it worth it? It's gonna look different, but is it worth it?" G, unwilling to commit, shrugged as he said, "Somewhat. Possibly." Still, G spoke positively of the program during one of his interviews. We spoke about Alice and laughed a little about how much she liked to talk. He enjoyed participating in the group enough to say, "It would have been nice if they had extended [the program] for a longer period of time [. . .] It took [until] the closing point to get people to feel open enough to talk."

G, at forty-eight, was older than many of the men in the program and had spent long stretches in prison, yet his desire to be a father and his belief that he had failed in the endeavor were shared by many men. The program's emphasis on communication spoke to this tension. Even men who had limited contact with their children could try to make improvements. Some men, like Paul (thirty-three, Puerto Rican), found that the program pushed them to rethink how they had interacted with their children on the outside. Frowning as he spoke to me, he said, "I exposed [my daughter] to my lifestyle [. . .] I used to have my drugs on the table, cutting it up. She comes up. And I be like, 'What?' Talking to her. She see me cutting all this whole bunch of cocaine all over this table and everything. She seen me do drugs. I wasn't ashamed to hide or nothing. I'd do it right there, right in front of her." In retrospect, Paul thought that being open with his daughter about his unwillingness to be monogamous and his involvement in the drug trade wasn't good. The messaging of the fatherhood program coincided with his recently rekindled religious faith. At the same time, he struggled to balance this with his unwillingness to lie to his daughter. He was particularly concerned that his daughter's mother was always ready to speak badly about him to their daughter and "throw [him] to the floor." For Paul, being honest with his daughter also meant showing her parts of his life that other people frowned upon.

Paul only talked in the group when the group facilitator pressed him to do so. At the end of the cycle, Star (the group facilitator) asked all the men to tell her what they had learned from the program that was most useful. Nearly all the men mentioned communication and Paul was no exception. Speaking carefully, he stated, "I can still keep communication with my daughter even though I'm in here. I can keep building that." Putting this into practice, however, was still difficult, since Paul felt he was essentially starting from zero. When he wrote to his daughter, she rarely wrote him back. It was difficult to stay motivated when Paul didn't even know if his daughter was receiving letters and refusing to respond or if his coparent was blocking his child from getting his notes or not providing the necessary materials for her to respond, such as stamps.

Paul wasn't alone in this struggle. Twenty men talked about writing their children in their interviews (57.1 percent), and most of them had issues of one sort or another (n = 14). The most common reasons men expressed frustration were that their children didn't write back, their coparents refused to help their children write, or the cost of stamps and materials was too high. Gregg (thirty, white) and his daughter's mother were together for three years. Gregg was clear that he didn't think he'd been a good boyfriend. He believed that he and his coparent were now friends but that he sometimes had to "spaz out" to get her to send school reports or bring his daughter up for a visit. He wrote to his daughter as often as he could and tried to talk to her three times a week (fifteen minutes for each call). His daughter was a year old when he got locked up, and he felt both surprised and blessed that she loved him, wanted to talk to him, and replied to his letters. The contact, however, relied on his daughter's mother to accept and pay for phone calls and to drop the letters her daughter wrote in the mail. His daughter's letters often sat for weeks before the mother could (or would) send them. Gregg sent his daughter envelopes with prepaid stamps on them in an effort to keep the communication flowing, but that only partially resolved the problem.

Maintaining phone contact was even more difficult. Fifteen men were in semiregular contact with their children (42.9 percent), and all of them reported that phone calls were difficult. By far the most commonly reported problem was the cost. Some men like Aeneas (early thirties, Puerto Rican) said that they didn't even bother with phone calls because the financial burden was too high. As Aeneas said, "I don't get to talk to [my son] on the phone because the bill is expensive. So I try to stay away from that." Other men reached out to their families despite the cost and did their best to manage the guilt that came from increasing the burden they placed on loved ones. Malik (forty, black) was married to the mother of his two youngest biological children.[33] Malik joined the program to make sure that he was in good shape to qualify for parole as soon as he could and to get access to the special visit. The phone calls were important to him as a strategy for remaining part of his wife and children's lives, but they were also a burden: "I try to speak to them at least once a week. But I sometimes run the phone bill up, calling every day, two and three times a day. So since I've been incarcerated, we might have spent over five thousand dollars on the phone bill."

Malik had been incarcerated when he was young and turned his life around when he returned home: working legitimate jobs, following through on the tenets of his Muslim faith, and striving to be a good husband and father. He returned to prison when he got into an altercation with an acquaintance over religion. The man in question was, according to Malik, engaged in a multiweek harassment campaign that culminated in a physical fight that ended when Malik shot and injured the other man. In his interview, as he told me the long and involved story of the events, he shook his head and blew out his breath, then said, "I didn't go the police." Instead, he had tried to handle the problem himself with devastating consequences for everyone. Malik considered his incarceration a mark of his failure as a father: "Where I came from [. . .] two little babies at home, [a] wife. Now I'm back incarcerated. Family's out there in need. They need me as a father, as a husband, and I'm not there. So I see myself, I guess, as a failure." The cost of remaining connected to his family was high, both financially and emotionally.

The special visits were the second most commonly mentioned positive aspect of the fatherhood program. Nine men mentioned the special visit as the best aspect of the fatherhood program. The level of contact in the special visit was an unusual privilege; only one other program in the prison facility offered anything similar. Gregg, for example, enjoyed the special visit with his daughter and felt grateful to have had even a brief opportunity to "be there" for his child. While he enjoyed the program, he felt that being a good father was about giving his child "unconditional love" and that this wasn't something that could be taught. His greatest regret was choosing drugs and alcohol over his child during his preincarceration life. Several times over his interviews, Gregg expressed shock that his daughter was willing to love him: "It's like I wake up, [and] I feel like a scumbag for that—for not being there, not being able to tuck her in, not being able to make her breakfast, or whatever. You know? Just not being there for her. And for her to love me—sometimes I feel I don't know why. You know what I'm saying? But she does. And I'm blessed for that. 'Cause that's, you know. That's my heart right there." He valued his connection to his daughter over almost anything else. Halfway through a fifteen-year sentence, he was already worried about his ability to be a good father once he returned home.

Men also stated that they hoped their participation in the fatherhood program would look good to the parole board (n = 4), that programs of any kind keep you busy (n = 4), that the program would help them gain access to extended visits (n = 3), and that the special visit would allow them to get a photo with their child (n = 1).[34] None of the men offered up significant criticisms of the fatherhood program during their interviews. The most significant criticism of the fatherhood program occurred during the fourth cycle I observed in a group setting. Damian was a tall, thin black man who always wore a kufi to group. He often spoke during the meetings and engaged with other prisoners, as well as the group facilitator. During a video on the importance of fatherhood, Damian shook his head, muttered under his breath, and finally put his head in hands and refused to watch any more.

Once the video was over, Katelyn (the group facilitator) pointed at him and said, "You think it was biased because there weren't any black people." After a pause, Damian replied, "I think the whole curriculum is biased." Blinking in surprise, Katelyn said, "From start to finish?" Damian nodded: "It's for white folks. Doesn't mean I didn't get anything out of it." A buzz of low conversation broke out, and over the next several minutes, the group debated Damian's claim. The discussion quickly became one focused on when, where, and if parents should use physical discipline with their children. Growing increasingly frustrated as he tried to make his point, Damian added, "I just don't [see] a typical black, Spanish family using the methods this curriculum gives us."

The conversation transitioned briefly to a discussion of their own fathers and how many of them had used physical discipline. Malik stated this his father hadn't been one for baseball games, but that "when it was time to fight, shoot someone, he was there." Malik continued, saying he thought that if his father hadn't beaten him, "[I] probably would have been worse."[35] In frustration, Damian tried to make his point again: "This curriculum is about class things." He waved a hand at the television screen. "[The father in the video's] success is his family . . . his pride, his legacy." Damian stopped for a moment and then suggested that the curriculum made it seems like "you've failed as a man" if your family is struggling. Changing directions, he referenced a handout from the previous group that featured a quote from George Washington—a man, Damian pointed out, who owned slaves: "For this [quote] to be in the curriculum, that's bias right there." Wiso (twenty-three, Puerto Rican) rolled his eyes and made a dismissive sound as he asked, "What the hell does that show?" Wiso argued that the quote was too old to think about it like that. Damian, pressed his lips together momentarily and then replied, "You done missed the point." Katelyn, seeing that group had gotten off topic, redirected everyone's attention to a handout that asked them to think about the "bumps in the road" they faced in their relationships with their children and their strategies for dealing with those challenges.

These frustrations didn't resolve for Damian over the course of the twelve meetings, and he was transferred before I could interview him. At the end of the group, Katelyn had the men talk about what they had liked about the program. Damian thanked us both for our input and then said that the group hadn't taught him to be a parent but had shown him something else: "How I haven't been a good parent. I came to prison early." He waved his hand around to include the group. "[We] haven't been beautiful to our children. [We've] been stressed because we haven't fulfilled our promises to our kids. Everyone knows how much I feel about this curriculum." The whole group laughed at that. "But like Mustang [another member of the group] said, we have to keep trying, not to be a parent but to be a voice." The program's emphasis on communication was successful, even for a man who thought the overall curriculum was deeply flawed.

Damian's struggle to identify his issues with the curriculum demonstrates how deeply embedded the "responsibilizing ethos" of neoliberalism is in our cultural understandings of parenthood and socioeconomic status. That is, the video the group watched highlighted a happy white, middle-class family, presenting methods of communication with little consideration for the ways limited resources increase stress and decrease parental choices. Similarly, Damian sought to identify the broader, more structural patterns in the ways that race, ethnicity, and socioeconomic status overlap with one another. Neither the material nor the group facilitator was prepared to respond to these kinds of criticisms. Katelyn quickly redirected the conversation to safer, more individual-oriented grounds: how the men could prepare for the inevitable and fairly predictable challenges they would face as they sought to remain connected to their children. And Damian, despite his dissatisfaction with the curriculum, still felt a high level of personal responsibility for the ways that he had failed to father his children.

BEING A "MAN OF HONOR" AT SY

About halfway through my fieldwork at the Southeast Youth correctional facility, the group facilitator, Jasper, showed the movie *Men of Honor* across two group meetings. The movie is based on the true story of the first African American master diver in the U.S. Navy. Cuba Gooding Jr. plays Carl Brashear, the black protagonist. Robert De Niro fills the role of Billy Sunday, the cantankerous, racist diving instructor who eventually comes to respect and support Brashear. The young men arrived for the second day of the movie in an excited clump. They liked watching movies and often asked, suggested, or demanded more of them.[36] Before starting the film, Jasper reminded them that they were supposed to be writing down scenes that demonstrated courage. He commented that he had liked what they wrote in the last meeting. One of the young men, sounding surprised, asked if he really read them. Jasper smiled and nodded as he said, "You bet I did." Smiles broke out across several of the young men's faces.

The young men talked to each other in low murmurs throughout the movie. At a pivotal moment, Brashear is threatened with death if he continues his pursuit to be a diver. As he suits up to take the final diving test anyhow, the young men focused intently on the screen. Chris (eighteen, black) leaned forward in his seat with an intense expression on his face and said, "He gonna do it anyway." As the diving test went on, it got harder as it became clear that Brashear's equipment had been sabotaged, and the longer the diving test went on, the worse the cold got underwater. Brashear continued with the test, determined to finish. Stewie (nineteen, black) said loudly, "I'd be outta there." A chorus of young male voices agreed with him. "I'd quit," someone said. When Brashear successfully passed the test, the young men laughed and smiled in relief.

At the next group meeting, Jasper talked about the movie. He had difficulty getting the young men to focus and scolded them several times. Chris, in particular, seemed to have difficulty focusing. He shifted in his seat, talked to the young man next to him, and wanted to look at my notebook and generally do anything other than listen. Jasper asked for Chris's attention several times. When Chris muttered that he was paying attention, Jasper frowned and snapped, "Well, then, look at me!" When Chris did, Jasper thanked him. Jasper asked the young men, "Did you see that family relationship [between the protagonist and his wife]?" The question was rhetorical, as Jasper continued without pausing, "He had his son there, his wife. Let me tell you something. I don't know how you guys feel about this. If you're gonna do anything important, you're gonna have to put some extra time [in]. You might have to work two jobs, three jobs. You wife might work three jobs, or go to school, and you'll still have to take care of your child. And you will." He nodded firmly. "When everyone went downtown [to party], where did [Brashear] go? The library." Jasper slapped the table for emphasis. For Jasper, the important takeaway message of the movie was one of grit and determination. At one point, he revealed that he and his wife watched the movie any time they were feeling down. The commitment demonstrated by the main character in the movie inspired Jasper, and he wanted to extend that feeling to the young men in the group.

This example captures Jasper's approach to the fatherhood group at the youth facility. Rather than focusing on communication, he emphasized the importance of being a good man. In some ways, this reflected the very different population of men at SY as compared to NCI. Most of the young men at SY were serving sentences of fewer than five years and would be home in the near future. Their children were much too young to talk on the phone or read letters. Only one of the fourteen young men talked about writing his child. Ricky (eighteen, Puerto Rican) was one of the few young men serving a longer sentence. With almost nine years left, he expressed an intention to maintain contact with his daughter: "She gonna get older, so when she get older, I can write her." The rest of the young men did not mention talking to their children on the phone. Instead, the young men talked about being in contact with family or friends (n = 6), and the mothers of their children (n = 6).

Jasper used seventeen handouts, far fewer than the ninety-two provided by the NCI program over the same time period. Eleven of these handouts focused on becoming an accountable and responsible "man of honor." The only handout that appeared more than once reflected Jasper's perspective on the ties between manhood and fatherhood:

> A man is created for challenges. He is equipped to overcome, to run the gauntlet, to stand firm as a well-anchored post. Men are the benchmark in life, society, and family. It is part of the masculine responsibility to demonstrate strength and responsibility, to protect and provide for those within their sphere of influence. This is the hallmark of manhood. (Gillham 1999)[37]

Jasper handed this quote out three times (roughly every six months). For Jasper, Gillham's message resonated with his own expectation that men can and should be the cornerstone of the family, but only if they are prepared to take on the work that comes along with that responsibility. And while part of being a good man is talking to your child and coparent, at the root of it, being a man of honor is about overcoming challenges with dignity.

The young men at SY liked Jasper. They joked with him, asked his opinion about situations in their lives, and spoke positively of him during their interviews. Three of the fourteen young men I interviewed specifically stated they were grateful that Jasper arranged individual visits with their children. Others listed specific things that they felt Jasper had taught them that they valued. For example, Ricky said that Jasper had taught him to "keep his promises" not only to his daughter but also to other people. During his interview, Stewie told me that Jasper had helped him learn to "be patient." Laredo (eighteen, black) was the most effusive, talking extensively about how much he valued the things Jasper had taught him, such as the importance of pursuing a good life for his children, even if Laredo hadn't had that as a child, and how to express emotion to his child. He also valued Jasper's help in his preparations to go home and have a relationship with his child. Summing up his feelings about Jasper, Laredo smiled and shrugged before saying, "He's a good dude."

There was, however, an enormous disconnect between the lessons Jasper wanted to impart and the young men's priorities and experiences. For Jasper, being a man of honor didn't require a big paycheck. A man who persevered through difficulties would likely end up employed, but it was the act of overcoming challenges and difficulties that mattered to Jasper. The young men, on the other hand, were quite certain that they needed money. Their hopes and dreams for the future, both their own and their children's, hinged on having an income. They certainly believed that the mothers of their children cared about whether they earned enough money.

Luis was eighteen when I interviewed him. He was multiracial with a white mother and Puerto Rican father, though he self-identified as Puerto Rican. He had long hair and often wore a large silver cross. His relationship with the mother of his daughter was contentious and a source of stress for him. They were no longer romantically involved, and Luis struggled to get even basic information about his daughter. His requests for a photograph, for example, had gone unanswered. His daughter's mother was romantically involved with another man and had written Luis shortly before the interview to tell him that she didn't want him involved with their daughter. Luis was incensed and had written her back to tell her that he wasn't going to abandon his daughter. Relating the contents of the letter to me, he explained what he'd told his daughter's mother:

> "Like, it don't matter what you think. When I get out, all I'm gonna do is I'm gonna go to the judge. He gonna see that I'm doing good. We can go. You can try to put child support on me. Don't matter." I was like, "It don't matter. That child support ain't holding no weight. You can put child support on me. I'll make sure I get my visiting rights. That's it. You can't stop that. I'm not abusing drugs. Feel me? As long as I have a stable environment, I'm not committing no crimes. And they see that I'm trying to better myself, [and] they are gonna let me see my daughter, regardless of what you say."

This future plan, however, required that Luis have a "stable environment" that hinged on his employment. Later on in the interview, I asked him what he planned to do for his daughter when he went home, and the first thing Luis mentioned was getting a job. Employment was the root of his future capacity to build a relationship with his daughter.

Luis already knew this would be difficult. His ease with the illegal options of the street and his difficulty getting legitimate employment had already contributed to his incarceration:

I swore on my daughter, I wouldn't get locked up again. Like, that's the only thing I regret. I ended up getting locked up again [. . .] I was trying to get a job. I was out there. That, that's what I think it was right there . . . I realized this world sucked. [*Laughs.*] I had to get money somehow. I was trying to get a job. I put in applications everywhere. I was going out every day, waking up early, eight o'clock in the morning. Putting on a button-up, looking nice, presentable. Going everywhere asking, asking, filling out applications [. . .] Really trying to change my life, like I could do this. Feel me? [I could] prove myself wrong. And nobody was hiring me. Everybody looking at me like, "Oh, you want an application?" That got me mad too. "What do you mean? Yeah. I want an application." [But] nobody's calling me back. I'm going back there, filling out another application. And that got to my head. Like, "Damn I can't make it." Like, "I'm used to the street life. I can't. I can't. I can't survive without selling drugs." And then I didn't have no money at all. So I ended up robbing somebody.

While Luis was particularly explicit about his concerns for future employment, he was not alone. In addition to Luis, four young men expressed concerns that they wouldn't be able to find legitimate work, five stated that selling drugs had provided income and a lifestyle they liked, and six directly stated that access to their child hinged on getting a job.

The concerns voiced by these young men weren't imaginary. Economic shifts over the last forty years decimated the employment possibilities for all teenagers and young adults. This not only affects their short-term earnings but also results in lower levels of work experience that impact their long-term employment possibilities. The un- and underemployment rates increase for those who belong to young at-risk groups such as minorities, those without a high-school degree, and those with a criminal record.[38] The young men in this study experienced a cluster of disadvantages that made any sort of legitimate employment difficult to access and a good job that included benefits and a living wage almost impossible to get. And while it is difficult to definitively state that young mothers deny unemployed fathers access to children, we do know that employed low-income men are more likely to marry their partners[39] and that employed disadvantaged fathers who have either a flexible work environment or higher pay are more likely to be involved with their infant children.[40]

The young men at SY liked that Jasper believed they could be better men, and during their interviews, they indicated that they were, in fact, listening to his exhortations to model out good behavior for their children, work hard even when there was little reward, and recognize the importance of spending time with their children. In some ways, Jasper's willingness to wave away the importance of employment offered the young men relief from the anxiety of locating a legitimate job that would allow them to financially support their children. At the same time, these young men had more experience with the difficulties in locating legitimate work and less faith that working hard would result in closer ties with their children.

THE SPECIAL VISITS AT NCI

At the end of the twelve-week cycle at NCI, men who successfully completed the program were supposed to receive a special visit. During a special visit, the regular rules of visitation were suspended, and men were allowed to visit with three children instead of the usual two, an adjustment that men with larger families in particular valued. Prisoners were also allowed to sit on the same side of the table as their visitors, play games, and, in theory, eat snacks with their families.[41] Additionally, the special visits lasted two hours instead of one. The group facilitators mentioned the special visit early on, and the subject came up multiple times over the course of all of the cycles. Men expressed anticipation and excitement, asked questions about what kind of games and food there would be, and often started working on persuading family members to come up for the special visit as soon as the cycle began. Nearly all the men spoke highly of the visit and suggested that it was one of the primary reasons they participated in the group.

Of the fifty-one men who participated in the five cycles, thirty-one ended up participating in the special visit (60.9 percent). The most common reason men didn't get their visit was because they were transferred to another facility (n = 9, 17.65 percent), followed by their family being unwilling or unable to come up for the visit (n = 3, 5.9 percent). Transfers often happened abruptly and with very little warning. Even men who expected to be transferred because their security levels were dropping didn't know exactly when it would happen. Five of the men (9.8 percent) didn't receive their visits for unknown reasons. They declined to be interviewed, or I spoke to them before the special visit and didn't have an opportunity to follow up.[42] I interviewed twenty-three of the men who received special visits, many shortly after the event occurred. For the men who successfully received a special visit, the high level of contact with their families was a unique and rewarding experience.

Clayton was a skinny white guy with short, dark hair. He was in his early twenties, and his only child had been born during his current incarceration. The special visit was the first time Clayton had been able to hold his son for more than a few seconds. When I asked him what it had been like, Clayton got a dopey smile on his face and said, "I was great. It was great. It was finally, basically, the greatest thing in the world." While Clayton was the only father with a child that young at NCI, the overwhelmingly positive emotional reaction was common. Aeneas, for example, received regular visits from his preteen son and still described the special visit as "quality time that we never got to have before." Indeed, Aeneas felt so strongly about the visit that he struggled to find words to describe the event.

Brown was in his midthirties and seven years into a thirty-year sentence.[43] He had four children with four different women and was committed to being connected to his children. Early on his cycle, there was a long discussion about "fathers" versus "dads." Men disagreed about which term differentiated a "sperm donor" from a man who was there for his kids. Hotdog (early forties, black) vociferously argued that you "never know what's in a man's heart" and that they shouldn't judge other fathers as a result. Brown frowned at Hotdog as the other man complained that women just wanted money for child support rather than an involved father. Finally, with an impatient shake of his head, Brown leaned forward, pointed into the air in front of him with an admonishing finger, and said, "If you aren't doin' everything you can, wrong, point blank, period." He leaned back when he was done speaking with an expression that suggested the discussion should be over.

Brown practiced what he preached. He had a court order mandating visitation for his youngest daughter and was in pursuit of a similar order for his only son. He also managed to arrange for his mother to have temporary custody of his three daughters (again through the courts) so that all three could attend the special visit. Brown started working on the paperwork as soon as he joined the fatherhood group and was successful. All three girls and his mother attended the special visit, and Brown smiled the entire two hours. He was also very involved with all three of them, playing games and talking to each one. I interviewed Brown after the special visit. When I asked him how it went, he smiled and said, "I'm still high from that special visit. That special visit was beautiful because I never got to see all three of my daughters together like that. To have that for that amount of time, right then and there. That was good. It was definitely a good thing." Brown was already thinking of the next opportunity to visit with his children and had begun putting together the paperwork to apply for an extended family visit.

Hotdog had short curly hair and a goatee. He had been married to the mother of his children for twenty-three years and was four years into a thirteen-year sentence. Hotdog had been in and out of detention facilities since he was a teenager. He had two sons, one twenty years old and the other fifteen. He was also close with his niece, who also attended the special visit.[44] His youngest son was currently in juvenile detention, and Hotdog felt he had failed him, stating, "A man [is] supposed to take his son and teach him what it supposed to be to be a man. And I did that with my oldest son. I didn't get a chance to do that with my youngest son. When he was seven, I should have been there to grab him." Hotdog worried that he was too late to successfully father his youngest son. When his oldest son and niece left the special visit, Hotdog cried.

The successful special visits offered men the opportunity, for a few moments, to let go of the limitations prisons placed on them as fathers and focus on improving their connections with their children. As such, those who received their visits spoke highly of the program and expressed a renewed or strengthened commitment to fatherhood. Clayton, for example, was serving a short sentence and would return home while his son was still young.[45] He spent most of his interview after the special visit talking about his plans for returning home and forging a connection with his child. He and his son's mother had a tumultuous relationship and weren't together at the time of his interviews. His coparent was talking about moving to Florida to live with family to reduce costs. Shaking his head, he said, "I might be stuck without having my son when I come home because of a mistake I made. So that kind of kills me." Clayton was eager to return home before that happened, as he believed if he could offer more financial support, his son's mother wouldn't leave the state. With his parole coming up shortly, he was gathering letters of support from anyone he could (including me) with the goal of getting home. When we spoke last, Clayton was hopeful he could talk his son's mother into remaining in the state. While Clayton and the other men who participated in the fatherhood program were already motivated fathers (or else they wouldn't have applied to join the group), the special visit offered them a kind of hope that was hard to come by in prison.

For men who were blocked from the visit either because of an issue involving the DOC or because their family wouldn't or couldn't come up, the special visits undermined their belief in their value as fathers. Montana grew up in Puerto Rico and moved to the United States when he was twelve. He'd been in and out of detention facilities since he was sixteen and had been with his children's mother for close to a decade. They had two children together, a girl age seven and a boy age four. He was two and a half years into a ten-year sentence. While his children's mother wanted to stay together, Montana had doubts about their ability to do so, stating in one of his interviews, "She be driving me crazy, like, crying and complaining, and I can't do it. So I rather sometimes be like, 'You do you; no disrespect or nothing.' But it still hurt me. You feel me? It hurt me. Seeing her like that, and I got to suffer too. It's like, [I] can't do it." He frowned and shook his head as he spoke.

Despite the tensions in their relationship, Montana had little choice but to rely on his children's mother to make decisions for the family. His daughter was living with her aunt so that she could have access to a better school district. Though he thought it would be better for his daughter to remain with her mother, he shrugged as he told me the story and said, "She probably see something that I can't see. So I said, 'You know, [it's] your choice. I hope you made the right decision.'" When things were going well between him and his girl, he saw his children twice a month.

Montana was looking forward to the special visit, especially the chance to hold his children and play games with them. He was, however, worried that his children's mother might not come; his coparent wasn't returning his phone calls. He was anxious that he had accidentally mixed up the letter he was sending to his girlfriend with the letter he was sending to another woman with whom he was exchanging letters. Montana had several brothers who were also incarcerated, and as the oldest, he felt strongly that he shouldn't ask his mother or other family members for any assistance, particularly monetary, while in prison. He was also concerned about asking his children's mother for money (though he did sometimes) because she was financially strapped and raising two children alone. Montana met the other woman through his brother and the two had been exchanging letters and photographs for a couple of months. The woman sent Montana money, something Montana did not worry about because "she work. She be having fun. She go to clubs. All that money she spending, she can send it to me." He laughed as said this and then frowned. While he knew his girlfriend would be angry if she found out, he expressed confusion as to why, stating that the other woman meant nothing and it was just a letter. He explained, "I lie [to the other woman]. You know, I wanted the money . . . and I wrote some—some stuff, you know. What she want to hear." The idea that exchanging letters with another woman would count as cheating frustrated him since doing so allowed him to avoid being a financial burden on his family.

When the special visit came around, Montana's girlfriend and children did not show up, despite telling the group facilitator that they would be there. Montana, along with a couple of other guys, was called up to the visiting room even though his girlfriend had not yet arrived. As other men received their visits, Montana sat to one side with a scowl on his face. As the minutes continued to tick by, Montana hunched over with his elbows on his knees, staring at the door as if he could will his family to appear. After thirty minutes of waiting, Montana stood and, with his hands balled into fists and his shoulders bunched up around his ears, said, "I'm leaving. They can call me back down if she gets here." The group facilitator, Star, suggested that he stay because she had talked to the mother recently and had been assured they were coming. But the volunteer coordinator, Baxter, shook his head, saying, "Let him go. We'll call him down again, when his family arrives." Baxter continued, "There was some miscommunication between myself and the correctional officer. They usually get called when their families get here. That way, they aren't embarrassed like this."

I didn't see Montana again. Though he attended the first support group that focused on organizing the special visit, he didn't attend any of the three additional support groups that occurred for his cycle. I don't know if his girlfriend didn't appear on purpose or if there was some bureaucratic mix-up. What I do know is that Montana, already feeling like a burden to his family on the outside, looked like he might punch a wall and break a few fingers on his way back to his cell. His frustration, anger, and sadness were palpable as he left. The special visit created hopes and expectations that lifted men up when it was successful and hurt them when it failed.

The Special Visits at SY

Over the two and a half years I attended fatherhood group meetings at SY, I interacted with thirty-seven young fathers.[46] There were two special visits in that time period, both of which I attended, and sixteen of the men (43.24 percent) attended at least one of these events. The young men at SY vanished with little warning more frequently than those at NCI. Sometimes, even Jasper didn't know if they had gone home, been transferred to an adult facility, or were in solitary confinement ("seg"). Eight young men (21.6 percent) were definitely transferred before they could participate in a special visit, and three (8.1 percent) went home. The remaining ten were transferred, went home, were in seg, or couldn't get their families to attend the special visit. Over the full span of my fieldwork, thirteen of the thirty-seven men were transferred to an adult facility (35.14 percent), and eight (21.62 percent) went home.[47] Six of the young men (16.22 percent) were still at the facility when I left.

Special visits at SY happened less frequently than at the adult facility, but it was easier for men in the program to get individual contact visits with their children. Jasper oversaw these visits, and fathers received as many as Jasper could arrange with the caretakers of the children. For some, this meant weekly high-level contact visits with their children. For men with uncooperative or busy caretakers, visits were more intermittent. Jasper pointed out that as long as he was willing to do the legwork, Healthy Connections and the DOC were willing to work with him to schedule contact visits. When larger special visits occurred, they were often run in combination with other programs that emphasized keeping young men in contact with their children.

On Father's Day in 2008, a large special visit took place for the young men in the Healthy Connections fatherhood group at SY. Participants from another program, Father Reads, joined the visit. In the lobby, the high-pitched voices of small children rose up over the murmuring of adults. In order to enter the visiting room, where the special visit would take place, each person had to go through the metal detector, enter through a sliding door, wait for that door to close, and then go through a second sliding door. The visiting room at SY was a large, nearly rectangular room, and the northeast corner of the room was glassed off. Short metal stools stood in a row in front of two banks of phones, one set behind the glass for the prisoners and the other on the outside for visitors to use. That day, the special visit took place in the southeast corner of the visiting room.

Staff from the various programs and the prison itself had already done quite a bit of setup by the time I entered the visiting room. One wall had been decorated with paper flowers and the words "We love our kids" in big cutout letters. One table had books on it, and someone had decorated with paper flowers and garlands of paper streamers, and a second table—covered in a blue plastic tablecloth, paper flowers, and paper streamers—had apple juice and a tray of cupcakes. The cupcakes were brightly colored—oranges, blues, yellows, greens, and reds. Each cupcake had a plastic ring stuck into it decorated with soccer balls, flowers, butterflies, Dora the Explorer, footballs, and Spider-Man. As I walked over, one of the staff from Healthy Connections commented that it would be fun for the children to take the rings with them when they left. Several minutes later, a male CO entered with a wheeled cart and added orange juice and ice to the table.

The families began filling up the visiting room, and once everyone had entered, the young men began trickling out from the far side of the room, near the entrance to the prison. The room was soon a cacophony of sounds. One little girl demanded access to her father's lap and remained there for the entirety of the visit. Other kids focused on the cupcakes and soon had frosting smeared all over their faces and fingers. Some children wanted their parents to look at books with them, while still others seemed to want to run in circles and scream. For a few minutes, the room settled down when a woman from a nearby library sang children's songs and played the guitar.

For the young men in the fatherhood group at SY, access to their families hinged on their status as juveniles rather than adults. This meant that the administrators and social workers hoped the young incarcerated fathers would take responsibility for their children—for example, by signing paternity papers at the special visit. No staff member I interacted with at the adult facility evinced any desire to help prisoners claim their paternal role. Despite the desire on the part of staff at SY to help young men take responsibility for their actions, it was difficult for the fathers to enact any kind of adult fathering role in the visit. One example captured this tension clearly.

Spots was lanky and told me that while he was technically both Native American and African American, he considered himself black. He was a part of the fatherhood program for most of the time I conducted my fieldwork and was one of the young men I got to know the best. During group, he alternated between dynamic engagement with the material, the group facilitator, and the other young men and silent withdrawal. Spots was curious about what I was doing and often wanted to look at my notebook as well as ask me questions about my project. He often brought his artwork to the group and would show it to me either before group started or afterward. Additionally, Spots and I would talk informally about his experiences in prison and out in the world. Spots was excited about being a father and regularly talked about his hopes for his relationship with his son and his son's mother.

Shortly after arriving for the large 2008 Father's Day visit, Spots's little boy needed his diaper changed. The baby's mother set him on a chair away from the group and started to change him as Spots wandered away. Thinking about our conversations where Spots discussed his uncertainty about what his son's mother wanted from him, I looked at him and suggested he "go on over there and help her change [your] son." He looked at me blankly for a second and then walked back over. He hovered nearby while she changed the diaper. Then she handed him the dirty diaper. He looked down at it with a startled and confused expression on his face and then began to look around uncertainly. After a moment, I realized that he was looking for a trash can.

The baby now changed, the baby's mother, her mother, and the little boy went back to the main group and found a place to sit. Spots remained standing, looking around, eyes narrowed and licking his lips nervously. On the far side of the room, where the door to the main prison facility was located, there was a desk with a male CO behind it. Spots looked over at the CO a couple of times, then back down at the diaper, but remained standing still. After a minute, I walked over to Spots and said, "Come on." I motioned him to follow with a wave of my hand.

I walked over to the CO, who was white and in his forties, and asked him if he had a trash can. Spots stopped about fifteen feet behind me and shifted from foot to foot, dirty diaper in hand, as I talked to the CO. The CO said "Yes" with a grin and held the one by his desk up. With a smile, I told him, "It's for a dirty diaper." His grin faded and he said, "Oh." He thought for a minute and then opened up a door behind to reveal a janitor's closet. The CO pulled a thin, white trash bag out of the closet and shook it open. I carried it over to Spots, who threw the diaper in it. Spots smiled in relief as he got rid of the diaper, thanked me, and then walked quickly over to rejoin his family.

Spots's story illustrates just how different the juvenile system managed young fathers compared to how the adult system treated older fathers. The men at NCI would never have had the opportunity to feel stressed about what to do with a dirty diaper because children in need of a changing had to leave the visiting room with an adult and have their needs dealt with elsewhere. The only nod that the COs made to the special status of the program visit at NCI was that the child and adult would be allowed to reenter the visiting room, something that was not true during normal visiting hours. Even though Spots had more access to his child, he remained reliant upon the goodwill of COs and volunteers in order to provide even a basic level of care for his child. His uncertainty as to whether the CO would help him deal with the diaper left him trapped among roles: prisoner, adult, teenager, and father.

CONCLUSION

The state prevents incarcerated fathers from directly parenting their children. As a result, the best an incarcerated father can do is develop (or maintain) a positive relationship with the coparent and be in verbal and written contact with his children. The Healthy Connections fatherhood programs attempted to help men achieve this and were partially successful. In particular, men responded positively to the emphasis on communication at the adult facility and the special visit with their children (at least, those who received their special visit did). The fathers at the youth facility responded positively to having an adult consistently and honestly believe in their ability to do right by their children. The Healthy Connections programs were, however, hobbled by their inability to address systemic barriers in improving men's ties with their children.

In her analysis of two motherhood programs in women's prisons, Lynne Haney argues that the refusal of the staff to consider the outside social forces framing poor women's lives accomplishes two things. First, focusing on individual responsibility makes these programs appealing to public and private actors who control funding decisions. Second, "there are very real dangers to bracketing the social from these women's lives—not only does it psychologize their troubles and distort their lives, but it denies them a potential source of alliance."[48] Though male prisoners have very different experiences than female prisoners, the neoliberal ideal of self-governance also impacts paternal parenting programs.

On a broader level, the security apparatus of the prison creates profound barriers that no individual program can overcome in a large-scale, meaningful way. Some structural changes to improve incarcerated parents' connections to their children, such as decreasing the cost of phone calls, are easier than others that would require a significant shift in how we think about security in prison facilities. None of these larger-scale structural fixes, however, fit with the "responsibilizing ethos" that assumes individuals can and should be held responsible for systemic inequality. While I do not advocate changes that would leave correctional officers vulnerable to violence, making it easier for prisoner's families to visit and for men to be in contact with their children is a worthwhile goal and one that cannot occur without a willingness to make such structural changes.

CHAPTER 2

Little Me versus My Princess

FATHERS' EXPECTATIONS ABOUT GENDER

MOST PARENTS HAVE GENDERED expectations for their children, and organizations often mediate these expectations. For example, sociologist Michael Messner examined how the structure of children's sports organizations and the agency of parents and children combine to make gender differences between boys and girls appear "natural."[1] Gender also matters when it comes to parenting styles and responsibilities. Mothering and fathering are substantially different roles in the family, with mothers primarily responsible for nurturing and fathers' obligations linked to providing financially.[2] Furthermore, parents express different worries, concerns, and obligations to children of different genders.[3] Sociologist Emily Kane pointed out that parents both undermine and support "normal" gender identities. Among the parents with preschool-aged children in her study, many parents encouraged their daughters to participate in athletics and their sons to be nurturing through play with dolls. That said, there were limits to parental acceptance for nonconformity, particularly for boys who wanted to wear pink, play with Barbie dolls, or wear makeup. Beyond the academic work, a massive number of how-to books aim at helping parents learn how to properly raise sons and daughters. These texts, while focusing on larger issues of self-esteem and the influence of media, tend to start from the position that there are innate biological differences between boys and girls.[4] Children's gender can even affect parental relationships, with men slightly more likely to marry the mothers of their sons.[5]

Much of the research on gender socialization and parenting in U.S. families focuses on white, middle-income families and draws on cross-sectional data. Because the research on gender socialization focuses on white families, there is a limited amount of information on how race mediates gendered patterns of child-rearing. The limited research on black families indicates that there are different patterns of gender socialization when compared with white families, though these differences are not consistent between studies.[6] In some studies, racial inequalities have a profound effect on how parents socialize their children in regards to gender.[7] For example, African Caribbean fathers in the United Kingdom considered teaching their children, regardless of gender, how to respond and deal with racism to be an important parental responsibility.[8] It is worth noting that the gender socialization patterns in these studies reveal some of the ties between gender and responses to the challenges of race and class. Some of the gender socialization techniques among black families were contradictory (e.g., training daughters to be both "warriors" and "ladies" or having more traditional expectations for sons than daughters), but most studies find that black parents seek to prepare their children to face specific problems such as racism in the workplace and the challenges of economic class mobility.[9]

Teaching children to navigate racism was an important element of parenting both sons and daughters, and it was surprising that such conversations didn't emerge in my discussions with incarcerated fathers.[10] Indeed, when the fathers discussed their expectations for their sons and daughters, they sounded startlingly alike regardless of race or age. Instead, the men raised concerns primarily about what constituted the successful performances of both masculinity and femininity. The men considered physical and emotional strength important aspects of successful manhood. A responsible father raises his son to be a man—strong, emotionally distant, and heterosexual—at least in part because boys will be expected to fight and stand up for themselves. At the same time, many of the men experienced anxiety that their daughters would be tricked into having sex or would be hurt by men who cared little about them. In short, many of the interviewees felt they had to protect their daughters from the kind of men they were raising their sons to become. Sons and daughters offered men different ways to embrace being a "good" man and father and resist the worst aspects of enacting dangerous masculinity even as the distinction between boys and girls reinforced a gendered binary that emphasized the importance of aggression for men.

In group meetings and interviews, men discussed raising boys as something that was enjoyable. Daughters, on the other hand, were most often discussed as sources of great anxiety. In particular, men expressed concerns that other men would take advantage of their daughters. Men's discussions of raising sons tell us about their understanding of what makes someone a man worthy of respect as well as their understanding of the challenges they expect their sons to face. Specifically, while men were more willing to express worry about daughters, many of the men recognized that their sons would have to be able to fight and be tough and were also at risk for ending up in prison.

For many of the fathers, fatherhood served as an important connection to the outside world and provided a way for men to resist at least some of the negative assumptions about prisoners that serve as the bedrock for the organization of prison life—specifically, the institutional expectations that male prisoners are disconnected from families and of little value to their children. At the same time, fatherhood as an identity undermined the aspects of prisoners' masculine performance that emphasized emotional distance, independence, and strength. The expectations for manhood are more limited within prison (as compared to many structures and institutional frames in the outside world), and the cost of deviance is both overt and high. Prison compressed men's gender performance to such a degree that nearly all the men, regardless of their racial identities, presented similar concerns and rewards for fathering boys and girls. A good father taught his son to be strong because his son would have to be tough in order to be successful (or really, not victimized). At the same time, men experienced anxiety about the vulnerability of their daughters as they considered, perhaps for the first time, the costs of particular aspects of masculine gender performances.

"Little Me" versus "My Princess"

In the fatherhood groups at both NCI and SY, the men brought up their concerns for their children without prompting from the group facilitators. In fact, even when the various group facilitators wanted to talk about something else—such as improving communication with coparents—the men in the fatherhood groups would derail the conversation in order to talk about their personal concerns about their sons and daughters. Men did discuss their worries about how they would successfully raise their sons to be men, but they were much more likely to talk about their sons with other prisoners by telling humorous stories about their sons' sexual precociousness or toughness. When men discussed their daughters, they highlighted girls' vulnerability to manipulation by men. During their interviews, seven men (14.3 percent of all interviewees) referred to their daughters as "fragile" or "vulnerable," twenty-four men (48.9 percent) stated that their daughters needed to be protected, and thirteen men (26.5 percent) described raising a boy with either the word "rough" or "tough." What was most interesting was the absence of any cross-over use of these terms. Girls were never described as "tough," nor were boys ever described as "fragile," "vulnerable," or in need of "protection."

A group of researchers interviewed young fathers in prison and found that most of the young fathers expressed a preference for a boy, in part because young men were more confident that they could teach their sons important life lessons.[11] In doing so, they could be better fathers than their own fathers and raise "hypermasculine and self-reliant" sons.[12] As with any discussion of the outside world, there was always an element of fantasy in thinking about the future while incarcerated. A son offers the opportunity to imagine oneself as an ideal father (e.g., "being there," going to sporting events, teaching a boy to be a man), and because a son is not yet grown, the possibility remains that he will become an ideal man. Girls, on the other hand, mostly present challenges: How does a father teach a daughter to become the ideal woman?

Achilles was tall and broad shouldered and often wore his hair tightly braided. He was still involved with his daughter's mother at the time of his interviews. He self-identified as black, was nineteen, and was serving a short sentence at SY.[13] During one of his two interviews, we discussed whether Achilles and his girlfriend would have another child. Achilles told me that he was close with his nephew and that he wanted a son of his own. When I asked him why, he replied,

> Another person I can just . . . He's a boy, so I can rough him up; we can play ball together like—he's not a girl, so you can't be so fragile— "Come here . . ." [*Makes grabbing and wrestling motions with his arms.*] Like it just be like, like a son. [*Laughs.*] He's a big boy; I just treat him like my nephew—not rough but just like play with him, tickle him, I don't know—I can't describe it. Just have fun with him, but I don't gotta treat him like a little fragile . . . you know, 'cause he's a boy. He can take it . . . I just want a boy. I can't really describe it. I just want a little me, that's it.

Achilles was excited about the possibility of raising a child without the worries of fragility or vulnerability that came with having a daughter. Instead, this story highlights the qualities that Achilles enjoys or respects in men—that is to say, toughness, the ability to "take it" and enjoy rough play.

Achilles was not alone in expressing this difference between raising sons and daughters. Both older and younger men often emphasized that while they may have been worried about some aspects of raising a boy, they were mostly excited to roughhouse and play with their sons. Interviewees often discussed game playing, particularly physical games, as a way to teach sons to be strong. Tyler was thirty-six, and though he claimed Irish, Native American, and black ethnicity, he referred to himself as black when telling stories about life in prison. He was serving a short sentence at NCI and had been in and out of prison for most of his life. When I asked Tyler how many children he had, he replied, "It's questionable." He was sure he was the father of six children and felt closest to his three youngest, two of whom he'd had with the same woman.

When I asked Tyler about the differences between raising sons and daughters, Tyler put substantial emphasis on the connection between rough games with his sons and teaching his sons to be strong. His daughters were a different story:

TYLER: The son, you have to teach him to . . . With me, my daughter's a princess. You know? And I treat her like she's delicate. She's my little flower.

My son is my bag of potatoes. I beat—I'll punch my son. I used to beat my son up when he was eighteen months old.

ANNA: What do you mean, beat him up?

TYLER: Punch him in his chest and stuff, knock him down a little. [*Taps himself on his chest.*] You don't understand; you ain't got a kid. You just tap him in the chest, he falls, he gets back up, you push him back down. They start to get frustrated. He don't let nobody push him around then. [. . .] But I've never put my hands on none of my girls. I don't believe that the man should beat his daughters because there's a tendency at times for, especially in the urban areas, the woman to feel like [her] father beat [her] and then, at the same time, he telling [her] he loves [her]. Now they have problems disassociating that with their boyfriends: "Oh, he gave me a black eye, but he said he love me." You know what I'm saying? And they stay in it for the wrong reasons. Listen, he don't love you; he's beatin' your ass. That's not love. [. . .] The daughters, I treat them like they're fragile. You gotta protect them. [. . .] A daughter, the way you raise her up, she usually stands straight. But the son is like, you know, he gotta explore. He gotta experiment. That's the American way.

Tyler was particularly clear that his obligations to his children were different based on their gender. In part, this was a reflection of Tyler's fairly rigid understanding of the differences between men and women. His own value as a man was rooted in his ability to provide through both legal and illegal means, and he stated that he'd always worked more than one job since he started working at sixteen. Tyler also emphasized that he was good at fighting, though he was quick to reassure me that he only did so when it was absolutely necessary. He also differentiated between "good" women who were not promiscuous, did not get abortions, and were loyal to their men and "jump-offs" who were always in clubs looking for a man and "chickenheads" who "do whatever for whatever."[14]

Many men expressed how much they enjoyed playing rough-and-tumble games with their sons. These games were presented as something that sons offered that daughters could not. The descriptions incarcerated fathers provided suggested that men felt that they were helping their sons develop physical and mental strength through play. When it came to their male children, men emphasized training their sons to be independent, physically and emotionally strong, and heterosexual. The emphasis on these masculine qualities meant that men didn't have to wrestle with the reality that their sons were as—and, in some ways, more—vulnerable than their daughters. Girls are certainly subject to high rates of abuse all over the country, but boys face high levels of risk as well. Boys, particularly younger boys, are more likely to be on the receiving end of violence from other boys, more likely to be expelled from school, and more likely to be incarcerated than girls are.[15] This is particularly true for low-income, black and Latino boys.

Stewie was an enthusiastic participant in the fatherhood group at SY. He attended class for more than a year and talked in nearly every group he attended. Stewie was a skinny young man who used his entire upper body to emphasize the points he was making. At nineteen, it was unusual that he hadn't been sent to an adult facility, and Stewie stated that he wanted to finish his short sentence at SY because it meant more visits with his child. During his interviews, he self-identified as black and Puerto Rican. He was also roman-tically involved with the mother of his son during the time I interacted with him and occasionally discussed the possibility of marrying her. At the same time, Stewie was clearly uncertain about his ability to be a father or a husband. In large groups, this meant he vacillated between expressing concerns about being a good father and confidently stating that he knew what to do.

After a few months, Stewie began asking me questions about what I expected from a boyfriend or a husband and, on one occasion, asked me to explain his girlfriend's behavior to him. One day after group, Stewie sat down at the table I was sitting at and told me he needed a "woman's opinion." After I told him to go ahead, he looked around to make sure no one was close by, leaned forward with his shoulders hunched, and asked me what women "look for in a marriage partner." I blinked in surprise at him, not expecting this question, and Stewie began to talk rapidly, stating that he was engaged to his son's mother and did not know what she wanted him to be. When I sug-gested that he ask her instead of me, he threw his hands up, saying, "I did! [But she] don't want to answer through the glass [during a noncontact visit] or in a letter!" Stewie was motivated to be a good husband and father but didn't seem entirely sure what that meant or how he could enact such roles.

During a group at SY, as we discussed showing affection to children, Stewie commented that he was glad he had a boy. Stewie added, "There's more to worry about with girls." Another guy in the group, Spots, nodded in agreement. Spots, like Stewie, had only a son. Later in the group, Stewie started to laugh and, when pressed by the other guys in the group, said, "My son, he had a grabbing problem." He held up his hands and made a grabbing motion in front of him. Most of the guys broke into laughter. The two guys who did not laugh leaned forward and demanded to know what the joke was. Someone muttered quietly to them and made the same hand motion, which set everyone off laughing again.

I frowned and mimicked the motion, asking him what he meant. Stewie laughed and repeated, "A grabbing problem." He started to giggle and began a story. He was at the mall with his son, and they were eating at the food court. The woman sitting next to them was big—Stewie sat back and held his hands in front of his chest, which prompted a chorus of giggles through the group. Stewie, grinning, said that his son looked over once, then twice, then he reached out and groped her. The woman laughed, and Stewie was surprised she didn't get angry. At the time of this story, Stewie's son was just under two.

Achilles, who had one daughter, said, "That's a good sign," and Stewie agreed with him. I asked, "A good sign of what, exactly?" Stewie did not answer my question directly, though he continued, telling the group that as he and his son walk down the street, "My son watches every woman that walks by. Sometimes, he'll turn around and try to follow them!" Stewie laughed as he said this, and other men did as well. With a shrug, he said, "I'm not sure what to do about it." He paused for a moment and then added, "It's a good sign because it means he's not gay . . . but it seems like it might become a problem." The other men in the group told him, in a chorus, that his son would be fine. Stewie's story of his son's fascination with women was presented as both funny and a signal that Stewie was doing something right in raising his son. During group, men often told humorous stories about the things their sons did. The stories often resulted in a group dialogue and laughter, and it was a chance for men to both celebrate their value as fathers (because they were raising the right kinds of sons) and also reiterate the important elements of being a man (e.g., heterosexuality).

When fathers did express concerns about their sons, they listed specific problems. G was a short, wide-shouldered African American man in his late forties. His hair was mostly gray, and he had a small round belly. He had four sons and one daughter. G often expressed worry that his children would lose their way because he had always been more of a friend than a father. G stated that he joined the group to help him do a better job with his youngest child, a ten-year-old boy. He regularly expressed concerns that his youngest son wasn't doing his homework. G made sure to ask his son about school every time they talked and spent time considering how he could encourage his son to value academic success.

Similarly, both Steven and Angel had sons with behavioral problems, and they worried whether their children's mothers could effectively discipline "wild" or "crazy" boys. Steven was white, in his early thirties, and serving a short sentence at NCI. He attributed his incarceration to a drug addiction that got out of control. Prior to his incarceration, he'd worked with the local power company and had a fairly traditional marriage with his now estranged ex-wife. He described his son as "basically me" and believed his ex-wife was having a difficult time handling the boy. Steven's son was experiencing many of the same problems Steven had had while in school: difficulty paying attention and holding still. Steven was frustrated with his inability to parent his son, stating, "I can't control him, and there's nothing I can really do behind these walls. Even that two-hour [special] visit—I can't make any changes in two hours [to] the way he acts." When I asked about his daughter, Steven said that while he worried, she was better behaved, and he primarily wanted to teach her about men: "I know how boys are, and I want my daughter to not need a man. I'm not saying that she shouldn't have a relationship, but I'm saying that too many women build their futures around the guy instead of building their own future and his future together. That's what I'm trying to instill in her. That's what I'm worried about." This was an easier lesson to teach from prison, and Steven felt his relationship with his daughter was better than his relationship with his son.

Angel was thirty and had short buzzed hair and crooked teeth. I assumed that he was white when I first met him, but during one of his interviews, he told me that he was both Italian and Puerto Rican. While growing up in the foster care system, Angel started getting locked up at the age of thirteen; he was emancipated at seventeen. When I spoke to him, he was most of the way through a seven- to ten-year sentence for robbery. He had two children with the same woman, though his son and daughter were almost eight years apart. When I asked him what made a man a good father, he struggled to answer, telling me, "Some men ain't good fathers . . . I don't have patience. I'm not the type of father that plays games or none of that. And it sounds bad, but I've never been that type of person . . . Plus I'm a big kid myself, so it's kinda hard . . . As long as you take care of 'em and support 'em, that's good enough for me." Both of his children had also spent time in the foster care system. His son was briefly removed from the home when, after the boy struck his grandmother with a skateboard, Angel violently punished his son. His daughter was removed from the house for more than a year when she was an infant. Angel was incarcerated at the time and so was a little fuzzy on the details. According to the children's mother, the baby had broken her leg. This went undiscovered for several days. When the mother brought the child to the hospital, the medical staff reported the injury to child protective services (CPS). The mother blamed the injury on her son, and CPS refused to return the baby until the boy had undergone extensive psychiatric treatment.

Despite his uncertainty about how to be a father and his violent relationship with his son, Angel was more worried about fathering his daughter when he returned home, stating, "I'll probably end up killin' a guy. Mmm-mmm. [*Shrugs.*] I know I'm a whore, so I don't want my daughter with somebody like me." When I asked if he was worried about raising his son, Angel replied, "Nah. I was with him for two years. So I know what he has to do, and I'm not worried about it. Her . . . I never raised no girl." In another interview, as we discussed the special visit, Angel pointed out that "girls are hard [to take care of because] you can't hit 'em 'cause they're too fragile." Angel did express concern that his son's behavioral issues were too extreme for the mother to handle, and yet when pressed, he worried most about protecting his daughter from men like himself.

Protecting Daughters

When men discussed daughters, they most often highlighted their anxiety that other men would mistreat, manipulate, or abuse their daughters and how they did not want their daughters to have sex. In expressing this concern, my interviewees sounded like fathers on the outside. Much of the research on gender, parenting, and discussing sexuality indicates that fathers discuss sexual topics with their children less often than mothers, that American parents generally are uncomfortable with their children expressing sexual identities, and that protecting daughters from other men and the consequences of sex is one of the primary responsibilities of fathers.[16] Of course, the assumption that it is girls and not boys who bear the consequences of sexual activity relies on the belief that girls are passive and unable to defend themselves and that boys are active pursuers of sex who won't be held responsible for either aggression or pregnancy.

At both NCI and SY, during group meetings and in interviews, men suggested that one of their primary goals for their daughters was making sure their daughters were not sexually active until they were much older. Some men suggested twenty-one as an appropriate age; others declared thirty to be their preferred outcome. Derek was eighteen and served most of his short sentence at SY before being sent to an adult facility; he was solidly built, not particularly tall but wide across the shoulders, and taciturn.[17] During our one interview, he seemed restless, and when I asked him what race or ethnicity he considered himself to be, Derek cut me a scornful look and said, "Black." Derek spent a chunk of time during my field observations in segregation for getting into a fight with another prisoner, and he often seemed reluctant to speak up during group. During a group discussion of things that can blindside a person, the group facilitator, Jasper, mentioned the possibility of your child contracting AIDS. Derek muttered that he didn't want to think about that and then stated firmly, "My daughter not having sex. Ever." Though Derek has both a son and a daughter, his concern that his daughter might engage in sex was his top anxiety. Indeed, Derek never expressed any fears for his son to me or in the group.

Men were far more likely to express anxiety over their daughters having sex. As Stewie's story in the previous section demonstrates, men tended to boast when their sons demonstrated heterosexual inclinations. The stories men told, both in the fatherhood group and during interviews, presented their sons' behavior as a source of pride and amusement. A daughter's sexual behavior, however, was a source of immense anxiety. For example, during one group at the adult facility, as the guys discussed when it was appropriate for children to begin dating, Big Cheese (fifty, multiracial) quipped, "When you have a son, the only penis you have to worry about is his. When you have a daughter, you have to worry about everybody else's." The room broke into laughter, and Big Cheese grinned. This sentiment—that daughters' sexual activity was anxiety producing—was commonly stated in both group meetings and interviews. During group meetings, a mix of laughter and nods of agreement met expressions of this sentiment.

Clayton was twenty-three, white, and serving a short sentence at NCI for driving with a suspended license and no insurance and for violating his parole. He had one son and, though the relationship was rocky, expressed hope that he and his girlfriend would be together when he went home. When I asked Clayton if raising a daughter was different than raising a son, he asked me if I ever watched the daytime television show *Maury*. When I said I didn't, he launched into a story about fourteen-year-old girls who wanted to get pregnant. Finally, he stated, "I'm scared to have a daughter. I really am. Not in the world, just nowadays . . . A boy—you know what I mean?—he can handle himself . . . A boy's always—ah, they're. I don't know . . . It's different, I know that . . . I see these girls out there, twelve years old, walking around with shorts up to here. [*He touches his leg up near the hip.*] If my daughter ever tried leaving the house like that. [*He shakes his head.*] She ain't leaving the house ever again." For Clayton, even the challenges of a hypothetical daughter were stressful, and he expressed relief that he had a son rather than a daughter. Additionally, Clayton linked wearing revealing clothing ("shorts up to here") and the risk of pregnancy. And yet if he had a daughter, he would have been unable to do anything about either concern until he returned home.

Pedro was eighteen and serving a short sentence at SY. He didn't want to discuss the reasons he'd been incarcerated but implied that it was drug related. Both his parents were born in Puerto Rico, but he'd lived his entire life on the East Coast. He had a son and a daughter (with two different women), and during one of his interviews, we discussed the differences between raising a son and a daughter. Pedro declared that his daughter wasn't going to date until she was thirty-three. When I asked him why he didn't have similar concerns for his son, Pedro shrugged and said, "A son, that's my boy. That's my little boy, little Pedro, little Junior right there. [With] a son, you gotta be strict, too, 'cause you don't want them to make the mistake that we did. I love 'em both the same, but little boy, I'll be with him all day. Little girl, you gotta be stricter 'cause they could get pregnant ASAP. They could have sex ASAP, like we did." The underlying anxiety around girls' sexual activity reflected the real likelihood that girls who have children young would become single parents. Pedro, because he was incarcerated, was well aware that sometimes men cannot father their own children, even if they wanted to be connected to their families. He believed his son was better able to take care of himself without a father around but was not as confident about his daughter.

Exceptions to the Rule

Freedom was thirty-four and serving a thirty-five-year sentence for murder at NCI. Freedom claimed that while he had been present at the time of the murder, he hadn't been the one who pulled the trigger. Rather, the person who had actually committed the murder snitched immediately and placed the blame on Freedom. Despite this, Freedom considered himself lucky because he'd been incarcerated before the state enacted truth-in-sentencing changes to parole. As a result, he was eligible for parole after serving 50 percent of his sentence as opposed to 85 percent. Freedom was Muslim, usually wore a kufi, and self-identified as black. He had a son and a daughter with two different women. As we sat in the cinderblock ten-by-ten-foot interview room at NCI, Freedom told me, "I try to keep my ties with them [my children] very well knotted . . . they come here [to visit me], and I'll get to smile 'cause they got jokes. So it just makes my day. I'll go back [to my cell] and I'm all right for the rest of the day. It's like I'm not even in a prison anymore." Freedom spent a large portion of all three of his interviews discussing his children, often without prompting from me. Unlike many of the men, Freedom actively expressed concerns about his son's romantic life as well as his daughter's. That said, Freedom's primary concern for his son related to keeping his boy out of prison. For his daughter, like many of the other men in the group, he was primarily concerned about her having sex too early and being manipulated by "nasty" men.

With his son, Freedom was explicit that his concerns were related to keeping his son out of prison. As we were discussing how his children were doing, Freedom emphasized that it was important to stay in close contact with his son: "He's more likely to wind up in the streets than she is. So what I tell him is the truth about the streets. What [there] is, what's out there, how it's poison, and who's poison, and what to look out for." Freedom was also concerned that romantic relationships would distract both of his children from being academically successful and told me that he spent a lot of time emphasizing that there's "plenty of time ahead" to deal with dating for both of his children.

Other men did occasionally express their concerns about the risk of incarceration for their son during their interviews, but Freedom brought this worry up more than once during his interviews and during group. His willingness to bring up his worries about his son in front of the other men prompted several group discussions in which men expressed similar concerns. Compared to other groups at either facility, the men in Freedom's group expressed more concerns about their sons' risk for incarceration. Furthermore, Freedom told stories about his attempts to guide some of the younger men that he worked with in the prison, asking them, "Do you think your son is gonna survive this [incarceration]? Because this [*he motions around him with one hand at the prison*] is what's lined up for him. Now what are you telling him to avoid? What obstacles do you tell him to look out for?" Freedom presented himself as being something of a father figure for younger prisoners, and this was something he valued about himself.

At the same time, he felt he needed to protect his daughter more than his son. He was particularly concerned that the boys or men she dated would take advantage of her and that she would have sex too early. As he stated, "[I tell her] I was one of those little nasty boys. I said I know what they after and what they do." Freedom was simultaneously disassociating himself from the way he used to be (nasty) and suggesting all young men are only after sex and it is young women, not young men, who are harmed by sexual activity. Freedom captures in two sentences a tension that many of the men struggled with. The aspects of their masculinity that they valued, that they wanted to pass on to their sons, that allowed them to be successful and survive in prison were often the kinds of "nasty" behaviors that put their daughters at risk.

Aeneas was in the same twelve-week cycle at NCI as Freedom and was also serving a long sentence. Born in the United States, Aeneas still felt strong ties to Puerto Rican culture. He was also one of the few men who expressed concern that his son would exhibit sexual behavior too early, and he expended a great deal of effort to be overtly emotional with his son. Aeneas's mother brought his son to visit him almost every Thursday, and I often saw Aeneas bent over the rope in the visiting room, hugging both his son and mother. Aeneas's mother and the boy's maternal grandmother took care of Aeneas's son. According to Aeneas, his son's mother was not very involved in his son's life. Shortly before the fatherhood cycle began, Aeneas's son moved in with the maternal grandmother to get access to a better school. As a result of that move, Aeneas's son moved into the room where Aeneas and his son's mother had conceived their child.

During a conversation in the fatherhood group, the facilitator brought in a handout describing three styles of parenting: lenient, rigid, and flexible. During the discussion on lenient parenting, Aeneas said he "kn[e]w so many people" who were raised like that. Especially "girls. Especially in the suburb." Aeneas started to laugh and told us that once he was in the bedroom with a girl, and her parents came home. "I was freaking out," he explained, and then she said that her parents don't "come through [her] door unless they knocked." He shook his head and rubbed his face. "That's my son's mother." Aeneas continued, saying, "There was no structure in her life," and thanking God that "[his] son [got] structure from [his] family." He used to tell his son all the different ways he used to get into his son's mother's room. "Now he's living in the exact same room. I tell him 'Don't be trying [anything].'" Another prisoner, Alex, looked over at Aeneas, with a little grin, and said, "I think [Aeneas's] proud [that he got into that room]."[18] Aeneas nodded and a quick grin flashed across his face as he boasted that the window was "fourteen feet high!" Then he shook his head and muttered, "My son better not."

During his interview, I asked Aeneas if he was concerned about his son. Aeneas nodded and said that he tried to encourage his son to stay focused on school and not girls. "Not like me," he said, grinning. I asked Aeneas if his son was dating. Aeneas nodded, adding, "He's had a girlfriend, you know, but he's shy, and I like it like that. I was real free-spirited; I was never shy. He is, and I like it like that because I would rather him be a kid than try to be a grown-up. I [was] trying to be a grown-up at thirteen, and I basically was doing all grown-up things." Aeneas had a clear and direct concern that his son would become sexually active too early, and he perceived pregnancy as a problem for boys as well as girls.

What was interesting about Aeneas's concerns was the way other men in the group responded to his statements that he didn't want his son to get anyone pregnant. To be more accurate, it was their lack of response that caught my attention. While Freedom's worries about the possible incarceration of his son resonated with the men in his group, Aeneas's were usually met with silence or a change of subject. During one group meeting at the adult facility, the group facilitator, Alice, warned against treating children differently based on gender. When several of the men in the group frowned and shook their heads, she asked impatiently, "If we're congratulating our sons on sleeping with girls, well, who are they sleeping with?" Aeneas agreed and said that he felt sympathy for men with daughters: "[My son] can't get pregnant, but he can get someone else pregnant, and he's very young. Too young." As Aeneas spoke, two of the guys in the group began talking to one another quietly, and everyone else—except Freedom, who nodded and expressed agreement—remained silent. Alice agreed with Aeneas, and then the conversation changed abruptly to the different definitions of cheating among men and women. Men were prepared to express anxiety about their sons' chances of being incarcerated, though few seemed worried about their boys' sexual behavior.

CONCLUSION

The high numbers of incarcerated men with children, the negative consequences of incarceration on men's connections with families and employment, and the impact of parental incarceration on children all combine to make it important to examine how men in prison understand their obligations to their children. Prisoners struggled on an individual level to mesh their desire to be good fathers and men worthy of respect. This struggle highlighted how an identity as a father could simultaneously offer men resources that undermined their status as dangerously male and increased their emotional vulnerability within the confines of the prison. As is the case on the outside, differentiating their obligations by gender allowed men the space to value aspects of their masculine gender identities. This was particularly true for men with sons, who could, in effect, reward their male children for being "little mes."

In his analysis of middle-class, mostly white fathers, anthropologist Nicholas Townsend discusses the gendered aspects of parenting. Most of the fathers in Townsend's study felt anxiety about protecting both their sons and their daughters but were more concerned about what their sons would do (i.e., boys were considered active agents) and what would be done to their daughters (i.e., girls were considered passive). In short, "They did not attribute agency to their daughters."[19] Additionally, many of the men he spoke with preferred having a son over having a daughter, not only to carry on the family name but also because the men felt they had a better idea of what their sons would need and looked forward to roughhousing, camping, playing sports, and participating in other "masculine" activities with them. The context of the fathers in Townsend's study was quite different than the one on this study, yet the division between "active" and "passive" and the value of a son with whom a father can roughhouse sound quite similar.

Like men on the outside, these incarcerated fathers understood their sons to be "active" participants in the world and their daughters to be "passive."[20] Inside prison, the distinction between "active" and "passive" had a specific meaning: boys needed to be taught to stand up for themselves, limit their emotions, and pursue (heterosexual) sex; girls were easily manipulated and harmed by sexual activity and therefore needed to be protected by their fathers. The institutional setting of the prison had an effect on how men understood the value of the differences between boys and girls as well as the aspects of gendered parenting that the incarcerated fathers emphasized. In the case of sons, incarcerated fathers could validate their masculine performances in an institution (and oftentimes larger culture) that profoundly devalues them. Daughters, in more anxiety-laden ways, also validated the men's roles as protectors while simultaneously emphasizing the limits prison places on fathering. After all, it is difficult for a father to protect his daughter from the threats of other men while he is incarcerated.

Many of the fathers felt that their emotional connections to their children, regardless of the child's gender, were important but that connections to the outside world also made them vulnerable. Nearly all the men presented fatherhood as something they valued about themselves, though men were often private about the value they placed on being fathers, with the exception of humorous stories that allowed men to boast of their son's masculine accomplishments. During one of the NCI support groups, one of the fathers said that he had spent several years deliberately isolating himself from his family because "they [the DOC] use your family against you." In the fatherhood groups and the interviews, men discussed the various ways they attempted to balance their need to feel connected to their children with the realities of incarceration. Gender shaped this balancing act in meaningful ways for the men in this study. While I cannot speak directly about the experiences of the children of these men, it seems likely that how their fathers interacted with them impacted how children perceived, and potentially enacted, their own gender identities.

CHAPTER 3

Unruly Boys and Dangerous Men

SECURITY AND MASCULINITY IN PRISON

AFTER GROUP ENDED ONE day at SY, a CO named Rivera stopped Jasper, the group facilitator, and me in the hallway. Rivera was a big guy, around six feet tall with a bulky build, and in his late forties. Broad and muscular across the shoulders and chest, Rivera also had a fairly large and round beer belly. The CO seemed eager to talk, falling into step with us as we left and then stopping in front of the security station where we would exit and placing his body between the door and us. As we walked, he said that the COs had been having some trouble in the cottages (the housing units) and then brought up one of the men from the fatherhood group. At nineteen, Tarif was already older than many of the young boys and men incarcerated at SY. Technically, the facility was for offenders between the ages of fourteen and twenty-one, but most of the young men I spoke to were sent "up the way" to an adult facility shortly after turning eighteen. The only exceptions were those prisoners who only had months or weeks of their sentences left to serve.

Tarif kept his hair short and often wore glasses. From group to group, he would alternate between sullen silence and boisterous participation. He occasionally spoke about having difficulties with ADHD. On his neck, he had a tattoo in big cursive letters that said, "Fear No One." Tarif stated that he believed the system was stacked against people like him and worried about his ability to protect and provide for his daughter. One day during group, Jasper asked the guys to fill out a survey. One of the questions asked about their racial identity. Several of the young men started cracking jokes by suggesting they all claim false racial backgrounds. Tarif, unsmiling, said, "I'm Latino and black, but I'll put black. Fuck it. We're all brown." Of all the young men I interacted with at SY, Tarif was the only one who made direct statements about structural racial and economic inequality and the ways this disadvantaged him.

Rivera mentioned that Tarif had gotten into a lot of trouble because of the results of a drug test. Rivera's eyes narrowed, and his mouth puckered into a moue of disapproval as he stated that Tarif's counselor had tried to say that

Tarif was on a lot of medications and the results were a false positive. Rivera rolled his eyes as he said this last part. After hedging for a few minutes, Rivera finally said, "He tested positive for PCP." He lifted his eyebrows at us and shook his head. Jasper murmured something I did not hear, and Rivera replied, "Fuck him. He did it to himself"—"it" being a transfer to an adult prison. Jasper sighed, nodded, and said, "Yes, he's ruined his chances, that's for sure."

Rivera was one of the gruffer COs at SY, and his interactions with prisoners revolved around making sure that their shirts were tucked and pants pulled up, that they remained on the correct side of the hallway, and that volunteers and social workers did as little to disrupt the routine of the prison as possible. In short, he went about enforcing the rules of the facility with zeal and, for the most part, interacted with prisoners as though they were unruly young boys rather than dangerous men. Despite his "get tough" attitude, his exchange with Jasper and myself held a hint of regret. Rivera seemed to want us to confirm or agree that Tarif deserved what was coming to him. His disdain for Tarif reveals what happens when young prisoners cross the line: from an institutional point of view, they become "unsalvageable" and dangerous men who belong in an adult prison.

The juvenile justice system in the United States has existed for well over a hundred years. It is based on the premises that young offenders are categorically different from adult offenders, that the state has a moral obligation to protect children, and that rehabilitation should be the primary goal of the juvenile courts. For decades, juvenile justice courts operated more informally than those in the adult system, and dealing with youth offenders was considered treatment rather than punishment. In the 1960s, the juvenile justice system began to make a transition to a more "law-and-order" organization, partially in response to concerns that youths were being held indefinitely for "treatment" and that this kind of rehabilitation was ineffective. These changes, however, did not eliminate the strongly held belief that misbehaving juveniles were different from criminal adults. Instead, there was a concerted effort to develop ways to resolve problems for children outside of the juvenile facilities.[1]

The same social and economic changes that drove the expansion of the adult criminal system impacted juvenile justice in the United States: deindustrialization, unemployment, a spike in the crime rate, widespread institutional "get tough" legal changes, the War On Drugs, a global economic slump in the 1970s and then again in the 1990s, and neoliberalism. It just took longer for those changes to filter through the system. The War on Drugs extracted a particular cost on youth offenders in the United States. The hysteria over "crack whores" and their "crack babies" legitimated a whole host of punitive social policies disproportionately aimed at poor blacks.[2] Writing in the mid-1990s, political scientist John Dilulio Jr. popularized the term "superpredators," capturing, and in some ways contributing to, the public and political anxiety surrounding the remorseless offspring of "crack mothers" and absentee fathers.[3] The term allowed predominantly white politicians, policymakers, academics, and the larger public to talk about their racial anxieties without ever explicitly stating that the superpredator was black and male; the term was understood to refer to "young black thugs . . . holding handguns" without ever saying so explicitly.[4] Yet the anxiety about superpredators did not eliminate the long-standing commitment to saving children within the juvenile justice system.[5] Instead, these two understandings of young offenders now coexist in tension with one another.

Juvenile criminal facilities, for many young men, serve as important settings for learning what is "masculine" and what is not.[6] Young men like Tarif face significant challenges as they transition from teenagers to adults while under the supervision of the juvenile justice system. Both schools and penal facilities have changed in ways that assume certain kinds of young men—those who are poor, dropouts, and racial minorities—are inevitably going to end up becoming adults who threaten the social body.[7] Despite these shifts, many people still believe young offenders can be rehabilitated—but only if they adapt their behavior in ways that are out of step with the world many poor young men inhabit. Young men first learn that they must be strong, independent, and willing to hurt on the streets and in school. Heading to a juvenile facility offers new opportunities to enact these lessons. Young incarcerated men who are also fathers face yet another layer of challenges: the difficulty of enacting their role as breadwinner via legal routes.

In the eighteenth and nineteenth centuries, a political and discursive shift occurred in the legal definition of a criminal.[8] Instead of meaning someone who has chosen to commit a crime, a "criminal" became an inherently dangerous individual who, by his very existence, was a threat to the social body.[9] Criminological theories made a similar transition and increasingly linked the frequency of crime with the internal failings of dangerous offenders.[10] Until the 1970s, criminological scholars, law enforcement, and lawmakers were almost exclusively focused on poor men who commit crimes. While there has been some expansion into the study of female and white-collar criminals, the long-standing focus on poor urban criminals remains embedded in the U.S. criminal justice system. The neoliberal shift in economic and social policies in the 1970s subsumed the long-standing focus in the American criminal justice system on the internal failings of dangerous criminals. This marriage ensured that there was very little room for rehabilitation in the prison system; after all, why waste energy trying to salvage the unsalvageable? What resources exist for rehabilitation prioritize individual responsibility over structural changes.

By comparing the adult and youth facilities—both in terms of how the fatherhood groups worked and how correctional staff enacted security practices—we can examine the way that age informs the shared and taken-for-granted understanding of young male prisoners as a category of people. The presence of both beliefs—that some young men are superpredators in need of control and that juvenile facilities can rehabilitate their residents—affected how and when COs, staff, and social workers at SY enacted security measures. In some ways, the juvenile offenders in my study were more restricted than their adult counterparts. In other ways, particularly their ability to access their children, the young men at SY had more institutional support. Still, managing prisoners' bodies requires the use of particular techniques within a penal facility that rely on treating prisoners as a uniform group.

UNRULY BOYS AND DANGEROUS MEN

Much of this book focuses on incarcerated fathers' experiences in prison—as members of the fatherhood groups, as parents, and as men. That said, prisoners do not make the rules in prison, and as a group, they have little power over the day-to-day running of a facility. The assumptions COs and prison staff make about prisoners and the embedded gender expectations within the structure of prison itself create a specific context in which incarcerated men exist. Put another way, prison is an institution in which masculinity is (re)constructed, undermined, and reaffirmed. In this sense, it bears a resemblance to other institutions in which masculinity comes to be defined, such as school, the workplace, the military, nightclubs, and the street to name just a few.[11] As is the case in other institutional contexts, some elements of masculinity in prison are highly visible while other aspects are made invisible. Prisons, however, are a particular kind of institutional setting, one that actively resists the diversity of masculine practices and identities. The rules and policies in prison, particularly those around security, and the logic COs use to make decisions about rule enforcement rely on all prisoners possessing a uniform masculinity. The dangerous masculinity of adult male prisoners leaves little room for family ties and undergirds the fourth barrier men face: the primacy of security protocols.

When talking about the masculinity of adult men in the prison system, I use the word "dangerous" in order to capture the set of assumptions COs, prison staff, and the general public make about incarcerated men. As a category of men, prisoners are assumed to be hyperviolent, hypersexual, coldly rational, and lacking in emotional connections with others. I draw on two concepts, "hegemonic masculinity" and "hypermasculinity," to develop the term "dangerous masculinity." Hegemonic masculinity, a concept first introduced by Australian sociologist Raewyn Connell in the mid-'80s, emphasizes the impact of the idealized standard of manhood on men's experience of their own gender identity. In current Western constructions, some important components of hegemonic masculinity are authority and dominance over women and marginalized men, emotional self-control, heterosexuality, whiteness, and at a minimum, a middle-class economic position. Few men, if any, demonstrate all aspects of hegemonic masculinity. Instead, hegemonic masculinity represents the most valued or respected forms of masculinity that legitimate the patterns of gender hierarchies between men and women, and among men, through force, cultural norms, and institutional pathways.[12]

Despite its impact on men's individual lives and broad social patterns of inequality, hegemonic masculinity is neither static nor independent of the cultural forms of masculinity that came before; instead, masculine practices combine certain aspects that shift depending on different social categories such as race, class, or sexual orientation. Some men can more easily enact valued practices of manhood when compared to other men. Furthermore, masculinity is a continually contested identity, and a man's social position affects his ability to enact hegemonic masculinity. The more qualities of hegemonic masculinity an individual man can embody, the more likely it is that others will perceive him as a man worthy of respect.

Hypermasculinity emphasizes a subset of the qualities of hegemonic masculinity: callous sexual attitudes, high levels of violence, and the experience of danger as exciting.[13] In focusing on specific aspects of dominant or successful masculine gender performance, hypermasculinity offers some interesting analytic possibilities. For example, scholars have used hypermasculinity as a lens for studying cohesion in military units or the presentation of masculinity in television police dramas.[14] For men in the illegal drug market, the qualities of hypermasculinity overlap with the skills that are both valued and needed to deal drugs at the street level. The work on hypermasculinity offers tools for considering how men in prison link violence and sexual conquest with successful masculine performances. That said, hypermasculinity can be a narrow cultural lens through which to analyze masculine gender performance because it often obscures the influence of race and class on men's gender performances. This is especially true when scholars use hypermasculinity as a set of behaviors to study prisoners. Focusing on how prisoners enact violence and sexual aggression is important, but we must also pay attention to the profound vulnerability of incarcerated men—both in prison and in the outside world.[15] Using the concepts of hypermasculinity and hegemonic masculinity in combination allows for a more nuanced analysis of masculinity in prison.

The phrase "dangerous masculinity" draws on a larger set of widely held cultural beliefs about men—that they are more violent, more sexually aggressive, and less emotional than women; that these characteristics are more extreme among incarcerated men; that minority men demonstrate these characteristics in the extreme; that poor men demonstrate these characteristics in the extreme; and finally, that male criminals are intrinsically different from other people.[16] This last assumption in particular shapes the behavior and interactions among COs, prisoners, and outsiders.

I use the word "unruly" when discussing the masculinity of the young men in this study in order to reflect the two contradictory understanding of young men's masculinity—that they are both salvageable and potential superpredators. The term conveys an important component of young incarcerated men's experiences. In feminist writing, "unruly" women are potentially threatening as they seek to undermine the rules and structures that ensure that men, as a group, remain more powerful than women, as a group.[17] Similarly, although they are male, these young men are outsiders by virtue of their race and class positions; they do not belong to the "normal," ordered functioning society.[18] The term also serves to differentiate between the young men's attempts at enacting masculinity and the more stable and developed masculine identities of the adult prisoners at NCI. SY served as a space for young men to practice enacting adult masculinity and potentially transition from unruly to dangerous.

COMPARING SY AND NCI

The young men at SY and the adults at NCI shared many demographic qualities though they were born at different points during the War on Drugs and the legal changes that came along with it. Many came from the same or similar communities with high rates of poverty and a robust illegal drug market. Most were incarcerated for theft, possession with intent to distribute, assault, and/or weapons charges. They shared racial and ethnic characteristics as well. For example, the most common ethnic identity for Latino men at both prisons was Puerto Rican. A number of the men incarcerated at NCI had begun their interactions with the criminal justice system at a young age and had served time either at SY or at the less punitive juvenile facility in the state. In many ways, the young and adult men I spoke with shared a similar language for what was "masculine," what made someone a good father, and what the best ways were to do time. At both institutions, there was significant variety in the length of sentences. Most of the men at NCI were serving long sentences, though some men would return home within a few years. One or two men expected to be incarcerated for the rest of their lives. Similarly, some of the prisoners at SY had been tried as adults and would eventually serve the remainder of their sentences in adult facilities. Others had been tried as juveniles and were serving short sentences of fewer than five years.[19]

At the institutional level, the structures of the prisons also shared similarities. Both NCI and SY operated—in theory at least—under the same set of rules. Both had the same high security level (four out of five) even though SY housed juveniles between the ages of fourteen and twenty-one. The structures of both facilities, while not identical, relied on similar technologies (cameras, electronic doors, etc.) to maintain control and decrease the possibility of physical threats to COs. Additionally, both facilities shared physical characteristics, such as large-scale walls and hallways, resulting in claustrophobically high levels of observation, an industrially drab appearance, and difficulty in moving from place to place. Dealing with outsiders—visitors, social workers, and volunteers—presented challenges to COs at both facilities because people from the outside rarely understood the challenges of operating a prison facility and behaved in ways that disrupted the routine of day-to-day prison life.

The state where I conducted my research had contradictory and conflicting policies regarding juvenile offenders. On the one hand, like most other states, the juvenile justice system got progressively more punitive toward young offenders in the 1980s and early 1990s. Also similar to the national pattern, the school system in the state where I conducted my research became increasingly reliant on law enforcement for discipline, and the number of school expulsions rose. On the other hand, a fairly strong grassroots movement against this punitive shift emerged early in comparison to other states in the nation. Over two decades (the late 1990s to the early teens), these activists were successful at getting policymakers, DOC personnel, and law enforcement to at least partially scale back the punishments meted out to juveniles. SY reflects these two contradictory trends in the state. In some ways, SY is halfway between a juvenile training school (where young offenders serve very short sentences) and an adult facility.

Reflecting its position as neither a training school nor an adult prison, there were also important differences between SY and NCI. Indeed, the biggest difference between these two prisons was the age of the men incarcerated, a difference that softened the responses of the COs and prison staff and left room for a greater belief in rehabilitation. SY is smaller than NCI, housing almost a quarter of the number of prisoners. The DOC description of SY also emphasizes the importance of educating and mentoring young offenders so that they might successfully reenter society. The DOC description of NCI, on the other hand, emphasizes using education and vocational training to maintain a highly structured environment. Both facilities operate under the same set of administrative rules, but the security protocols were enforced in different ways.

One important aspect of a CO's job at a juvenile facility is to reign in the potentially threatening behavior of these young men and to discipline their bodies and minds into more socially acceptable, docile forms. When compared with the men at NCI, it was easier for the young men at SY to access their families, and COs did not assume that all prisoners were on the brink of sexual assault. However, when the juvenile offenders at SY went too far and did things that, as one prisoner said, "We're not supposed to," they might finally misbehave enough to persuade COs and staff that they were becoming dangerous men no longer worthy of help.

COs and prisoners engaged in a mutually constitutive relationship, with each group trying to define the other in ways that glorified themselves (usually at the expense of the other group). At the heart of this negotiation was a struggle over what it means to be a "real" man.[20] COs—and, to some extent, prisoners—treat masculinity as an inherent identity, although all identities are constructed in day-to-day interactions. Treating masculinity as a static identity—whether it is unruly or dangerous—simplifies security protocols within the prisons. Assuming adult prisoners are dangerously masculine and young prisoners are all similarly unruly boys serves three main functions for COs. First, it provides a clear logic for controlling female outsiders. Second, it elevates and legitimates security as a priority over incarcerated men's connections with family. Third, it helps maintain the divisions between prisoners and COs. In combination, these three functions form the fourth barrier men must navigate to connect to their families—the bureaucracy and security apparatus—a barrier that the fatherhood group facilitators and material were ill-suited to address.

HYPERHETEROSEXUALITY AND THE FEMALE OUTSIDER

Triston was in his midthirties, was quick to smile, and identified himself as Jamaican though he'd been born in the United States. As we exited the cafeteria at the end of a fatherhood group meeting at NCI, he told me, "[My son's] mom wants him to go [to college] someplace around here; I forget where. I want him to go to Florida." The last part of the group discussion had focused on ways incarcerated fathers can still encourage their children to succeed from prison, and Triston was clearly enjoying thinking about his son's future. Triston's son was a freshman in high school, and so the possibility of college was still far away and mostly imaginary. "Why Florida?" I asked. Triston grinned and told me that he really liked Miami: "You can go lots of places for cheap. I'll join him." As we entered the wide, echoing hallway, Triston's smile dropped away. Three COs waited outside of the room. The COs motioned for the men to line up against the wall.

One of the COs, wearing blue rubber gloves, frisked the inmates as another CO searched through their folders. All the inmates were subject to the search. Alice, the group facilitator, asked the third CO, Guy, what was going on. Guy shrugged, saying that this kind of search was normal and he suspected one of the guys in the group was passing "kites" (illegal notes). Guy was white, in his late thirties, and always wore his brown hair in a ponytail. Both prisoners and staff had pointed Guy out to me as a tough but fair CO. After an awkward pause, Guy hunched his shoulders, leaned in, and speaking in a low voice, said, "I had [the] control [room] tape the whole thing. I was in the room next door so I could come in and catch him." As he continued talking, I realized that he also suspected one of the men in the group, Alejandro, of masturbating. When Alice finally understood what he was saying, she replied, "I didn't see anything." Guy shrugged. "They're pros. Unless you're in here eight hours a day, you don't see it." He said that Alejandro was acting suspiciously the week before, his hands in his pockets, looking around for a CO: "When they're looking around, you know something's wrong. [*Points to his eyes with two fingers on one hand.*] You've got to be always watching. These are the bogeymen you warn your children about."

In the end, however, the COs did not find any kites, nor did Alejandro ever get pulled out of class for inappropriate behavior. In this interaction, the CO presented himself as a particular kind of man, one who possessed rational skill ("it takes a pro to catch a pro") and offered masculine protection to female volunteers. However, the part that most interested me was the foil that the CO was constructing his masculinity against: the masculinity of the "bogeyman" prisoner. COs and staff alike assumed that male prisoners possessed a *particular kind* of capacity for aggression and sexual assault, one that was dangerously masculine and unique to prisoners. In doing so, the CO was suggesting that he was protecting not only the female volunteers but also all women and children in society. The assumption that inmates are bogeymen was used regularly to legitimate searches, write tickets, and deny visitors entry. The understanding of the prisoners as bogeymen was an important organizing principle for the relationship between the prisoners and correctional officers as well as prisoners and the larger society; it helped reinforce the division between dangerous (male) prisoners and normal people on the outside.

Alice, one of the group facilitators at NCI, faced constant scrutiny about her clothing. She was an attractive African American who dressed professionally; a number of the women who ran groups at NCI could be described in the same way, and Alice dressed no differently than they did. She was covered from neck to ankle and in ways that fulfilled the written rules regarding clothing at the facility. And yet Alice was subjected to regular conversations with different sets of COs about her clothing. Alice was different from other group facilitators in one key way: she did not behave as if prisoners were more dangerous than other men. In doing so, she rejected an important organizing principle of prison, one that is rarely stated explicitly but is nonetheless fundamental: male prisoners are more dangerous than anybody else.

Alice's brother had been incarcerated when she was a teenager. Alice knew what it was like to enter prison as a visitor, and as many visitors do, she had some unpleasant interactions with COs. As an adult now working in the prison system, Alice was coolly polite with most COs. There were a handful of COs with whom she had warm interactions, but mostly she did as they asked and tried to, as she stated, "Keep it moving." She had run the fatherhood program at NCI for a couple of years and knew a number of prisoners in the facility. She smiled, waved, and said hello to these men as she walked down the hallway.

She saw her work in the prison as giving back to her community. Alice believed that the men in the fatherhood program could contribute to their families and that it was important that they remain connected to them. She often talked about how important her brother was to her as she grew up and how much she valued his efforts to stay involved with her despite his incarceration. Alice did not believe that all prisoners, by virtue of their status as prisoners, were significantly different from other men; she rejected the application of dangerous masculinity. It was clear that her behavior irked the COs. Alice was bothered so much about her clothing that it was common knowledge throughout the prison facility. For example, during my security orientation, the issue of appropriate dress came up. Baxter, the volunteer coordinator, used Alice as an example, mentioning that she often had problems with appropriate dress because she was "curvy and the material of her clothing clings." From a practical point of view, this was not a very good example, since he was unable to follow up with effective advice on how to avoid being curvy. Instead, he pointed out that Alice was cooperative and took the COs' concerns seriously. Of course, Alice had little choice but to cooperate. Getting angry with the COs would have done nothing but confirm their belief that she did not take the prison rules seriously. Focusing on her clothing allowed the COs to discipline Alice, and the issue of her friendliness with prisoners was transmuted into an unsolvable problem: her body. None of the other group facilitators, who shared both stylistic and physical similarities with Alice, experienced this level of interference. COs discussed every aspect of Alice's clothing, and they did so publicly, frequently, and unpredictably. The combination of frequency and unpredictability kept Alice on edge, since she never knew whether there was going to be a problem with what she was wearing.

Staff and COs commonly used the expression "those are the rules" or some derivative when confronting visitors and volunteers. Of the seventy-three group meetings or special visits I attended at NCI, "the rules" came up twenty-six times (35.6 percent of the time). Despite the regularity with which this phrase was uttered, the specifics of "the rules" changed frequently, though the discussion of them usually centered on one of two issues: clothing or paperwork. Prison staff regulate the clothing of visitors, particularly women's clothing that is deemed "too revealing."[21] The facilities I attended were no exception, and female visitors, of any age or race, were subject to an intense level of clothing monitoring. During every special visit, at least one family member had to have an extended conversation about whether her clothing was appropriate. This often resulted in clothing being added, removed, or borrowed from another visitor. In some ways, this changing set of rules can be read as COs struggling to navigate the often contradictory policies set down by administrators, as well as power plays on the part of COs. Underlying "the rules," however, is an assumption that male prisoners are simply unable to control themselves at the sight of female flesh.

One example brought this vividly home for me. At the last special visit I attended, one of the children, a small two-year-old girl, was wearing a tank top dress. Her clothing technically violated the rules regarding clothing that specified that women could not wear tank tops. There was a huge fuss at the front desk, with the COs insisting that neither she nor anyone with her could enter for the visit. Eventually, one of the other women produced an enormous black T-shirt. Once the little girl was "properly covered" from neck to toe, the COs allowed her and her family to enter the visiting room. What makes this example especially troubling is that one of the prerequisites for participating in the fatherhood group at NCI was an absence of any history of committing physical or sexual crimes against children. That is, no one was allowed to participate in the program if they had been convicted of causing harm to a child—theirs or anyone else's. However, the assumed masculinity of *all* male prisoners sexualized a two-year-old girl while simultaneously casting all prisoners as sexual perverts.

At NCI, the COs behaved in ways that assumed all prisoners, regardless of their crime, were sexual predators. The presumed sexuality of prisoners was not connected to the actual real-time behavior of prisoners, and this attitude simplified how COs controlled and managed them and their visitors by creating clear boundaries between prisoners and nonprisoners, between prisoners and COs, and between COs and female volunteers. On the surface, the issue of women's clothing is about female vulnerability and sexual availability. However, this issue does not make sense without the concomitant assumptions that men are unable to control themselves around women and that incarcerated men are particularly violent and hypersexual. By basing the conversation about women's clothing on the presumed dangerous masculinity of male prisoners, COs legitimated what would have been, in the outside world, the sexual harassment of female visitors and volunteers. Furthermore, COs need to control both prisoners and female outsiders for their own good.

At SY, the COs seemed less convinced that male prisoners were sexual predators and were less inclined to believe that prisoners would sexually harass or assault female outsiders given even a sliver of a chance. Instead, COs and administrative staff expressed to Jasper their skepticism about how dedicated the men in the program really were to fatherhood, proposing that the prisoners were likely only interested in contact visits with their children so they could spend time with their girlfriends. Jasper had a quick reply to this critique, responding that he told the guys to focus on their children and usually tried to get someone other than the children's mothers to oversee the visit (such as the prisoners' mothers). Some version of this conversation happened as we entered the prison facility every couple of months. Sometimes, Jasper and the staff person would exchange laughter about the young men's disappointment when they saw their mothers instead of their girlfriends. If he believed COs were sympathetic, Jasper would also discuss his own positive experiences watching young fathers bond with their children. Other times, the staff person was not convinced by Jasper's proposed solution and implied that the young fathers either lacked a sense of responsibility or were too committed to violence to be a good influence on their children.

The COs at SY also seemed less concerned than those at NCI about my being alone with prisoners. For example, the two main places where the fatherhood group met, the library and the conference room, were off the regular path that COs walked as they kept an eye on the facility. And while there was a camera in the library, there wasn't one in the conference room. It was common for groups at SY to occur without a CO walking by the windows of either room, though some COs made a point to walk past the conference room or library several times over the course of a group. In comparison, the cafeteria at NCI had four cameras, and the CO assigned to the part of the hallway that housed the cafeteria would walk by at least once during the hour-long group and usually more often. Though no CO at SY ever said so explicitly, their behavior suggested they weren't worried that the young men they oversaw were on the brink of sexual assault.

The differences in the processes of entering and exiting SY and NCI are also revealing. In particular, although the two facilities had identical levels of security on paper and were governed by the same set of administrative policies, the procedures at SY were significantly less sexualized. This suggests that the COs did not perceive the prisoners in their care as always hovering on the edge of assault. This is not to say that it was easy to enter SY, only that the COs spent less time judging the suitability of visitors' clothing as compared to the adult facility. At NCI, the COs' issues with the "appropriate-ness" of women's clothing was a routine ritual for women visiting the facility and a regular occurrence for female social workers and volunteers. At SY, I never saw a woman denied entry to the facility, and no CO ever hassled me about my clothing, though once, as I chatted with a couple of women in the visiting room, an older woman told me that she'd been asked to leave and buy "appropriate" clothing at a nearby department store because her shirt showed her shoulders.

The COs at SY were still stringent about the clothing of everyone, including social workers and visitors, but their focus was less on how "sexy" the clothing was and more on whether any given item would pass through the metal detector. The COs I spoke with at SY swore that all the metal detectors in the state were set by someone from the central administration and that all the detectors should be at an identical level of sensitivity. And yet the metal detector at SY was finicky and unpredictable. Correctional officers grumbled throughout the process of getting visitors through, though their complaints were usually aimed at the machinery instead of the visitors. Despite the sensitivity of the metal detector at SY, the underwires of bras rarely set off the alarm. At NCI, the physical shenanigans female visitors had to go through in order to get their bras through the metal detector were both funny and depressing. I once saw a woman change bras with her sister in order to get through the metal detector at NCI.

As I stood in line at SY one afternoon, I overheard a conversation between the CO at the front desk and a female visitor. The CO was on the phone, holding the mouthpiece down and away from his mouth. A thin, blonde white woman wearing a yellow T-shirt with a white tank top underneath it and camouflage Capri pants, leaned against the counter and frowned. The CO asked her if she had something she could wear over her tank top, and she replied, "No." He shook his head: "That's two things wrong that [mean] I shouldn't let you in." He lifted the phone up to his mouth and said, "She's got all this metal and shit on her pants." I looked at the pants and noticed they were covered in decorative zippers.

At the time, I was quite certain she would not be allowed into the facility. As the CO talked on the phone, the woman in the yellow shirt turned around and talked to the person in line behind her, a black woman in black pants and a black tank top. The white woman said that, since she had two tops on, she "[didn't] see the problem." Then she looked the black woman up down: "You might have some problems, too." The black woman shrugged and replied, "They never give me trouble about my clothes." I tried not to raise my eyebrows in surprise, as she was very curvy and I could see the band of her underwear sticking out of her pants. Additionally, her top did not meet her pants and a small band of skin showed at her waist. I was certain that at NCI, neither woman would be allowed into the visiting room. After a couple of minutes, two COs came out, one male and one female, with a metal detecting wand. As I left, the white woman stood next to the metal detector, her arms out, while the male CO moved the wand slowly over her pants. The black woman had already entered the visiting room. When compared to the example at NCI, in which a two-year-old was not allowed to wear a tank top dress into the special visit, the differences between the two facilities were substantial, even though both facilities were closely monitoring visitors.

Much like the treatment of black men as hyperheterosexual in the outside world, ascribing excessive sexual urges to all male prisoners is a way to legitimize the use of force and coercion to control and subdue them. Sexual predators, the assumption goes, do not possess emotion or value ties to their families, and they cannot be trusted to behave responsibly. This construction of dangerous masculinity serves as the rationale by which COs control and dominate female outsiders as well as male prisoners. More than that, this construction makes it seem *sensible* to do so.

ACCESS TO FAMILIES

The visiting room is the public face of the penal facility. The bulk of prisoners' time in prison is spent in the deepest areas of the facility: on the cellblock, in the gym or in the chow hall. While some prisoners interact with volunteers in a variety of programs, the most common point of contact with the outside world is the visiting room. At NCI, there was a single U-shaped table that took up most of the space in the room; prisoners sat on the inside of the table and visitors sat on the outside of the table. Prisoners could receive up to three visitors at a time, and children had to be accompanied by an adult (both in the lobby and in the visiting room). Normal contact visits lasted around an hour. Along one side of the visiting room were the glassed-in phone bays where noncontact visits occurred; prisoners spoke to their families over the phone with a glass barrier between them. COs oversaw both kinds of visits. For families, this meant providing paperwork and documentation, stowing personal items, and passing through the metal detector and traps. For prisoners, this meant navigating their way through the prison and providing the COs on duty with appropriate paperwork. For contact visits, prisoners had to keep their hug and kiss greetings brief (less than five or six seconds) and undergo a strip search after the visit. Visitors and prisoners were not allowed to make contact with each other over the table (for example, no hand-holding). COs applied a set of basic assumptions in managing visits: (1) prisoners would try to, in the words of one CO, "cop a feel" even though it was against the rules; (2) prisoners would drag their feet in order to extend the visit or would in some way try to bend the rules; and (3) prisoners could erupt in violence at any time. In these ways, COs ascribed a uniform gender identity to the adult prisoners—one that is hyperviolent, hypersexual, and dangerous.

On busy nights, the visiting room was packed, with roughly twenty prisoners receiving visits at one time. The noise level was deafening, and prisoners sat fairly close to one another (two or three feet apart) in order to make sure as many prisoners received visits as was physically possible, given the space and time constraints. As I moved in and out of the room where I conducted my interviews, I listened to the COs chatting with one another. They often grumbled about the work involved with the visits, promising one another they would wrap up on time and occasionally telling each other to keep an eye on a particular prisoner. The complaints were almost always about the managerial challenges of the visits. Prisoners were seated in the order in which they arrived, the seats closest to the COs filling up first.

The special visits received by the men who successfully completed the program at NCI disrupted the regular routine of daily prison life and exemplified the institutional barriers that prisoners face when trying to maintain connections with their family. To start, these types of visits were of such a low priority to the prison administration that they were canceled unpredictably, moved, and delayed, with the end result being that some men received a special visit and some men did not. Some of the COs expressed frustration about having to deal with special visits, asking me whether I believed the men I talked to had anything useful to say, and occasionally expressed surprise at the level of emotion prisoners displayed during the special visits. Though it was clear that at least some imprisoned fathers were motivated to remain in contact with their children, these men were considered the exception rather than the rule. This was true even though the fatherhood programs in the facility were always full and had long wait-lists. Most staff didn't acknowledge how difficult it is to maintain contact with children while incarcerated, even when prisoners are motivated to do so.[22]

Special visits also caused administrative headaches. The special visits required that the prison facility adjust to the needs of families, and this made a number of staff uncomfortable. Because special visits took place during the same time slot as general visiting, prisoners who were not part of the program couldn't receive visits during program events. As a result, these men complained about being denied visits, and their families sometimes arrived for visits only to find the facility closed. Furthermore, even though general visiting was shut down for the night, the same numbers of COs were on duty regardless of how many men received visits. Unlike a general visit, COs working the special visit had time to stand around and chat. Despite the increased downtime, special visits were stressful for COs because the increased physical contact between prisoners and their families meant there were more opportunities for contraband to move into the prison.

In all of the special visits at the adult facility that I observed, at least one CO would spend a portion of the evening in front of the families wearing the blue plastic gloves used for the body cavity searches they would conduct on prisoners after the visit was over. During regular visiting hours, COs did sometimes come into the visiting room with the blue strip-search gloves on; however, it was usually to ask a quick question of another CO before returning to the hallway—out of sight of families—where they conducted strip searches. In one of the special visits, a CO spent close to forty-five minutes out in the visiting room, staring at families and intermittently snapping his glove against one wrist. In other visits, the COs simply stood around for the two hours, wearing the blue gloves and chatting loudly to one another. Special visits presented challenges to the established routine and required COs to deal with elements of prisoners' lives that were messy and emotional.

The volunteer coordinator at NCI, Baxter, having to explain himself to those positioned above him, was always concerned there wouldn't be enough prisoners at the special visit. It was never clear—to me, anyway—what constituted "enough." In the first special visit I observed, only five men participated. Baxter spent the next two years referring to that group "where only five inmates showed up": "And to shut the whole facility down, visits, everything—I just do the math on that one." The solution Baxter proposed— and implemented—involved combining the special visits of different cycles. In this way, Baxter hoped there would be more men in the visits, thus justifying the headache of shutting down regular visiting hours and keeping so many COs occupied for such a small number of prisoners.

However, combining the visits did little to ensure the groups were larger because prisoners were regularly moved from facility to facility. The special visits of the second and third group I observed (the second and third cycles) were combined to try to make sure that "enough" men received the special visit. But by the time the combined special visit occurred, only two of the ten men from the second cycle were still in the facility and, therefore, allowed to receive their visit. This meant that this special visit included about the same number of men (roughly ten) as most of the other visits I observed. Despite the limited increase in the number of men participating in the special visit and the high number of prisoners who did not receive their visit as a result of this policy shift, Baxter told me that the higher-level administrators considered the combined special visit a success.

The differences between the family visits at adult and youth facilities, however, were significant. At SY, fewer COs were on duty during the special visits (one as compared to four or five), suggesting that the visits were less of a burden on COs and also that the security protocols assumed that one CO, in combination with cameras, could oversee a large group of juvenile offenders and their families. The COs on duty also interacted more pleasantly with the visiting family members, social workers, and volunteers at SY than they did at NCI. Though the COs at SY could be grumpy and impatient with the large number of visitors at the special visits, the more relaxed clothing rules meant that most visitors weren't anxious they were going to be denied entry. This improved the overall interaction between visitors and the COs. Additionally, not once during the special visits at the youth facility did a CO interact with families while wearing strip-search gloves. In fact, I did not spot a CO wearing those blue gloves in the visiting room at any point during my two and a half years at the youth facility. After one of the special visits, a CO pulled on rubber gloves and began looking over the area where the visit had occurred in order to make sure that nothing had been left behind, but by that point, the prisoners and their families had exited the visiting room.

The special visits at SY were overall quite different from the five special visits I observed at NCI. For example, the food offered to families at NCI slowly declined until Healthy Connections staff could not even offer children gift bags on their way out the door. At SY, the food was never an issue at the large special visits. The special visits often had juice, milk and some kind of snack (such as cupcakes). Correctional officers and staff at SY also exerted less rigid control over what the volunteers and staff from Healthy Connections could bring in, as compared to NCI. For example, at one of the special visits at SY, staff from Healthy Connections brought in a printer so that they could print paternity paperwork for the fathers to fill out. Additionally, it was possible to bring in outsiders to the special visit in much higher numbers. The COs and other staff at SY were willing to make more room for the fatherhood visits, and the administrative staff often seemed quite enthusiastic about them, laughing and smiling as they watched the visits.

Us versus Them

In his classic description of total institutions, sociologist Erving Goffman points out that contact between the large managed group (the inmates) and the supervisory staff has to be highly restricted in order for the total institution to work. More important, any total institution has a series of formal and informal mechanisms—such as rules guiding interactions—to maintain the distance between groups.[23] Despite the necessity for clear and formal divisions between staff and inmates, total institutions are intimate in unexpected ways. A CO supervises prisoners' food provision, toiletries distribution, bathroom behavior, visits with family, masturbatory practices, leisure time, and conflicts. During the year he spent as a correctional officer as Sing Sing, journalist Ted

Conover found himself drawn deeper into the institutionally carved pathways that encourage COs to dehumanize prisoners in order to get the job done as safely as possible. The division between COs and prisoners, "us" versus "them," comes through in his book as his audience learns next to nothing about the personal lives of the prisoners. Indeed, rules of the institution encouraged Conover to learn as little as possible about the men he guarded.[24]

In some ways, it was easier for COs at SY to maintain the division between themselves and the young men they oversaw. The age difference alone made it unlikely that the young men would consider themselves on the same footing as the COs. I could see the impact of the age difference on maintaining control and institutional divisions in the tactics that COs used to manage prisoners' clothing and movement within the facility, particularly when compared with similar protocols at the adult facility. At both facilities, the COs enforced rules regarding the appearance of prisoners' uniforms. At NCI, this primarily meant that prisoners tucked their shirts in when they walked down the hallway. However, once prisoners were no longer moving—for example in the cafeteria where the fatherhood group occurred or in the visiting room—many men untucked their shirts, and COs allowed them to do so. Almost without fail, as the men in the fatherhood group stood to leave, any man who had untucked his shirt placed it back into its institutionally correct position. As a result of this unspoken agreement between prisoners and COs about clothing, only once in the entire time I moved in and out of the prison did I hear a CO shout "Tuck in your shirt" down the main hallway of NCI.

This is in direct contrast to the situation between the COs and the prisoners at SY. The refrains "Pull up your pants" or "Tuck in your shirt" echoed in the large hallway of the main part of the prison nearly every week. While young men had control over whether their shirts were tucked in and clearly engaged in testing the COs by untucking their shirts, the issue of their pants was less clear. Many of the prisoners at SY wore uniforms that were too large for them, their oversized pants, shirts, and jackets swallowing their narrow not-yet-entirely-adult frames. The size of the uniforms made it quite difficult to keep the pants at the height COs seemed to think was appropriate. The staff at the prison facility provided prisoners with their clothing, and it seems unlikely to me that the prison facility staff provided their young charges with larger-sized uniforms for "style" purposes. It seems more likely that the uniforms came in a limited number of sizes, many of which were too large for teenagers.[25]

No matter the source of the problem with oversized pants, controlling how the young men wore their clothing offered an opportunity for COs to exert authority through the routinized micromanagement of day-to-day rules.[26] While at the adult facility, the micromanagement of prisoners relied on the assumption that all prisoners are dangerous sexual predators, at the youth facility, the COs linked routinization to the expectation that young prisoners were unruly and unable to obey simple commands. In order to maintain the division between COs and prisoners, the staff at SY infantilized young men by drawing on larger cultural anxieties about wild and disorderly teenaged boys.[27] In some ways, the COs' response to the juvenile prisoners' uniforms mimicked the behavior of school administrators enforcing dress codes.[28] The added element of prison security also meant that COs were training young men about how prisoners should behave.

Similarly, how COs at NCI and SY controlled the movement of prisoners highlighted the ways youth impacted the organizational logic of facility security protocols and the maintenance of the divisions in prison. The hallways at both facilities were about twenty feet across. At NCI, prisoners were expected to keep to the right half of the hallway in whichever direction they were headed. As result, any prisoner moving down the hallway had roughly ten feet of space to move in, prisoners going different places had room to space themselves apart from one another, and there was no opportunity for prisoners moving in opposite directions to run into one another. Prisoners at NCI also had to go through metal detectors every hundred yards or so, suggesting that COs considered prisoners dangerous enough that they could, in the space of a hundred yards, get their hands on a contraband item while also minimizing how many COs needed to be on duty in the hallway.

The only exception I saw to these rules at NCI was when a large group of prisoners moved from the gym back to the block that contained their cell units. At that time, COs stopped other smaller groups of prisoners at security checkpoints while the men returning from the gym were allowed to spread out over the hallway. A number of prisoners would speed-walk, hoping to get back to the unit first to use the showers before anyone else. A group of three or four COs walked behind the large group, shouting at men not to run and speaking into their walkie-talkies to notify the security guards along the hallway that a large group of prisoners was headed their way. For an outsider, this looked remarkably like border collies herding sheep.

At SY, there was significantly less movement of prisoners in the main facility as compared to NCI, and the rules for prisoners were stringent in different ways. About six weeks after I began conducting fieldwork at SY, a painted yellow line appeared on one side of the wide hallway. The distance from the wall to the yellow line was roughly three feet wide, enough for two people to walk side by side though they would have to be almost touching at the shoulder in order to remain inside the line. Prisoners were required to remain inside the yellow line no matter which direction they were walking, something that caused occasional awkwardness as prisoners tried to pass one another within the narrow confines. The rest of the hallway width (approximately seventeen feet) was reserved for traffic by COs, volunteers, and other staff. Prisoners were to remain inside the yellow line even when the rest of the hallway was empty. The narrow space "behind" the yellow line suggested that the COs and staff were more concerned about prisoners having too much space to move around rather than prisoners' getting into fights, since prisoners walking different directions would run into one another. Additionally, the yellow line facilitated COs' management of both prisoners and outsiders.

One day after group, Jasper and I stood in the hallway talking with one of the fathers from the group. Eric was the only white father who participated in the SY fatherhood program during my fieldwork. He was eighteen and had a mop of red hair. The three of us were standing by the door to exit the main part of the prison and enter the lobby, to one side of the security station. Eric hadn't been in the group long, about four or five months, and was close to his release date. Eric talked wistfully about "being somebody" when he got home within the next couple of months; he was considering joining the military. He was not sure if it was better to join the military and support his daughter or if he should try to stay close by so that he could spend time with her.

As he talked, he shifted his body weight several times and ended up with one foot outside of the yellow line. Almost immediately, there was a crackling sound from the security station, and a CO said through a loudspeaker, "Get behind the yellow line!" Eric hunched his shoulders and gave us a chagrined smile as he pulled his foot back behind the line. I realized with a start that the CO must have been watching and listening to us the entire time. Shortly after managing Eric's position in the hallway, the CO buzzed open the lock on the door. The loud sound clearly communicated that the CO thought it was time for Jasper and me to exit the facility. As Jasper waved goodbye, Eric frowned and rubbed the back of his neck. I got the impression that Eric wanted to continue the conversation. The yellow line served to remind all three of us of our place in the prison hierarchy: Eric's at the bottom, volunteers and social workers above him, and COs managing everyone.

Dana Britton's work on the prison as a gendered organization offers a more nuanced view of COs' perspectives on the division between prisoners and everyone else. In particular, Britton focuses on the intersection of race and gender identities in order to capture the nuances of COs' experiences at work. If I had interviewed COs rather than prisoners, I undoubtedly would have seen similarly nuanced understandings of their roles inside prisons. However, what COs think privately in their own minds, in casual conversation, or in the outside world has only a small bearing on what they do, and are expected to do, at work. Whatever their personal feelings, COs must maintain the division between prisoners and everyone else. It is one of the central requirements of the job, and it is remarkably difficult to accomplish.

CONCLUSION

Gender is an inescapable element of organizational structures.[29] Before COs make choices about enacting discipline over prisoners, other actors and institutionalized pathways have already divided the incarcerated population into two groups based on gender. This is part of the reason transgender prisoners cause so much consternation among prison staff.[30] Transgender prisoners undermine the "naturalness" of the gender binary. Similarly, female gender identities and roles as mothers impact the organization of women's prisons. One of the central themes of sociologist Lynne Haney's book *Offending Women* revolves around how the staff at the two programs she observed used motherhood (and children) as both a reward and a punishment for female prisoners. Though it was quite problematic for the children, particularly in the program Haney observed in 2002, it is worth pointing out that the women in both programs lived with their children while incarcerated. No such program exists for incarcerated fathers.

COs tend to view male prisoners as both more violent and easier to deal with than female prisoners because their violence is more rational and therefore more predictable.[31] Sociologist Jill McCorkel points out that while there are similarities between men's and women's prisons (in particular, the decline of the rehabilitative ideal, increasingly punitive policies, and a rise in the number of black and brown prisoners), women are treated as less-than-rational actors within the prison system.[32] Where the staff in men's prisons focus on maintaining control over the violence men's bodies can enact, women's prisons focus on the "habilitating" the mind and ordering the disordered self. Seeing men's violence as relatively rational stems from the idea that male prisoners have little or no connection to the outside world and few emotional needs. In fact, the entire structure of prison, as well as the attitude of many staff members, is built on the belief that incarcerated men have little emotional connection to their families and are of little value to their children.[33] On this basis, prison staff routinely exercise control and discipline over male prisoners by ignoring or minimizing their connections to children, romantic partners, and family. This is particularly true for adult prisoners.

Many young boys are literally becoming men behind bars, in terms of reaching the age of majority but also by becoming fathers. Estimates suggest that roughly a quarter of young men in prison are also fathers, but we have no national-level information on how many of those young men were incarcerated at the times of their children's births.[34] Drawing on data from Transition

Research on Adjudicated Youth in Community Settings, education researchers at the University of Oregon found that the juvenile fathers in their study were at a higher risk to return to prison than nonfathers. If previously incarcerated fathers had access to employment and community resources, however, the young men were less likely to recidivate than their nonfather counterparts.[35]

Sociologist Anne Nurse tracked young men as they entered and left prison and focused on their experience of prison and its effect on young men's life chances once they leave. Nurse finds that while the spirit of rehabilitation remains, lack of funding, overcrowding, and understaffing undermine the likelihood that young offenders will have access to the resources needed to prevent their recidivism. For young fathers, the difficulty of keeping the promises made to the mothers of their children during incarceration, particularly promises to locate legal work and desist from crime, has a significantly negative effect on young men's relationships with their children.[36] Nurse also points to a pervasive fear of violence, from both staff and other prisoners, and the link between this fear and violent and misogynist masculine performances. This last point is particularly important, as it suggests one thing that young men might find rewarding about a dangerously masculine performance: diminished vulnerability. In this, young offenders resemble their adult counterparts, drawing on institutionally and culturally accepted masculine practices to manage their experiences in prison.

In this chapter, I have outlined how COs responded to unruly boys and dangerous men and the ways that this simplified when and how they enacted security practices. There were clear links in the assumptions COs and institutional policy made about these two groups: both were in need of discipline (both internal and external), and neither group could be trusted. For many COs (like Rivera at the beginning of this chapter), though young offenders had more opportunities and programs to rehabilitate, it was more likely that they would fail and end up incarcerated dangerous men. This partially reflects the larger social context in schools and neoliberal policies that decreased state investment in rehabilitation and increased resources for incapacitation. In the next chapter, I discuss masculinity and incarceration from the perspective of the prisoners as they struggle to balance the demands of fatherhood with their need to be men who are respected by other prisoners as well as COs. Most prisoners, like most Americans, have absorbed the message that they are individually responsible for their failure and success. The contradictions between being a father, which requires emotional vulnerability, and being respected, which requires the will to hurt, created problems for the incarcerated fathers in the program—problems that the fatherhood program material and group facilitators could do little to resolve.

CHAPTER 4

Game Faces and Going Up the Way

ENACTING MASCULINITY IN PRISON

AENEAS WAS INCARCERATED AT the age of seventeen on a felony-murder charge. In the course of robbing a gas station, one of his coconspirators shot and killed the clerk working that night. Under the felony-murder law in the state, Aeneas was found as culpable as the shooter and sentenced to thirty-eight years without the possibility of parole.[1] Now in his thirties, he talked about how difficult it had been to adjust to life in prison. Shaking his head, he told me, "I came in here and was like—man, the first thing I did on my first day [in prison] was make a weapon . . . Because I didn't know what the hell to do. I didn't know what to expect. All these prison movies that I used to watch—*American Me, Blood In Blood Out*, these movies that they had out there . . . I'm thinking, 'Oh, my God, I got no chance.'" Indeed, the first several years of Aeneas's life in prison were marked with violence and conflict. During an altercation over whether he would become affiliated with a gang, another prisoner broke Aeneas's jaw. After six weeks in the hospital, with his jaw still wired shut, Aeneas had to engage in a lengthy battle with the prison administration to ensure he wasn't returned to the same facility where his attackers were housed.

After he recovered from the assault, Aeneas was even more willing to fight: "It was rough when I first came in here, especially when you came here young. And little. That's why I was putting up my dukes quickly. I was like this"—he held up his fists, then laughed and rubbed his hand through his short dark hair. "'The next person that says something . . .'" He shook his head and shrugged. "I received a lot of disciplinary actions [infractions]." Aeneas fought with other prisoners as well as COs. Once, as a result of a verbal argument he had with two COs, he ended up in segregation for seventy-three days.

Aeneas's story, as well as many of the remaining stories in this chapter, is what most people expect to hear about when they pick up a book on prison. Our cultural images of prison emphasize prisoner-on-prisoner assault and sadistic prison guards.[2] These images are so powerful that it can be difficult to see past them and into the specific context of the prison. In chapter 3, I focused on understanding the commonsense assumptions that COs develop about prisoners as a group of men that help them maintain order within the prison. Imagining prisoners as a group that shares a singular dangerously masculine identity allows COs to minimize certain kinds of risk, even as the security protocols intensify prisoners' isolation from their families and thereby increase the costs of backing down from conflict.

All male prisoners, not just the ones convicted of violent crimes, are perceived (by prison administrators, staff, and society at large) as violent, dangerous, and in need of inflexible regulation.[3] And yet prisoners who are unwilling or unable to enact violence increase their chances of victimization within the penal system. The narrow confines of prison mean that the opportunities to enact masculinity are severely curtailed. A prisoner can't even take a shower or go to the bathroom exactly as he pleases. Nearly every aspect of prisoners' lives occurs at the whim and will of the prison administration. As a result, masculinity in prison is a constant battle to remain dominant. Given the few resources a prisoner can dominate, control of sexual resources (namely, other men) becomes pivotal. In the isolated, all-male environment, sexual orientation becomes meaningless or, perhaps more accurately, the meaning of homosexuality is redefined in a context where there are no women against whom masculinity can be shaped. How an inmate demonstrates his sexuality (i.e., engaging in sexual assault, becoming the victim of sexual assault, or carving out the space for neither) can become his social role within the prison.[4]

This reality is part of the reason that sexual assault between prisoners is usually one of the first things that come to mind when people think about incarceration. Reliable rates of sexual assault in prison are difficult to collect, but the *threat* of sexual assault is prevalent.[5] Prison staff often do little to prevent assaults, and in some of the worst cases, COs use the threat of sexual assault to keep prisoners in line.[6] The Prison Rape Elimination Act of 2003 (PREA) prioritized the creation of programs aimed at decreasing sexual assault in prison, but to date, it has had limited success.[7] Furthermore, nonsexual assaults between prisoners and between COs and prisoners are equally difficult to quantify and remain as pervasive a threat as sexual assault.[8] Avoiding victimization, then, often hinges on demonstrating "a will to hurt" in order to gain respect and reduce the chances of assault.[9] The will to hurt, in turn, feeds into and confirms the expectation that prisoners are dangerously masculine.

Masculine gender performances occur in both private and public spaces. For many men in prison, before they were incarcerated, successfully enacting masculinity was closely linked with their public presentation of self on the street. On the outside, most men have other arenas of life (for example, domestic relationships) where they may find rewards for masculine behaviors less valued than they are in public settings. Life in prison, however, is both heavily observed (by other prisoners and COs) and isolated from the rest of the world. By design, prison compresses the possibilities for performing a number of valued aspects of self and places limitations and pressures on prisoners to engage in violence in particular ways. Some of these ways echo outside patterns of behavior on the street, and others are specific to the prison system. The need for imprisoned men to enact violence as part of their gender performance is not unique to either prison or prisoners.[10] All men negotiate how and when they are willing to enact violence and do so in numerous institutional settings.

The men in this study talked about enacting masculinity—particularly violence—in ways that confirmed their status as dangerous men who should be separated from society. At the same time, men drew on their status as fathers to try to carve out space to be more than an "animal." These two aspects of their identity—as violent men who should be respected and as nurturing fathers—did not mesh particularly well and created stress for incarcerated fathers. When it came to masculinity, the men presented themselves, the prison, and the COs along a continuum of "hard" and "soft." Someone who is "hard" is tough and worthy of respect and therefore not a victim. A key element of claiming "hardness" in prison was finding ways to dismiss or denigrate the power COs held over basic, everyday needs. The men were also aware that getting caught violating one of the numerous rules of the facility meant decreased access to their families.

This Prison Is "Soft as Hell"

Incarcerated men, like many people on the outside, define masculinity along a continuum that links weakness with femininity and strength with masculinity.[11] The men discussed "hard" versus "soft" masculinity in the fatherhood groups as well as in one-on-one interviews, and the terms came up dozens of times. Many of the men described the prison system of the state where the facilities were located as "soft as hell," with the exception of the two maximum-security facilities, one of which housed prisoners the DOC considered gang-affiliated. Describing the prison as "soft" meant several things. First, the men agreed that there were fewer fights as compared to the state's prison system in the 1990s, as well as fewer prisoner deaths, and that sexual assault happened but was not pervasive. When I first began discussing the prison with my respondents, all three of these things seemed like positive developments to me, so I didn't understand why so many men curled their lip as they called the prison "soft." The prisons in California and in the South were considered to be the toughest places to be incarcerated, though no prisoner expressed a desire to be incarcerated there instead of the state they were currently in.

Although the DOC staff had a high level of control over prisoners, a world of activities and power struggles existed out of sight of the COs. Much of this centered around the underground food market and the disputes that emerged while men played cards and other games. For instance, even though prisoners resented the policy change and sought to get around it, the prison administration and COs had managed to almost entirely eliminate cigarette smoking in the prison facility. Cigarettes became a highly sought-after item on the black market and increasingly difficult to acquire. Based on my conversations with prisoners, it seemed to be easier to get scheduled drugs than cigarettes.

Perhaps more important to daily life was the treatment of "snitches," prisoners who told on other prisoners. The topic of snitches came up in every twelve-week cycle at the adult facility and multiple times at SY. During a group at NCI, one prisoner suggested that snitching was not acceptable and another man, Big Cheese rolled his eyes as he said, "Everybody in the joint [prison] be doing it." Several men made noises and nodded in agreement. Big Cheese's assertion, that prisoners got away with snitching, was a widely held belief at the adult facility and one that older prisoners pointed to when they suggested that life in prison had changed in ways they didn't like.

G had been in and out of prison over the past thirty years, mostly on drug and assault charges. During one of his interviews, G commented that the level of snitching that went on in the prison today wouldn't have been tolerated twenty years ago. The snitches in the facility would have been beaten and ostracized, but nowadays nothing happens to them. G felt that it used to be easier to keep to yourself and do your own time, but COs now felt empowered to talk to prisoners in ways that were not acceptable. He stated, "You [a CO] would have got hurt, you would have easily got stabbed, for just the way they talk . . . [The] officers around here, they don't have a clue. I mean, I'm glad they're in [this state] 'cause if they went somewhere else, they'd probably be dead [. . .] They come from a [place of] 'I'll say anything and do anything,' 'cause that's the space that they're given." It was unclear if G thought the issue was that prisoners had become too tolerant of snitches or that COs were more effective at monitoring the facility.

Interestingly, the young men at SY were more likely to complain that their codefendants were snitches and were more likely to end up in segregation for engaging in fights with other prisoners over snitching. Laredo was black and serving a short sentence at SY on charges related to selling drugs. He wore his hair buzzed short and had a neatly trimmed goatee. During one interview, Laredo commented, "It can get crazy in [the prison]. Two guys just got beat up [. . .] for bein' snitches."When I asked him how common that was, he shrugged and wouldn't answer the question.[12] Over the course of two and a half years of fieldwork, four of the young men in the fatherhood group at SY ended up being caught and punished for assaulting a prisoner they thought had snitched on them. None of the men at NCI were removed from the group for the same reason.

Messiah, who was in his late forties and born in Aruba, thought the issue lay with the prisoners. He had been incarcerated early on in his life, been out for a number of years, and then returned to serve a fourteen-year sentence. He stated that NCI was "lenient" and the prisoners were too comfortable.With a disappointed head shake, Messiah told me, "People in here, they so scared.You got guys in here with a hundred years, and the CO say, 'Yo, sit down and shut up.' And they go sit down and shut up."When I asked him why that was the case, Messiah shrugged and said that it used to be easier to get certain things through the commissary. Now only snitches could "get privileges; they get radios and hot pots, and you know, they get little—oh, their main thing is this oil . . . It's cologne, but it's oil based." Even though Messiah asserted that it was the flaws of the prisoners that allowed for snitching, the ability of the COs to limit what prisoners could access successfully created space for prisoners to inform on one another.

This tension between the effect of the individual flaws of prisoners and the COs' reliance on institutional power highlights an important debate over masculinity within prison.That is, COs had power over prisoners not because of their own individual strength but because they were willing to use technology and blackmail to gain control.This opened up the possibility for prisoners to claim strength and personal "hardness" in the face of "soft" institutional power. Power in prison is more a constellation of practices than a linear application of force, though the physical barriers of prison—the concertina wire, fences, locks, and gates—do operate as direct applications of coercion. Similarly, when COs break up fights, catch prisoners breaking the rules, and move individuals into segregation, they are using direct force to control prisoners.Without such direct force—"hard" power if you will—COs would be unable to maintain control inside prisons. And yet it would be equally ineffective to rely solely on such physical power. The use of technology—such as body alarms and cameras—is efficient and does not require COs to put themselves in direct danger. Similarly, by controlling prisoners' access to resources, COs can punish and reward behavior and elicit obedience without direct physical coercion. This particular set of techniques, "soft" power, is arguably the most effective tool COs have for maintaining control over prisoners.

After a while, I began to hear something different in the prisoners' description of the prison as "soft."The word itself is highly feminized, suggesting that this was not a prison system that could handle "real" men. The word "soft" allowed prisoners to denigrate the capacity of COs to control the prison because their manner of control was rooted in technology and blackmail rather than physical strength. Prisoners presented their masculinity as being in conflict with the masculinity of the COs. Put another way, prisoners could, and did, highlight that they were strong in the face of the limitations of prison, a quality that made them "harder" than the COs. Was the willingness of a prisoner to fight for respect a sign that he was a violent, dangerous bogeyman or that he was someone with strength, dignity, and honor? Was the dedication of a CO to rational skill and "the rules" indicative of his or her successful enactment of the masculine requirements of the job or an indication that COs have, as one prisoner put it, "power issues"? Prisoners and COs offered up different answers to these questions that hinged on contestations over what it meant to be a man.[13]

At the end my fifth twelve-week cycle at the adult facility, there was a last-minute change to the scheduling of the special visit. In the tenth meeting (out of a total of twelve), the group facilitator, Star, announced that the special visit wouldn't occur until almost six months into the future and that their group would be combined with two other cycles that had yet to happen. Men in the group shouted their disapproval, a couple of them got up and started to pace, and there was much arm-waving and frowning. A number of men in the cycle were well aware that their chances of being transferred to another facility over the next six months were high. As Star and I left that night, Baxter, the volunteer coordinator, joined us in the hallway. One or two men tried to stop and talk to Baxter, but the volunteer coordinator told them they would have to contact him formally by writing a complaint. Two COs hovered nearby and told the men who had stopped in the hallway that they needed to get going. Star reported that the prisoners were "some kind of unhappy when they found out about the special visit." Baxter nodded and said he could tell just from her face and that she should be sure to direct any complaints to him. He added, "You be sure and tell them it isn't up to you; you'd have the visit right after the group, if you could." Star said she was going to do just that.

When the prisoners did complain to Baxter, he too pointed further up the chain of command and, like Star, suggested that he was sympathetic to their position but that there was little he could do. In fact, the chances of one of the men speaking directly to the person or committee who made this decision were virtually nonexistent. In this way, the hierarchal authority structure in the prison created a diffuse kind of power that was almost impossible for prisoners to directly confront. They could write letters and complain to the social worker or volunteer coordinator, but their actual ability to enact change was quite limited. At the next meeting of the program, one of the prisoners walked into class and directly over to the table where Star was sitting. She looked up in surprise as George, a heavyset white man in his early twenties, demanded to know how he could get a "hold" put on him to make sure he remained in the facility long enough to receive the special visit. Star suggested he speak to Baxter, and George replied with an impatient huff, "I did. [Baxter] dirtbagged me in the hallway. He looked at me [and said]"—George twisted his mouth into a tight line and said in a nasty tone—"'Ain't nothin' gonna change.'"

One of the other men called out, "At least he was tellin' you the truth." There was a round of laughter and hisses. George stuck to his guns: "Homeboy trying to dirtbag me. I was staying out of trouble to see my child, and now you're gonna take that away from me." Star held up a hand and shook her head: "He was just trying to avoid an awkward situation. Do you know how hard it is to tell someone something like that?" George made a snorting sound of disbelief: "Tell a criminal no?"

Another man in the group, Eustis, started snickering. Eustis was tall and thin and wore his hair in long dreadlocks.[14] Eustis tapped the table in front of him with his knuckles and said, "Baxter was afraid of the beatdown; he was nervous." Other men in the group started laughing, and Eustis grinned. He pointed with his chin at me: "Star and Anna know." I realized that he was referring to his own attempt to talk to Baxter at the end of the tenth class. Raising the pitch of his voice slightly and drawing his body up into an upright position, he impersonated Baxter offering to escort Star and me out of the facility: "'I have to walk these ladies down.'" Eustis laughed and shook his head. His mocking impersonation of Baxter directed attention away from the diffuse institutional power and onto the possibility that Baxter should be afraid of a physical altercation with one the prisoners from the group. Because it was couched as a joke, Eustis's comment wasn't a direct threat and was, therefore, unlikely to garner official punishment.

Well aware of their subordinate position in the prison hierarchy, prisoners actively pursued available avenues of reclaiming power, dominance, and respect. For example, prisoners emphasized the methods of dominance most available to them—direct coercion or strength of will—as markers of a man worthy of respect. Prisoners sought to redefine the indirect methods of control COs relied on, particularly when and if prisoners can access material resources, as inferior, weak, and "soft." In other words, COs used strategies that were feminine and therefore unworthy of respect in the highly masculine atmosphere of a men's prison.

"GOING UP THE WAY":
ACHIEVING MANHOOD AT SY

The young fathers at SY also presented masculinity along a continuum that echoed the "hard"/"soft" division at the adult facility. It was their status as adults that captured most of the young fathers' attention. The prisoners at SY wanted to be perceived as men rather than boys—by me, their families, COs, and other prisoners. For the young men at SY, men were "hard" and boys were "soft." They reflected, accurately, the larger cultural beliefs about the differences in strength and "hardness" between boys and men.[15] Though SY technically housed prisoners between the ages of fourteen and twenty-one, men were often sent to an adult facility around eighteen or nineteen. The prisoners and social workers called this "going up the way." Not one father in the program I observed was over the age of twenty, and being transferred to an adult facility was the most common way men left the fatherhood program at SY.

Many of the young men in the group wanted to "go up the way." The men at SY sought to resist the institutional understanding that their youth meant they were in need of constant supervision and their ability to enact manhood should be severely curtailed. The young men in the program sought to differentiate themselves from other youths in the facility, particularly the youngest offenders, calling them "young minded," "youngins," and describing SY as a "little kid jail." Their desire to go to an adult facility remained strong even though they would likely have less access to their children as a result of no longer being in Jasper's fatherhood program. In addition to arranging special visits, Jasper arranged individual visits between men and their children as often as prisoners' families were willing to make the trek. The level of access fathers at SY had to their children was very high when compared to NCI. Furthermore, moving to an adult facility would decrease their access to educational and job-training programs and, potentially, increase their exposure to violence from other prisoners. Nonetheless, "going up the way" was a desirable outcome for many of the young men at SY.

As young men entered the room where the fatherhood group occurred at SY, they would exchange greetings, slapping each other's backs, laughing, and exchanging gossip about who had gotten put into segregation and who had gone up the way. The only thing that elicited more expressions of jealousy or curiosity was when other prisoners were released into the outside world. One day, after the group at SY was over, Jasper, myself, and four of the young men from the program stood around chatting. I told two of the young men, Stewie and Achilles, that I was trying to schedule an interview soon because I was concerned they might be transferred to an adult prison. Stewie shrugged and told me that he was turning nineteen soon and couldn't promise anything. Achilles nodded in agreement. The four then began discussing how they each wanted to go up the way. With a frown, I asked them why. Raphael, just shy of eighteen and black, looked at me from the corner of his eyes and said slowly, as if he couldn't understand why I'd ask such a question, "There's little kids here; we grown." For the young men at SY, separating oneself from the "little kids" was essential to establishing one's identity as a man.

Though men over the age of eighteen were regularly sent up the way as a result of age, a number of the young men in the group believed they would get sent to an adult facility if they misbehaved. During one group at SY, as we waited for Jasper to arrive, I got to chatting with the group about where they worked. Four of the young men worked in the kitchen. Of medium height and build, Chris was one of the most talkative men in the group. He seemed to enjoy bantering with Jasper, cracking jokes, and was quite open about his love for his daughter and stepson.[16] When I asked how many people worked at the kitchen, Chris laughed and leaned back in his chair. "I quit," he said loudly. He waggled his eyebrows at one of the young men who had their hand up as an answer to my question. Someone asked where he was working, and Chris's smile broadened: "Nowhere. I don't want to get used to having money." This prompted a round of laughter, and young men nudged one another with their elbows and nodded.

Once the laughter had stopped, Chris set the front legs of his chair back down and added, "I want to go up the way." Several of the young men start grinning, and I asked him whether that's something he can decide to do. Chris nodded in response to the low chorus of chuckles and said, "I can [if I] do stuff I'm not supposed to." Someone muttered, "Trouble," and Chris laughed and nodded. Not long after this conversation, Chris was sent up the way, though I don't know if it was because he made the right kind of "trouble," the kind that painted him as dangerous and therefore adult, or if it was simply that his bed was needed for someone too young to justify sending to an adult facility.

"He's Just Floating": Dismissing COs' Power at SY

The technique of dismissing or insulting COs also helped younger prisoners manage the frustrations of incarceration and avert conflicts while also affirming, or attempting to affirm, their value within the prison system. Many prisoners, both adult and juvenile, were loath to admit the level of power COs and the technologies of the prison had (i.e., the prison is "soft as hell"), but they were also highly aware that conflicts with COs meant the loss of privileges and access to the outside world. Nearly all the fathers, at both NCI and

SY, agreed that getting noncontact visits "behind the glass" was unpleasant, hard, and often emotionally painful. As a result, prisoners usually attempted to undermine COs' power without getting caught.

During a group meeting at SY, a CO strolled through the library. Linde, the CO, was white, male, and in his midthirties, and I had never seen him before. Jasper, the group facilitator, nodded politely to the CO. Linde smiled and said, "I'm just floating." He exited the room through a different door than the one he'd arrived from. As soon as the door closed, Chris turned his head to one side and said, "That's why, before he come to work—" he sniffed loudly and moved his head as if he were snorting a line of cocaine. It was a small group that day, only five young men, but they all cracked up. Chris was talkative, and the other young men in the group often agreed with the things he said. Chris had several tattoos, including the words "thug" and "life" in heavy gothic lettering on his forearms. Pedro, a skinny young Puerto Rican man who always seemed to be bouncing with nervous energy, asked with a wide grin, "You can tell?" Chris nodded: "He's just lost in the moment." Luis, who was heavier set and wore his long black hair in a ponytail, also nodded and added, "He's just floating." The young men cracked up again.

Jasper sighed and repeated his question about the kinds of masculinity they see on television: "Are there traits of masculinity you want to pass along to your son?" The conversation continued as the young men bantered back and forth about how men pretend to be something they aren't when they're trying to impress women. Luis made a *pssh* noise and said that happened in prison too: "Guys are in there for a parole violation, and they say it's a gun charge." He shook his head and made another dismissive noise before adding, "[They're] fronting [self-aggrandizing]." Jasper began listing different kinds of men (football players, rappers) and asking the young men in the group to list off the images that came to mind. When Jasper listed "politician" the room broke up into a round of hissing, dismissive sounds. Luis leaned forward and rested his forearms on the table, "[They] act like they know everything." Other young men in the group nodded in agreement. Luis continued, "They're taking away parole for violent crimes. That ain't gonna work. And they wonder why COs getting stabbed." He shook his head and leaned back in his chair.

As Luis was talking, Linde walked past the bay of windows at the back of the library. The windows overlooked a hallway that housed administrative offices and other rooms where vocational and educational training occurred. Linde kept his eyes on the group and a small smile on his face for most of his walk. Pedro nudged Chris and pointed with his chin at the CO: "He's floating by." Chris snickered, "On a boat." Chris began to mime like he was paddling in a canoe. Pedro and Luis cracked up and nudged each other. Jasper, impatience beginning to thread into his voice, called the young men's attention back to the conversation on media images of masculinity.

The parallel between Luis's discussion of politicians who "think they know everything" and, in his estimation, contribute to violence toward COs and the mocking suggestion that the CO was high captures the tensions between individual agency in the prison and the structural limitations placed on life on the inside. Luis's comments suggest that the roots of violence inside prison can be found on the outside. That is, politicians make decisions that increase the possibilities of violence for both prisoners and COs. Chris, on the other hand, was more interested in the immediate power negotiations occurring between prisoners and COs in everyday interactions. Stating that a CO snorts cocaine, particularly in front of a social worker and a volunteer, implies the guards are no different from, and certainly no better than, prisoners.

Dismissing COs as weak was also an effective way to defuse the tension created by the sheer amount of power COs as a group had over prisoners. During the time I spent at SY, Achilles was released on parole. He then violated the terms of his parole and was returned to prison. Not long after his return and our interviews, he was sent "up the way" to an adult facility. Achilles was generally laid-back, always ready to make a joke, and one of the first young men in the group to make friendly overtures toward me. I only saw Achilles get angry once. Toward the end of one group meeting, Achilles asked Jasper if he could go to the bathroom. Jasper told him to go ahead. Achilles was back a minute later stating that the guard wouldn't let him go to the bathroom. Achilles said that the guard told him to go back to his cottage and that the CO had also told him that he should not "approach [the CO] like that." Achilles's hands were bunched into fists, his shoulders up around his ears, and he stared straight ahead with his eyebrows pulled down tight. A long, tense silence ensued. The young men began looking at one another nervously before several started a chorus of complaints about COs. So many people were talking that I couldn't really follow any of the stories, but Chris stated loudly that COs always do "crazy shit." Jasper shook his head and told them that he should end group anyhow so Achilles should go back to his unit and take care of business. Achilles nodded once and then stood up to leave. Chris walked with Achilles, talking to him in a low, quiet voice as they exited the room.

In the moments between when Achilles returned to the room and the young men began complaining, the possibility of violence felt high. I don't know what happened when Achilles returned to his unit, but the dismissive complaints and insults about COs momentarily defused the tension. Achilles was not alone in his frustrations with COs, as the other men in the group sought to remind him. Rather, the fault lay in the internal failings of the CO, who was resoundingly declared "crazy."

PUTTING ON A "GAME FACE" AND "BRAWLING"

Prisoners also had to maintain and manage their relationships with other prisoners and often discussed (both in group and in their interviews) their strategies for doing so. Managing negotiations with other prisoners and the COs was a learned skill. When I asked the interviewees about what it was like when they first arrived in prison, a number of them talked about how difficult their first few months (and sometimes years) had been. Conflict with other prisoners that spiraled out of control was one of the main reasons men ended up in segregation and lost privileges, including access to their families. Men stated that it was sometimes necessary to show a willingness to fight and to get caught, though many men also highlighted the importance of self-isolation as a tool for decreasing their chances of getting into conflicts with other prisoners. The only exception was the basketball court, which served as a sanctioned site for public physical confrontations.

Aeneas walked a fine line between embracing a new way of practicing masculinity and maintaining a reputation inside prison. Over the course of his interviews, Aeneas disassociated himself from his previous masculine identity, stating, "I was an asshole. I'm not afraid to say it." Similarly, he expressed how much he wanted his son to grow up to be a different kind of man than he had been and not go through the same things Aeneas had. Carving out space to practice a less aggressive, more emotionally open masculinity was at least partially built on his prior reputation for violence and aggression. During the early years of his incarceration, he regularly got into fights. Shortly after arriving at the county jail, he saw "a man performing fellatio on another man for a pack of cigarettes." He told me there had been a large group of other prisoners watching and "hooping and hollering." Being sexually assaulted was his "biggest fear" when he arrived, and avoiding victimization meant being proactive about fighting and defending himself. As he described it, "People talk junk to you, [and] you can't back down. It was horrible. Sometimes I look [back] at that, [and] I don't even know how I survived two years—my first two years. They were bad." Aeneas talked at length about how long it took him to develop the ability to walk away from a fight, to "keep [my] hands open instead of closed" in a fist. Eventually, he figured out the rules of the facility and learned how to avoid fights with prisoners and COs.

Part of how Aeneas managed to avoid fights was to severely limit his interaction with other prisoners and correctional staff, though he still engaged with the staff-sanctioned site for aggression and violence between prisoners: the basketball court. Most of the prisoners described the basketball games as more violent in prison than on the outside, and Aeneas referred to it as "brawl" rather than "ball." Aeneas, like many of the prisoners, was often injured during the game (including a severe ankle sprain and a broken finger) but continued to play because it "release[d] so much." As I drove to the facility in the evenings, I often saw men playing basketball outside, and the bulk of the outdoor space that I could see from the road was made up of basketball courts. Aeneas went to great lengths to minimize his chances for violent interactions and sought opportunities to emotionally connect with both other prisoners and his son, though the basketball court remained a place where he could, and would, fight. Aeneas took part in a prison-training program to become a grief counselor and help other prisoners deal with their emotional reactions to incarceration. He was trying to get his college degree while incarcerated, although, given the barriers to college education for prisoners, he had found it difficult to do so. Many of the courses he had taken were not accredited, meaning he had spent money and learned but would not be able to get an actual degree.

Messiah had three biological children and two stepchildren with two different women. He had served a short sentence when he was younger and was then home for a number of years before ending up back in prison. He'd served four years of a fourteen-year sentence at the time of our interview. Messiah described his first time in prison as "crazy" because he did not know anything. He attributed avoiding fights, currently and during his first bid (or prison sentence), to his skills as a "people person." Despite his ability to talk with people, he spent a large portion of his interview discussing his frustrations with his cellmate, a man he'd lived with for close to a year. In Messiah's estimation, his cellmate talked too much: "I'm in a eight-by-twelve environment. I don't want to talk. There's nothin' to talk about. We come in, 'How you doin'?' We wake up in the morning, 'Good morning.' The buck stops there." This self-imposed isolation extended out of the cell as well. For example, he avoided playing card and board games because he felt that those kinds of interactions caused conflict.

The only group activity he expressed excitement about was playing basketball, and even in this, his cellmate caused problems. Messiah stated, "I play basketball with [my cellmate], and he's very annoying . . . When I go play sports, I like to enjoy myself. When I come back I want to say, 'Yeah I had a good time.' Not come back with a headache because you been jabby-jay-jibby-jabbing in my head all day." The cellmate also caused problems for Messiah with other prisoners. The basketball court may have been a sanctioned site for low levels of interpersonal violence, but it could also spawn fights that bled out into life in the unit. Messiah's cellmate's inclination to "jibby-jabby" annoyed other prisoners as well, and Messiah felt obliged to talk these men out of "jumping" his cellmate. As he told me a story about his cellmate mouthing off to another prisoner during a game, Messiah laughed, sighed, and rolled his eyes. Finally, he summed the situation up with a shrug: "He's a mess, you know?"

Ricardo had short dark hair shot through with gray, and most days, he wore glasses. In his early thirties and Puerto Rican, Ricardo was serving a long sentence at NCI. During group, he sat with an acquaintance, and the two of them often made jokes to one another, sometimes in Spanish and sometimes in English. At the end of his second interview, Ricardo talked about having to put on his "game face," the expression he used to show other prisoners and COs that he was serious and not worth messing with, before he left the interview. For Ricardo, it was important that other people didn't know much about his business. I asked him if he ever talked about his kids with anyone else in the prison. He replied, "Not really. I really don't. I got a cellie [cellmate] now, and he knows, and he [. . .] he like forty-eight. And we talk and stuff, but you know, I really don't like getting into it too much 'cause I get emotional and stuff, and then I get mad at myself, and then I start cryin' for . . . not cryin' literally cryin', but then—I call it cryin'—I start talkin' about stuff that I don't even wanna talk about and some . . . I just don't wanna let people know more things about me that they should not know." Ricardo was quick to say that he doesn't "literally" cry but that any display of intense emotion or personal information left him feeling vulnerable. At the same time, Ricardo drew on his identity as a father to motivate himself to participate in groups and to focus on the time, far into the future, when he would leave prison. As he stated, "It's [fatherhood] what's keepin' me [working] every day to live and to go out there and do better." Ricardo, like many men, valued his role as a father but also sought to keep his emotional life private.

"Behind the Glass" and Remaining Connected to Family

When prisoners received tickets for infractions, they lost a whole host of privileges. If they weren't moved to segregation, they were moved to what the men called the "ticket block." They lost their current cellmate (which might be a plus or a significant loss as finding a good cellie was important for doing time comfortably), their jobs, access to educational programs and training, and most importantly, their ability to receive contact visits. Normal visits lasted an hour and men were allowed to hug and kiss their visitors at the start and end of the visit. Noncontact visits, on the other hand, meant that visitors remained on one side of a glass wall and the visit took place over a phone. The subject of noncontact visits came up in the groups at both SY and NCI, and they were universally disliked.

Nine men discussed noncontact visits in their interviews, all of them from the adult facility (25.7 percent of the men interviewed at NCI). Two of the men brought it up because they had recently gotten a ticket and had lost their contact visit privileges. Angel was one such father. He was caught with marijuana and, as a result, lost not only contact visits for several years but also the two-hour special visit he was supposed to receive for participation in the fatherhood group. Well versed in the ways of the prison administration, Angel hadn't told his children that the special visit was occurring and was relieved his children didn't know they'd lost out as a result of his misbehavior. In fact, because only one child could come to a noncontact visit, he thought it was unlikely that he would see his children for some time.

Five of the men brought up the loss of contact visits as they discussed adapting to prison. Gregg was white, thirty, and had one daughter. As he discussed what it was like to come to prison for the first time, he told me, "I was a little bit of a knucklehead at first. . . . I had a few years with no contacts . . . My daughter used to have to stand up behind the glass." He told me that when he first came to prison, he got regular visits from his daughter and his daughter's mother. Once he lost his contact privileges, the visits "slowed down," and by the time he was able to receive normal visits again, the relationship with his girlfriend was over. Similarly, Shawn talked about how difficult it was to receive noncontact visits. In his early thirties, black, and serving a short sentence at NCI, Shawn stated, "At first, when my daughter would come up . . . she didn't understand [why I was behind the glass]. She be like, 'Let me come with you.' [I'd say], 'You can't,' and she'[d] start crying. Then there's a piece of glass . . . she banging on it. [I'm] trying to [say], 'You can't come.' I tell my brother, 'Grab her or something. Take her, she going crazy.' Oh, brother. I didn't like that much. I had to cut that out." Shawn spent most of his interview talking about how important being a father was to him. He was also the only prisoner I ever saw successfully persuade the DOC to let him have a special visit with a group other than his own when, due to a miscommunication over the date of the event, he didn't receive his own group's special visit. He spent the next several months campaigning to be included in the next special visit for the group that followed his own. That he was successful was a testament to his patience and dedication.[17]

Ricardo treated the material in class seriously and spent quite a bit of time talking about how it was important to him to learn to be a good parent to his two daughters (ages fourteen and twelve). He also had a son with another woman, about the same age as his youngest daughter, with whom he had no contact. Ricardo blamed himself, saying that he had been heavily into drugs at the time the boy was conceived and that he and the child's mother had a violent and negative relationship. The mother of his son wanted nothing to do with him and the mother of his daughters wanted Ricardo to have nothing to do with the mother of his son. As a result, Ricardo focused his attention exclusively on his daughters.

At the time of the interview, he had served thirteen years on a fifty-year sentence, and he described his early years in prison as filled with fights and gossip. He told me that participating in the fatherhood program was part of his attempts to get his "mind right": "I got my daughters waitin' for me out there. And I would never forgive myself if something happened to them while I'm in here and I can't be there for them. I can't live with that, you know?" Ricardo struggled to balance his desire to be connected with his daughters and the realities of incarceration. Particularly in the beginning, this was a struggle. For part of his sentence, he was housed out of state, and the fights he got into meant he was only allowed noncontact visits "behind the glass." He disliked having his oldest daughter see him like that but continued asking for visits because "I also wanted her to know that I always gonna be there, even though they put me underground, I'm always gonna be there for her."

CONCLUSION

Is dangerous masculinity really about microinteractions between COs and prisoners (i.e., the individual agency of both), or are these interactions simply reflections of the structural conditions produced in the total institution of the prison? The answer to that question is yes. As a number of previous works demonstrate, the prison is a site of social and structural violence.[18] The prison system is part of a much larger set of institutionalized responses that criminalize and punish poverty as well as reinforce racial and class inequality.[19] The prison places such limitations on the agency of COs and prisoners alike that the likelihood of violent interactions over scarce resources is high. The compression of options—for both gender performances and literal resources—means that violence is often one of the few possible methods for solving disputes. Despite this, most prisoners and COs prefer to behave in ways that diminish or avoid violence.[20]

Neither prisoners nor COs are automatons. Individual members of the prison community negotiate their relationships with prisoners, COs, staff and volunteers, and family members in a variety of ways. For COs, the worst punishment, incarceration, has already been meted out. What, then, does a CO do when prisoners refuse to obey the rules? A prisoner's incarceration hampers his ability to enact masculinity in the manner that feels most normal or natural, but it does not eliminate his desire to be both unharmed and respected. What, then, should a prisoner do if another prisoner steals his shoes? Calling on the COs will label him a snitch, but doing nothing will mean other prisoners think he's unable to defend himself. In this, the challenges of prison bear a resemblance to those individuals face when dealing with disputes in an illegal drug market. A drug dealer can't rely on legitimate avenues of violence to maintain his share of the market—he can't call the police if he's robbed. Leaving the offender unpunished, however, invites others to take advantage of your weakness. Disputes must be resolved quickly and violently. Many of the prisoners were familiar with the techniques for resolving conflict outside of the bounds of law and adapted these approaches to life on the inside.

Dangerous masculinity is an inescapable part of prison life that is linked to elements of masculine behavior on the outside. Both prisoners and COs (and other staff) import ideas about "normal" and "deviant" masculinity from the outside world. Once inside the walls, both groups attempt to define masculinity in ways that support their social positions within the institution. Incarcerated men have little choice about whether they will engage in individual negotiations around the "dangerously masculine" generic male prisoner. However, this does not stop incarcerated men from contesting, undermining, or seeking to redefine some of these expectations.

To claim personal "hardness" as a prisoner is also to claim a right to status, respect, and manhood. Most of the men had an opinion on the "hardness" or "softness" of the prison facility, COs, themselves, and other prisoners. By understanding people's behavior along this continuum, prisoners might disrupt the bright line between "us" and "them" that the COs and staff work hard to maintain. That is, a prisoner can potentially be a better man—a harder, more masculine man—than other prisoners and COs. Despite their attempts to contest or undermine the understanding that they are hyperviolent and hypersexual, prisoners have limited power over the terms by which they are judged, something that many researchers who discuss masculinity in prison often gloss over.[21] Dangerous masculinity remains an organizing element of prison life because the power of COs relies on institutional structures. Disrupting "the rules" of the facility is quite difficult, and prisoners are often helpless to resist the demand that they submit to the security routines of the facility. This interplay between COs and prisoners over the meaning of masculinity is integral to the internal organization of the prison, and it hinges on the dangerous masculinity of prisoners.

The limitations of incarceration mean that men must balance the conflicting demands of manhood and fatherhood. The negotiation in prison is different than it is for men in the workplace, though the institutional mediation in both instances tells us that fatherhood and masculinity are not easily combined. In many ways, being a "good" father requires reassessing what it means to be a "good" man, and organizations such as prison and work play a role in the process. The prison system actively limits men's opportunities for enacting manhood and fatherhood in order to simplify security measures; incarcerated fathers must similarly limit how they understand themselves as men and parents. Despite these constraints, for many of the men, being a father offers them a way to feel connected to the outside world and to understand themselves as more than dangerously masculine, as prison rules, administration, and many staff assume them to be. This remains true even as men point out how they must present themselves as aggressive and violent in order to avoid conflict on the inside.

The men in this study spoke at length about their love for their children, their hope to remain connected with their children, the work that goes into maintaining such connections, their desire for their children to take their advice, and the importance of keeping familial relationships private. Visits were opportunities to drop their "game faces" and instead emphasize their value as more than prisoners. In particular, men were able to express deep emotions about their children even as they acknowledged that there was little space for emotions within the context of prison.

Conclusion

THE CONDITIONS OF POSSIBILITY

ONE OF THE LAST interviews I conducted in the field was with Aeneas. He was also one of my earliest interviewees, and it had been more than a year since I'd last spoken with him. In the interim, he'd completed a certified nurse's assistant program and began working in the prison's hospital. It was more of a casual conversation than an interview, and we spent a good chunk of time discussing the challenges of moving forward or growing as a person while incarcerated. At one point, Aeneas told me,

> Some people just go with the flow in here. It's literally like [the] walking dead. Lot of guys, they just don't do nothing. Wake up, go and eat, play a little dominoes maybe, play a little cards. Gossip. Go back, go to sleep, wake up the next day, and do the same thing all over again. Just not moving forward . . . [Being] hopeless is just so easy in here. 'Cause you get up [and] you got a hundred some guys in your unit. Most of them don't give a flying *F* about you or about what you going through. And the same thing with the officers walking around. So you get a double dose of that. Some of these guys don't have families; some of them can't see their kids. So how do you feel human in that environment?

While he found the work at the hospital to be physically hard, the opportunity to connect and help others was something that was hard to come by in prison. As a result, he liked his new job.

Once men are incarcerated, their options for enacting masculinity are severely curtailed. This is a purposeful aspect of incarceration—isolating criminals in order to punish, deter, and possibly rehabilitate—and also a way for correctional staff to streamline security measures and simplify the difficult task of confining a large group of people against their will. The dangerous masculinity of the prisoner emerges from the negotiation among the DOC administration, COs, and prisoners within the confines of a total institution.[1] Because COs and staff start from the position that the inmates are "bogeymen," a heartbeat away from sexual assault, there was very little institutional pressure to take prisoners' bothersome feelings or connections to the outside world into consideration. Indeed, prisoners' dangerousness legitimated the level of control correctional staff had over volunteers' clothing and entrance to the facility, as well as over the prisoners themselves through strip searches and writing tickets.

While the prison is a unique setting, it is not as isolated from the outside world as one might expect. Specifically, ideas travel freely in and out of prison. The prison system borrows from and extends the same sets of negative and racialized assumptions about minority men's masculinity embedded in the structure of American legislature, policing practices, the courts, the judiciary, and the larger culture. Wider cultural understandings of what constitutes normal and deviant masculinity have a profound effect on COs' and prisoners' interactions and responses to prison. This is not to say that prisoners are not capable of violence and assault—statistics demonstrate that many men are capable of such aggression. Similarly, the desire for COs to be safe while they do their work is a reasonable one. And yet we must also consider the consequences of creating a place where prisoners are so isolated that they end up, as Aeneas described, "the walking dead."

The very logic of prisoners as a category of people draws on a powerful and long history of racist policies and ideology that assumes minority men are a threat to the social body. And yet in order for such assumptions to make sense in the current structure of prison, the masculinity of prisoners must be uniform and ubiquitous. Based on this set of behaviors and motives, the prison establishes rules and security protocols designed to protect COs, visitors, and the inmates themselves from the negative effects of this dangerous masculinity. Because the experience of prison as an institution is total, these rules tend to give rise to the idea that all prisoners necessarily embody this dangerous masculinity. The result is an image of all prisoners as dangerously masculine that appears to be race-neutral while, in fact, the version of masculinity attributed to these prisoners, regardless of race, is deeply racialized.

The racial order of the United States, however, overlaps and intertwines with class and gender inequalities. Prisoners are not excluded from the social body entirely on the basis of race but rather on the basis of a racialized identity that is also both male and poor. For female prisoners, such a gender-class-race nexus impacts the experience of incarceration, including how, when, and if they will be allowed access to their children. A number of scholars have pointed out that the assumption that the generic prisoner is male impacts the structure of female prisons and female prisoners' experiences. Only female prisoners have "troublesome" needs such as parenting responsibilities or identities, emotions, or a need for privacy.[2] Dana Britton points out that COs perceive the bodies of female inmates to be problematic and messy, their physical needs (such as feminine hygiene products) as more excessive, and female inmates to have emotional demands COs do not want to feel obliged to meet.[3] As a result, both femininity and motherhood are often overtly used to control and discipline female prisoners.[4] Like female prisoners, male prisoners' connections with the outside world and their families create disruptions within the day-to-day routines of the prison. For men, though their gender experiences are the "norm" for prison, the stereotypical male prisoner is a predator with little to offer society or his family. As a result, incarcerated fathers' connections with children and family are most often ignored or dismissed within the prison system.

The staff at Healthy Connections worked hard to carve out space for men to be connected to their families, even in the face of repeated institutional obstacles. The men in these programs, for the most part, recognized these efforts and responded positively to them. That is, as much as the men valued the lessons on communication embedded in the materials, many also valued the investment of time by the people from Healthy Connections. This was particularly true at SY, where Jasper actively sought to model the very style of manhood he encouraged. Indeed, the vice president of Healthy Connections once told me that Jasper's style was unusual and that, when she first started, his level of interpersonal connection with the prisoners concerned her. She added, "After a while, I realized that's what [the prisoners] wanted and needed . . . We pay him to be a daddy to fifty guys a year." The staff at Healthy Connections, however, were highly limited in what they could and could not address in the fatherhood programs. In particular, there was little support to address the structural challenges men faced.

In chapter 2, I discussed the differences in incarcerated fathers' perceptions of the risks, rewards, and obligations of parenting sons and daughters. These differences help show how incarcerated fathers negotiate masculinity and fatherhood. Incarcerated fathers, of varying ages and ethnic backgrounds, sound remarkably similar to one another as they seek to negotiate manhood and fatherhood on the inside. In some ways, fatherhood serves as a way for incarcerated fathers to resist the assumption that they are simply dangerous. At the same time, fatherhood highlights the costs of practicing masculinity inside prison. To be specific, men with children must make decisions about with whom they discuss their families and children, how they will deal with the emotional toll of losing contact with their families as part of the punishments meted out in prison, and the degree to which acting emotionally and physically strong requires them to behave in ways that alienate their families and children. The prison as a total institution has a significant impact on how men embody masculinity.

As laid out in chapter 3, age does appear to mediate the link between security enforcement and the raced and classed masculinity of prisoners. Many DOC staff and administrators behave in ways that suggest they retain some

hope that young offenders might still be prevented from becoming dangerous, unsalvageable predators. This does not mean, however, that the ways COs,
administrators, and the rules of the prison facility respond to young offenders
as a group are disconnected from patterns of race and class inequalities in the
larger culture. Instead, juvenile facilities are set up in ways that correspond
with the school-to-prison pipeline. The young men have the *potential* to enact
the same kind of dangerous masculinity found in adult prisoners and have to
be managed carefully as a result.

The impact of age, however, had real consequences on fathers' access to
children. For example, the state department for child protective services funded
the program at SY, whereas general state revenues funded the fatherhood
program at NCI. Toward the end of my field work, the state government's
goals changed to a focus on services for the children of incarcerated parents rather than the parents themselves. As I left Healthy Connections, their
focus turned to fathers who were about to be paroled or released and a more
general program focused on mentoring the at-risk children of incarcerated
men and women. As a result, Healthy Connections would no longer run a
fatherhood program at NCI, and the last cycle I observed was also the last
cycle run in the facility. The fatherhood program at SY, however, continued because its funding came from another source and was tied directly to
the juvenile status of the prisoners at SY. Though it was not without a cost, the
young men at SY had more access to their children than the older men
at NCI.

In chapter 4, I outlined the tension men experience between their identities as prisoners, men, and fathers. Incarcerated men cannot ignore the ways
that the assumption that all prisoners possess dangerous masculinity shapes their
day-to-day lives. One way or another, a prisoner must engage with aspects
of dangerous masculinity. As is the case with hegemonic masculinity on the
outside, an individual man can resist, attempt to redefine, or embrace different
aspects of dangerous masculinity. For many men, fatherhood offers an opportunity to define themselves in ways that resist the dominant narrative of prison.
Even in the act of resistance, however, the institutionally embedded assumptions about masculinity shape men's gender performances. For example, no
one resists the expectation that men are more violent than women by declaring themselves a time machine; the category of "time machine" makes no
sense in a struggle to articulate gender identity. Instead, the shape of resistance
reflects the dominant narratives. A man might, for example, position himself as
"not like other men" by asserting that he values nonviolent, nurturing behaviors such as caring for children, changing diapers, or being a good listener. For
the individual man, this resistance likely has value. As part of a larger pattern,
however, such resistance reinforces the idea that "normal" women are gentle

enough to care for children, to change diapers, and to love listening. Beyond hegemonic masculinity, the "dangerous individual" carries with it its own set of expectations. Examining the rise of the psychiatrist in the legal and criminal apparatus, Foucault argues, "Today, the crime tends to be no more than the event which signals the existence of a dangerous element—that is, more or less dangerous—in the social body."[5] In other words, dangerousness became linked to threats to the larger social order as the field of psychiatry began to claim that they could "cure" such threats.

Moving Forward

Finishing a book with suggestions about how we resolve the problems outlined in the earlier text is de rigueur among social scientists, and I am not going to break with the custom. In this section, I outline potential solutions that extend directly from my research as well as much broader, less directly connected potential solutions. I will not be the first nor will I be the last to suggest any of these solutions, but they bear repeating nonetheless. Many people already know what we must do if we want to reduce the negative impacts of incarceration. The political question before us is, do we actually want that? Or, to be more accurate, how many of us actually want to reduce mass incarceration? Change is expensive, hard, and unpredictable. And yet it is also inevitable. I see no reason not to outline the narrow and broad changes that would direct the United States to move in what I think is the better direction. Perhaps I will persuade some readers to agree with me. Even if I do not, I would like to at least prompt my readers to consider the possibilities.

Mass incarceration is a problem the American people must address. Though it has been slow to develop, politicians on both sides of the aisle and the American public are beginning to discuss prison reform.[6] The kinds of solutions that will emerge remain to be seen. Incarcerated parents are a subgroup of the prison population, and their time on the inside has a negative impact on their children, their coparents, and the communities in which they reside.[7] Making it easier for parents to remain connected to their children is one strategy for decreasing the social problems created by mass incarceration. That is, the most obvious takeaway from this book is the importance of fatherhood programs in prison. Imperfect though they were, the ones I observed offered incarcerated men space to discuss and consider their roles as fathers, prisoners, and men. Overwhelmingly, the fathers in this study emphasized how much they valued the special visits that gave them the ability to hug, hold, and play with their children.

A number of fatherhood programs have emerged over the last thirty years, though such programming remains haphazard and inconsistently used. For poor men on the outside, parenting programs proliferated under the neoliberal banner of "Responsible Fatherhood."[8] From the perspective of the state, the goal of responsible fatherhood programming is to increase men's financial involvement in their children's lives and to decrease the burden of welfare on state coffers.[9] Despite the emphasis on finances from state actors, staff and participants in responsible fatherhood programs often emphasize the value of social connections (especially those that emerge from the program itself) and the ways that caregiving is as important as breadwinning.[10]

In general, successful parenting programs use materials culturally appropriate to the target group, last long enough for rapport to develop among the group, and have well-trained, enthusiastic staff and high staff-participant ratios.[11] Fatherhood programs in prison, however, face challenges, including persuading the warden (or other high-level administrators) that the program is worthwhile, addressing security concerns, and training staff to adhere to the rules of prison facilities.[12] Failure to meet these additional challenges usually means the end of the program (or the inability to get a program started at all). Prison-based fatherhood programs also undermine the dominant neoliberal narrative of responsible fatherhood of the parenting programs that proliferated in the last thirty years. Incarcerated men cannot provide financially nor can they engage in day-to-day caregiving. Agencies running prison fatherhood programs must develop curricula that reflect these limitations and still provide incarcerated men with ways to remain engaged with their children. Despite decades of attempts, policymakers, social workers, and researchers do not yet have a consistent or clear answer to what these curricula should look like, though most fatherhood programs in prison rely on group discussion and improving interpersonal relationships with family.[13]

Part of the problem in choosing curricula that "work" is defining what success means. For example, if a researcher cannot prove that a specific fatherhood program directly decreased recidivism, does that mean the program didn't work? Is it enough that a fatherhood program helped the participants feel better? Or does success mean that participants contacted their children more frequently? A recent study of the InsideOut Dad program found that the curriculum used did improve fathers' confidence and knowledge about parenting as well as the frequency with which they spoke to their children.[14] Is that enough to deem the program a success? How one might answer that question is likely to reflect one's political position and belief in the rehabilitative possibilities of prison. Fatherhood programs remain, however, one way to begin reducing the impact of prison on families and communities.

It is also important to remember that the children of incarcerated parents are negatively impacted by the loss of their parents. In her book on parents in prison, Joyce Arditti argues that however we think about punishment, ignoring the impact of incarceration on children and families results in massive, unacknowledged damage. Indeed, she outlines what we know about the "disenfranchised grief"—the "loss [of something] that is not or cannot be openly acknowledged, publicly mourned, or socially supported"—that people with an incarcerated loved one experience.[15] Children often experience loss of stability due to decreased financial resources and increased caregiver stress. Many children are present for their parents' arrests and carry a specific kind of guilt and trauma as a result. If we are going to consider the success of a fatherhood program in prison, children are necessarily part of the calculation. And I argue that the standard for success—in this area, at least—should be low. If it makes a child feel better for even a moment, it's worth the effort.

There are also other potential solutions to enact while men are in prison. Such solutions are not directly related to fathering from prison but impact the likelihood that prisoners' can return home successfully. Lowering incarcerated fathers' recidivism can also mean decreasing the negative effect of parental incarceration on children. The limitations to prisoners' access to education (particularly college education) and decrease in investment in job training, as well as the utter lack of assistance for prisoners as they transition back to the community, all have an enormous impact on the likelihood of recidivism.[16] The 2011 May issue of the *Annals of the American Academy of Political and Social Science* wrestles with the issues facing young disadvantaged men, including incarceration, fatherhood, and employment. Steven Raphael, for example, emphasizes the importance of job training and providing more direct assistance for prisoners as they transition home.[17] Even something as simple as helping parolees get state identification before they return home could have a positive impact on lowering recidivism rates.[18]

Finally, someone concerned with reducing the incarceration rate and the negative impact of the penal system on American society could focus on how COs' training and behavior can positively or negatively impact the organization of prison and prisoners' reactions to incarceration. Dana Britton's *At Work in the Iron Cage: The Prison as Gendered Organization* outlines possible ways to improve COs' training around issues of gender and sexual harassment. Her work is primarily focused on the importance of acknowledging that female COs face different challenges than male COs (e.g., sexual harassment from prisoners) and that training could better prepare male and female COs for dealing with male and female prison populations. She also points out that treating the male CO as the "generic" CO actively contributes to creating a masculinized and hostile workplace. Other research indicates that COs' training and response to prisoners can have a significant impact on how prisoners adapt to incarceration.[19]

Solutions that occur in prison, however, can really only function as Band-Aids for much larger social problems. We must also address the issues facing our society outside of prison. A deteriorating educational system, a decimated industrial base, and an employment market that is sharply divided between high-skilled technology-based jobs and service work combine to create a society in which participating in the illegal drug market is a viable work choice for many.[20] That we declared a War on Drugs rather than addressing these social issues only served to deepen these problems. We must scale back or eliminate the War on Drugs and the sentencing structures that go along with it, such as mandatory minimums and truth-in-sentencing. These legal changes have done immeasurable damage to the fabric of our society, and decriminalization and increased treatment for drug addiction would do more to solve the social issues plaguing the United States than mass incarceration.[21] At a minimum, eliminating the massive racial disparities in sentencing guidelines around crack and cocaine would help ease part of the racial oppression that emerges out of the American criminal justice system. While Congress did reduce the difference in sentencing between crack cocaine and powder cocaine (from one hundred to one to eighteen to one) in 2010, the difference is still unfair and negatively impacts blacks more than whites.[22] While there is some indication that crack cocaine users commit more crimes than those who use powder cocaine, white crack users are less likely to get arrested than their black counterparts and face less severe sentences when they are caught.[23]

There is also work to be done creating political, social, and emotional space to redefine hegemonic masculinity in ways that allow for a wider range of men to enact a broader, less violent, more emotionally positive kind of manhood. Such solutions might focus on family-friendly policies for men and women in the workplace. There is a well-developed strain of public policy analysis that looks at the challenges of blending work and family both domestically and globally.[24] Someone interested in addressing the consequences of the current gender regime might focus on men's antirape movements on college campuses or in other large-scale institutions such as the military.[25] There is also worthwhile work to be done in providing resources for men of color to overcome significant racial barriers at work and in school.[26]

All these potential solutions, however, require the political will to enact such policies. The problem is, of course, that such solutions are expensive and difficult to execute and require restructuring our society in significant ways. Going to such trouble for "bogeymen" is, for many, a waste of resources. In the postindustrial, fiscally austere (at least when it comes to programs designed to improve social welfare), neoliberal political context of the United States in the twenty-first century, many such policy solutions *do not make sense*. It is the commonsense, naturalized, and unexamined understanding of what makes someone a criminal, how and when a person becomes unsalvageable and beyond help, and where and why someone no longer "deserves" the rights of U.S. citizenship that forms the discursive and ideological underpinning of American political, economic, educational, law enforcement, judicial, and criminal justice systems. All of these, not just the penal system, draw on a historicized understanding of minority men as dangerously masculine; the different ways systems draw on a similar cultural and historical discourse overlap, interact, and reinforce inequality and oppression along race and class lines.[27] These systems—or more accurately, the actors within such systems—do so because it solves a thorny problem: the need to balance demands for high levels of population control with limited resources.

THE CONDITIONS OF POSSIBILITY[28]

Over the course of forty years, the legal changes legitimated by the War on Drugs changed the American criminal justice system. The people who are most often swept up into prison are poor black or brown men, but the consequences of mass incarceration reverberate through the structures that delimit the boundaries of American life. Poor, uneducated white men have learned this lesson. Swept up in the widespread "get tough" policies of the last forty years, they constitute 40 percent of the American prison population and are what Michelle Alexander calls "collateral damage" in the racialized project of the War on Drugs.[29] In time, many Americans may look back on this time period and wonder how we let so many rights slip away. The shift in the last few decades in public demands for protection "*from* the state" to protection "*by* the state" reflects a change in how any number of agencies, institutions, and organizations provide safety and security.[30] These institutions must engage in more intensive regulation without spending excessive resources. In order to accomplish this, the definition of who belongs and who does not must necessarily become narrower. If fewer people deserve full rights, the state must provide less. Similarly, if the state can write off those who do not belong, the circumstances in which the underserving exist do not need to leave open the possibility of rejoining the social body. No one is exempt from the costs of incarcerating such an enormous proportion of our population, and nowhere is this clearer than in the American judiciary. Not only does the logic of dangerous masculinity continue to legitimate the reduction of civil liberties in America, but it has also been exported into the logic for the War on Terror.

In April of 2012, the Supreme Court of the United States of America handed down a decision in *Florence v. Board of Chosen Freeholders of County of Burlington et al.* that legitimated the use of strip searches for any individual entering the general population of a penal facility regardless of the severity of the crime and without the need for suspicions on the part of correctional authorities that the new inmate had contraband. The *Florence v. Board* case highlights some interesting, and concerning, issues around security, the unique dangerousness of prisoners, and access to family.

The judgment of the case hinged on the particular expertise of COs in assessing and managing the prison population. The majority opinion is quite clear that COs must have "substantial discretion" to devise solutions to the peculiar problems they face inside jails and prisons. It is this expertise that forms the bedrock for the majority's willingness to suspend the constitutional rights of citizens under the Fourth and Fourteenth Amendments as they enter prison and jail facilities as prisoners. Implicit in this presentation of expertise is that governing prisoners is different than governing any other group of people. That is, without "substantial discretion" that relies on the elimination or reduction of civil liberties, corrections staff will be unable to do their jobs. Prisoners are, in a basic way, not rights-bearing citizens for the duration of their stay. This remains true regardless of whether the prisoner has been determined to be guilty of the crime for which he or she has been charged.

Interestingly, in the majority's presentation of expertise, COs are simultaneously the final (or at least, most important) authority on how to create security measures inside the prison and also unable to enact any kind of nuanced implementation of strip-search policies. That is, COs should be able to strip-search everyone entering the jail facility because the officers are unable to draw any kind of distinction between incoming inmates. Justice Kennedy states, "Other possible classifications based on characteristics of individual detainees also might prove to be unworkable or even give rise to charges of discriminatory application. To avoid liability, officers might be inclined not to conduct a thorough search in any close case, thus creating unnecessary risk for the entire jail population." This emphasis on liability is an interesting one. By referencing the liability issues of strip searches, the majority opinion suggests that there are categories of prisoners COs might be inclined to search more than others. The worry about racial profiling leads the majority opinion to assert that it is better to treat all prisoners as dangerous than allow COs to decide which prisoners are more dangerous. In other words, in order to avoid strip-searching some kinds of prisoners more than others, COs should strip-search everyone.

In the dissent, on the other hand, Justice Breyer questions the reliance on COs' expertise, stating, "Nor do I find the majority's lack of examples surprising . . . The majority is left with the word of prison officials in support of its contrary proposition. And though that word is important, it cannot be sufficient." Instead, Justice Breyer draws on studies that have assessed the effectiveness of strip searches. The National Police Accountability Project, for example, examined the intake of seventy-five thousand new inmates over a period of five years and found that pat downs and searches of outer clothing captured the majority of contraband (thirteen out of sixteen cases) and that reasonable suspicion existed to legitimate full strip searches for the remaining instances. Similarly, Justice Breyer points out that the American Correctional Association standard "forbids suspicionless searches." Finally, he also points to laws in "at least 10 states that prohibit suspicionless strip searches" and implies that these states have not had significantly more problems than those states without such legal limitations.

Both the majority opinion and the dissent agree that prisons and prisoners are dangerous. The majority opinion relies on this to support the claim that COs must be allowed high levels of discretion, pointing out that "jails are often crowded, unsanitary, and dangerous places." The purpose of strip searches, according to the majority, is to decrease the spread of disease, identify gang members, and locate weapons and drugs. While the goal is to reduce the danger posed by prisoners to one another and to COs, the majority clearly believes COs will ultimately fail. The goal, then, is one of reduction or containment of danger rather than its elimination. Overcrowding, unsanitary conditions, and danger are simply part of the prison experience.

Justice Breyer does not appear to disagree. Instead, the dissent is primarily concerned that "someone with no criminal background arrested for jaywalking or another similarly minor crime" will be strip-searched and placed in the "dangerous world of the general jail population." Here, the primary cause for concern is that noncriminals or minor criminals (i.e., "normal people") will be subjected to the humiliation of a strip search and placed with a dangerous prison population. For Justice Breyer, too, the danger of the prison life remains both assumed and outside the scope of the case.

Finally, the majority draws on another Supreme Court case, *Block v. Rutherford* (1984), to support their claim that there is no need for "suspicion" when conducting strip searches of incoming prisoners. In *Block v. Rutherford*, the Supreme Court found that the "Los Angeles County Jail could ban all contact visits because of the threat [the visits] posed." The assumed dangerousness of prisoners legitimates, in this case, the denial of access to families and friends. The majority opinion, at least, sees no issue with denying prisoners the ability to see their families and, more important, assumes that the criminality of the prisoner *extends to his family members*. Not only is the prisoner so different he or she must be governed by a different set of rules than "someone with no criminal background," but such dangerousness extends beyond the confines of prison and out into the community. In some chilling ways, the reach of the penal system is beyond the literal confines of prisons—though, for some communities, this has been true for decades.[31]

There also appears to be no end in sight for mass incarceration in the United States. In fact, the War on Terror provides politicians, pundits, and the American public ample space to continue the disassembly of civil liberties in the name of security. Anti-immigrant sentiments are pushing punitive laws all over the country, and the events of the September 11 attacks provided public support for the rapid expansion of an already powerful security apparatus.[32] To quote Michelle Alexander, "Crack is out; terrorism is in."[33] The War on Terror is ushering in a whole new set of civil liberty losses. Some of the infringements that have caught public attention include the claim that the government has the right to engage in the targeted killing of U.S. citizens abroad without trial and with no oversight from the U.S. judiciary.[34] Similarly, the War on Terror has expanded the ability of the military to detain suspected terrorists, including U.S. citizens, without being charged and provided the National Security Agency with the wide-ranging ability to engage in warrantless wiretapping, again with very little oversight.[35] These losses of civil liberties are just the tip of the iceberg.

The next phase in the punitive orientation of the American criminal justice system will likely marry the gendered, raced, and classed category of the domestic criminal with the threatening foreigner. In fact, this has already begun as the political and criminal justice juggernaut begins to rumble that prisons are a "breeding ground" for Islamic terrorists.[36] The federal prison system has gone so far as to remove religious texts, which were unsurprisingly primarily Islamic, from prison libraries, though this has been contested.[37] In her book *Dangerous Brown Men*, Gargi Bhattacharyya analyzes how the vilification of black bodies in the United States extends, with some twists, to encapsulate dangerous brown men of the Middle East in order to provide legitimacy to the War on Terror. That Muslim men are predominantly not white according to the Western world means it takes very little to extend the constellation of images centered on portraying minority men within the United States as threatening to include dangerous brown men outside the borders of the American nation-state. In this way, the commonsense and unspoken understanding of "terrorists" as a group of people increasingly overlaps with the classed, raced, and gendered category of "criminal."

The American public continues to hand over some of our most culturally valued rights, such as the freedom from unlawful search and seizure or the right to privacy, in the hopes of utterly eliminating the possibility of danger. That this is an impossible task does not seem to be a cause of concern for far too many. Our prisons are proof of that. In the current political climate, the government must be seen to do everything possible to control the prison population (i.e., protection *by* the state). The issue is not that most people in power in the criminal justice system believe all prisoners will become terrorists but is instead the potential political fallout if the government did not appear to do everything possible to prevent prisoners from becoming terrorists and even *some* prisoners became terrorists.

It is difficult to examine "the prisoner" because he or she is at both the center and the periphery of the prison. The structure of a prison and its staff are entirely focused on maintaining control over prisoners' bodies but, in doing so, often ignore or avoid the individual experiences of prisoners. The governing of prisoners' bodies in the name of security, both within the prison facility but also as a part of the larger social fabric of society, requires a certain amount of willful blindness; this, however, is not just part of the COs' managerial style. Instead, it reflects a much larger response to mass incarceration, in which the public knows but does not know the far-ranging reach of the criminal justice system and is more than happy to leave dealing with prisoners to prison staff.[38]

The path forward is a difficult one. We face a troubling constellation of problems that will likely be addressed in a piecemeal fashion. For example, continuing the War on Drugs or extending the War on Terror ensures that large and expanding swaths of the American citizenry are excluded from society. The combination of diminishing citizens' civil liberties and a mushrooming security apparatus with the ability to invade personal lives silences political debate and those who oppose the status quo. There are also no solutions to the problems we face that will not create their own sets of new problems, power-knowledge relationships, and oppression. The list of potential solutions offered in the first half of this conclusion represent only a fraction of the potential ways we can attempt to redirect the criminal justice juggernaut and find a better path into the future, one that attempts to break apart the structures that (re)create race, class, and gender oppression. Finding the will to try out some of these potential solutions, however, requires the disruption of the too often unquestioned "commonsense" understandings that undergird what decisions and directions for the future "make sense" and who "deserves" resources and opportunities.

Appendix

Methods and Research Setting

In early February 2007, I began attending fatherhood groups at two prison facilities—one for adults (over eighteen) and one for youth offenders (ages fourteen to twenty-one)—in a northeastern state. The names of the prison facilities and the agency that ran the fatherhood facilities have been changed to protect confidentiality, and the location has been omitted. All of the names of staff, volunteers, and prisoners have been changed to protect anonymity. The prisoners chose their pseudonyms, and I chose the pseudonyms for the staff and correctional officers (COs). The adult facility, North Correctional Institution (NCI), and the youth facility, Southeast Youth Correctional Institution (SY), were both high security (level four out of five).

A social work–oriented nonprofit agency, Healthy Connections, ran these fatherhood groups as well as a number of other programs for prisoners and their families all over the state. When I expressed an interest in conducting research in prisons to a mentor, he put me in contact with the director of Healthy Connections. I presented the Healthy Connections' director with a short proposal, requesting permission to do preliminary research through their prison-based fatherhood programs. The director encouraged me to focus my attention exclusively on the fathers in the programs, both because this was a group she perceived to be underrepresented in the research on parental incarceration and because she believed my ability to access the families of incarcerated men would be limited.[1] Given the director's reluctance to give me access to the families of incarcerated men that were a part of Healthy Connections' programs, I focused my attention on the fatherhood programs.

I chose the two programs because they were located in different parts of the same state, providing geographical variety, and because the two facilities offered potential interviewees of a wide age range. Healthy Connections smoothed my path into the prison facilities because I first entered as a volunteer. In order to be considered a volunteer, I filled out an extensive array of paperwork for Healthy Connections, the central prison administration, and the correctional and administrative staff at both facilities. It took roughly two months before all the parties involved approved my entry to the prison facilities, and I began volunteering shortly thereafter. Once I was certain I had basic access to the fatherhood programs and the prison facilities, I began the process of procuring approval from my university's institutional review board (IRB) and the central prison administration's research unit (RU) to conduct interviews with prisoners from the program and, more generally, for my research project. The approval to conduct interviews took much longer than I anticipated, and I did not begin interviews until I had been in the field for almost eight months. I was, however, attending meetings of the fatherhood programs and collecting participant observation data during this time.

I drew on multiple approaches to qualitative research, though there is clear overlap among the techniques. For example, in terms of participant observation, I took extensive field notes in order to document as much detail as I could. When I began, it was not clear to me what would become important over time, and so I attempted to record as much as possible. As no one can actually record everything, there are flaws in such an approach. But I took as my guiding principle the importance of "thick description."[2] This approach served as the bedrock for my analysis as I developed analytic memos and coding schemes.[3]

As is often the case, my data collection choices directly impacted my analysis. For example, I began using the nVivo software well into my data collection. In fact, by the time I learned how to use nVivo, my data collection was nearly complete. The process of formatting and uploading field notes was time-consuming, and I ultimately decided to limit my use of the software. As a result, I only uploaded the first six months of my field notes and then used nVivo to develop the first set of key terms for coding. In other words, the software helped me establish broad patterns. For example, I used nVivo to establish the following codes for the ways incarcerated men talked about their sons and daughters: vulnerable, fragile, princess, protect, rough, tough, and little me. These codes formed the basis for my analysis in chapter 2. I then coded the remainder of my field notes and interviews by hand.

I took a similarly in-depth approach to my interviews, using a "focused life history" approach to create as much space for my respondents to tell their own narratives of their lives.[4] In approaching interviews as life history, I borrow heavily from what Francesca Polletta and her coauthors call "storytelling in institutional contexts."[5] This understanding of narrative builds on accounts and meaning-making, extending to treat stories as "social performances that are interactively constructed, institutionally regulated, and assessed by their audiences in relation to hierarchies of discursive credibility."[6] In other words, people tell stories that reflect their understandings of the institutional structures they interact with, agency and individual power vis-à-vis structural limitations, and the appropriate ways to behave.[7]

My approach to the interviews also drew on narrative inquiry approaches.[8] Though it was more time-consuming, the research proposal I submitted to the Department of Corrections requested multiple interviews with the men in the fatherhood program. Interacting one-on-one with the men in this study more than once allowed me to take a simultaneously more relaxed and focused approach in each interview. The first interview, in particular, was often free-flowing and followed the stories the men most wanted to tell me, with only minimal guidance from me. Afterward, I would go over my set of interview questions and check off the ones that came up in the interview. In the second interview, I would follow up with my remaining questions. This created the opportunity for me to think about what my interviewees had said (and not said) and, sometimes, ask the same questions more than once and see how their answers in one interview compared with answers in another. Additionally, more than one interview often improved rapport (though not always).[9]

I was mindful of the inevitable impact of power relations on how a researcher goes about collecting his or her data. Some researchers have examined the ways that race, class, and gender can impact qualitative data collection, particularly for interviews across gender and race lines. Mariana Sandoval and Lucia Trimbur suggest that when research relationships are based on mutual respect, the gender and race division do not necessarily hinder qualitative data collection. Other researchers have found the gender division, at least, to be more troubling. Terry Arendell, for example, suggests that her divorced male interviewees responded to her "on the basis of their expectations of me as a woman," and she found expressions of sexism and misogyny as well as romantic or sexual propositions to be difficult and challenging as an interviewer.[10] Much like Arendell, I circumvented or avoided innuendo and flirtation from both the prisoners and the COs to the best of my ability.

However, the impact of my position as a white female graduate student could not be avoided, and over time, I came to view the ways that prisoners, staff, and COs responded to me as valuable data.[11] The challenges of doing so in methodologically valid ways were extensive, and I drew on Pierre Bourdieu and Loic Wacquant's self-reflexive sociology, Candace West and Don Zimmerman's approach to analyzing gender as micropolitical support for social structure, and Dorothy Smith's approach to institutional ethnography to help me engage with my field site. In particular, I drew on Smith's analysis of the effects of power on ethnographic research as I conducted participant observation and interviews. My interactions with prisoners, volunteers, and COs all provided glimpses into the often unspoken power relations that governed the prison facilities.

Bourdieu and Wacquant's self-reflexive sociology emphasizes the importance of reflecting and engaging in a critical analysis of one's own social location throughout the research process and, most especially, as one considers the impact of the researcher on the subjects of study. I incorporated this approach in the ways I sought to use my own set of cultural assumptions and analytic frameworks to make sense of the lessons I learned while conducting my research. I was an outsider being inculcated into the appropriate ways to behave inside a prison facility, and my reactions to that training were analytically illuminating as I struggled to make sense of my observations. In particular, the ways that prisoners and COs responded to me as a woman and how, in turn, I responded to them as men (or in the case of female COs, as women) became an important analytic component of my research project.

In this study, Bourdieu's emphasis on critical self-awareness links with Smith's work explicating institutional ethnography. The expectation that a researcher must always interpret their work in "the ongoing, never-stand-still of the social"[12] directly affected how I conducted participant observation and interviews as well as how I went about analyzing my findings. In particular, I sought to begin from the day-to-day experiences of the people I interacted with in order to extend into an analysis of the prison as a social organization.[13] This was especially true as I considered the links between the prison system and the larger social world. From an institutional ethnographic perspective, my social location mattered, but the emphasis within this theoretical approach focuses on linking micro interactions with the large-scale functions of institutions.

West and Zimmerman's work on the ways individuals seek to perform normative gender ideals, or "do" gender, also informed my methodological approach to this study.[14] In part, the concept of "doing gender" helps bridge the gap between individual agency and the structural context in which people embody particular gender performances. As they state, "While it is individuals who do gender, the enterprise is fundamentally interactional and institutional in character."[15] While more recent work legitimately criticizes the original concept of "doing gender" for not allowing for the possibility of resistance and that ideal gender performances vary significantly by social location, the emphasis on the ways individual performances reflect and reinforce social structures is an important one.[16] For example, a number of authors have extended the original concept of how people "do" gender to the ways people "do" race.[17]

PARTICIPANT OBSERVATION

I observed and participated in the fatherhood programs and the special family visits that served as a reward for successful participation in the fatherhood program, and I interacted with COs and staff as I moved around the prison facilities. Group participation was not mandatory for prisoners and, while participation in programs could assist prisoners in the approval process for parole, group participation did not reduce their time. I collected roughly 280 hours of participant observation. I introduced myself to the participants of the fatherhood group, notifying them that I was conducting research on fathers in prison and that I was an observer and not an employee of Healthy Connections. I had fewer opportunities to introduce myself as a researcher to COs but did my best to be open and clear with them about who I was and why I was in the prison facilities. As an observer, I did not run groups or put together materials, lectures, or activities. I also limited how much I spoke unless the men in the group indicated that it was important to them that I participate. Usually, this meant I took part in "icebreaker" activities at the start of group and only spoke when someone in the group directly asked my opinion.

I took notes during the groups, invited men to look through what I had written, and made it clear that I would erase anything they did not want included in my field notes. While my note-taking initially elicited suspicion, the men's ability to examine my field notes and to question what I had written provided an opportunity to establish rapport with men outside of the confines of a program facilitator–prisoner relationship. In some groups, my note-taking became a source of amusement, with men instructing me to "write that down" whenever someone, especially a group facilitator, said something potentially embarrassing. Attending the meetings of the fatherhood program gave me a chance to observe how different groups of incarcerated fathers interacted with one another, with the group facilitator(s), with me, and oftentimes, with COs.

The fatherhood groups were also located as far into the prison building as I was ever allowed to enter. This offered me a particular view of the rhythm of penal life. During the time I spent in the programs, I observed prisoners not affiliated with the program moving down the hallway to and from work, the gym, or meals. I also observed COs escorting cuffed prisoners (under the observation of another CO with a video camera) to segregation, prisoners headed to offices to contest tickets they received for infractions, and once or twice, instances where the prison was locked down and no one was allowed to leave. In many ways, my participation in the fatherhood groups gave me the clearest view into life in a men's prison that I could have as a female outsider. While my participation in the program undoubtedly affected my research, being a volunteer smoothed my entrance into the prison and also provided me with a chance to sit and talk with incarcerated fathers. The opportunities for such a group interaction outside of a program are hard to come by in a prison facility, particularly for female outsiders.

I also observed the men interacting with their children in the "special visits" that served as a reward for successful participation in both of the fatherhood programs. These special visits were between an hour and two hours long. During the visits, men were allowed an unusually high amount of physical contact with their children. In normal visits, prisoners and visitors were allowed to hug briefly at the start of the visit; they were then expected to stay on opposite sides of a table with no physical contact. During the special visits, men could hold their children throughout, sit next to them, hug them at will, and play games that were unavailable during normal visits. The promise of these visits motivated many men to take part in the program. As a participant in these special visits, I helped set up games and decorations and then spent most of my time walking around, listening, watching, and helping fetch items (such as markers or stickers) for fathers and their families.

While I did not formally interview COs, entering and exiting a prison takes time. I chatted with COs as I signed in, as I waited in the lobby, as I waited in traps, and as they escorted me down hallways. It was the COs, not the prisoners, who sought to teach me official rules of the facility. I learned these rules through abrupt and impatient orders, through teasing and humorous interactions as I tried to get through the metal detector, and casual conversations as I waited to enter the facility, when COs pointed out the ways I made their jobs more difficult, as well as when they expressed concerns for my safety. I also had extensive time to observe how COs processed and interacted with visitors in the lobby and in the visiting room and to note the differences between how they responded to a volunteer and someone visiting a prisoner.

Conducting Interviews

I interviewed forty-nine incarcerated fathers for a total of 118 interviews (147 interview hours). Table 1 provides aggregated age and race demographics for the interviewees. Table 2 provides specific data for each interviewee (age, race, and the prison facility where they lived).

Table 1

Age and Race of Interviewees

Age	Number of Interviewees	Race	Number of Interviewees
18–19	14 (28.5%)	Black	21 (42.9%)
20–29	12 (24.5%)	Latino	15 (30.6%)
30–39	17 (34.5%)	White	8 (16.3%)
40+	6 (12.3%)	Multiracial	4 (8.2%)
Total	49	Total	49

TABLE 2

Interviewee Demographics by Pseudonym

Pseudonym	Age	Location	Race
Achilles	19	SY	Black
Aeneas	30	NCI	Latino (PR)
Alberto	34	NCI	Latino (PR)
Alex	28	NCI	Latino (PR)
Angel	30	NCI	Multiracial
Benny	30	NCI	Latino (PR)
Big Cheese	50	NCI	Multiracial
Brown	34	NCI	Black
Chris	18	SY	Black
Clayton	23	NCI	White
Country	early 40s	NCI	Black
Coyote	35	NCI	Black
Eric	18	SY	White
Eustis	37	NCI	Black*
Ezekiel	21	NCI	Black
Frank	35	NCI	Black
Freedom	34	NCI	Black
G	48	NCI	Black
George	23	NCI	White
Gregg	30	NCI	White
Hotdog	43	NCI	Black*
John	43	NCI	Black
K	29	NCI	Black
Kain	18	SY	Multiracial
Laredo	18	SY	Black
Luis	18	SY	Latino (PR)*
Luke	18	SY	Latino**
Magic	18	SY	Multiracial
Malik	40	NCI	Black*
Messiah	48	NCI	Latino**
			(continued)

Table 2. Interviewee Demographics by Pseudonym (continued)

Michael	33	NCI	Latino (PR)
Miguel	18	SY	Latino (PR)
Mikey	21	NCI	White
Montana	26	NCI	Latino (PR)
Mustang	28	NCI	Black
Patrick	29	NCI	White
Paul	33	NCI	Latino (PR)
Pedro	18	SY	Latino (PR)
Ricardo	31	NCI	Latino (PR)
Ricky	18	SY	Latino (PR)*
Shawn	30	NCI	Black
Spots	18	SY	Black*
Steven	32	NCI	White
Stewie	19	SY	Black*
Tony	39	NCI	White
Tyler	36	NCI	Black*
Vincent	27	NCI	Latino (PR)
William	18	SY	Black
Wiso	23	NCI	Latino (PR)

*Multiracial but claimed specific racial identity in the interview
**Referenced a Latino identity that was *not* Puerto Rican or did not mention a specific ethnic identity

Establishing race turned out to be surprisingly difficult. Far more prisoners described multiracial backgrounds than I expected, and then several of those men stated that despite having multiracial ancestries, they felt strongly linked to one particular racial group. In both table 1 and table 2, I have done my best to group men according to the racial identity they described as the most salient category. For example, Hotdog (forty-three, NCI) stated during his interview that he had Puerto Rican, Columbian, and black ancestry. Despite being able to claim a multiracial identity, he was firm that he saw himself as black. As a result, I coded Hotdog as black.

I conducted the one-on-one interviews in small rooms set off of the main visiting room. There were no COs or prison staff present during the interviews. Each interview was extensive, three to four hours each, and took place over two to four interview sessions. I combined open-ended invitations to speak (such as "Tell me about yourself."), semistructured questions organized around broad life categories (e.g., childhood, school, and family), and the extensive use of prompts (e.g., "What do you mean?" "How so?" and "Could you tell me a little more about that?"). I used my interview schedule as a checklist or guideline but did not ask the questions in the same order for every interview. Interviews were recorded and transcribed. Interviewees were informed of both actions and offered the opportunity to refuse to be recorded, and prisoners chose their own pseudonyms.

My ability to interview men more than once was invaluable. In addition to being able to interact with men during the fatherhood program, I also had an opportunity to observe how their relationship with me changed over the course of our interviews. For some interviewees, their willingness to talk to me increased over time. These men often presented themselves to me as guides, wanting to discuss their own lives and experiences in order to tell me how it is in prison and in the world. Other men were quite candid in their first interview but clammed up by the second, as if they had decided between the two meetings that they had opened up too much. Some men flirted; some did not. In a handful of interviews, it was difficult to get more than mono-syllabic answers (though one of these men told me at the end of his inter-view that he'd never had such a personal conversation with a woman before), and in still others, I could hardly get a word in edgewise—the interviewee started talking as soon as he entered the room and kept going until the door closed behind him.

I took notes before and after interviews in order to help contextualize the information I had gathered for each interviewee. This included conversa-tions and interactions with COs as I entered and exited the prison facility, as well as what was going on in the visiting room and the patterns of prisoners' entrances and exits. The dynamic between myself and the COs as I conducted interviews, in particular, was a valuable comparison for the ways the COs behaved as they escorted me, a female outsider, down the more central hall-ways of the prison facilities that led to the sites of the fatherhood programs. Part of the responsibilities of the COs watching over the visiting rooms was to interact with prisoners' families and legal counsel.

At NCI, I conducted interviews in small one-on-one rooms set off of the visiting area. The process for entering the visiting area was the same as the one I went through to enter the main prison. I checked in, put my stuff away, and went through the metal detector. Behind the metal detector there was a large wall that was mostly made up of thick, clear plastic. On the left side of this wall was a slider—a large, metal door with a small window in it that slid open and closed. A CO inside the main security station by the lobby controlled the doors that led into the facility as well as into the visiting room. Visitors walked through this door into another, smaller, waiting room.

The small waiting room had approximately fifteen plastic seafoam-green chairs. On the far side of the room was a single-occupant bathroom facility. The right wall of this small room was made up of clear material and had another slider. Once the first slider closed, the second slider could be opened. Visitors who had regular visits with prisoners waited until the prisoner had been called up to the visiting room. Because I was conducting a professional visit (or a visit in a one-on-one room), I was often allowed to enter before my interviewee had arrived. This meant I sometimes spent time overhearing conversations that went on around me, particularly those of the COs. In both rooms, I could hear the occasional shouted phrase from the hallway or the visiting room.

In the tan rectangular room, prisoners greeted families by hugging or kissing over a rope hung between two plastic poles. If people lingered too long at the rope, a CO told them to "move along." Along one side of the visiting room were the glassed-in phone bays where noncontact visits occurred. Prisoners receiving noncontact visits could not greet their families in person. Instead, families talked to men through a phone. COs oversaw these visits; for families, this meant providing paperwork and documentation, stowing personal items, and passing through the metal detector. For prisoners, this meant navigating their way through the prison, providing the COs on duty with appropriate paperwork, keeping their hug and kiss greetings brief (less than five or six seconds), and undergoing a strip search after the visit was over. Both contact and noncontact visits lasted approximately an hour.

At NCI, there was a U-shaped table, and prisoners sat on the inside of the table, visitors on the outside. Prisoners could receive up to three visitors at a time, and children had to be accompanied by an adult (in both the lobby and the visiting room). Visitors and prisoners were not allowed to make contact with each other over the table (for example, no hand-holding). On busy nights, the visiting room was packed, with roughly twenty prisoners receiving visits at a time. The noise level in the visiting room was deafening, and prisoners sat fairly close to one another (two or three feet apart) in order to make sure as many prisoners received visits as was physically possible (given the space and time constraints). As one entered from the lobby, there was a sizable desk on a platform on the left side of the room; the front of the desk faced the main visiting room and one end faced the slider that led to the small waiting room. There was a swivel chair in which at least one CO sat and observed the visiting room.

There were two one-on-one rooms, each one approximately nine by fifteen feet. One of the rooms was next to the CO desk. The other was closest to the entrance to the visiting room. I was almost always placed in the one-on-one room behind the CO desk. This room had a round plastic table and three plastic chairs. None of the chairs or the table matched one another in color. There was a door on either side of the room where I conducted interviews. Both were metal and painted tan; there was a long narrow window in each door. One door faced the visiting room, and the other door faced a hallway that led back into the prison. The door in the one-on-one room I was usually in looked out onto one of the areas designated for strip searches. This was not true in the other one-on-one room; that door faced the door where prisoners entered from the main facility. While I never saw anything below the waist, I was certainly engaging in a secondary assault of these prisoners, and I felt incredibly uncomfortable about it. I mentioned this issue to several COs, and eventually, the window was covered up with pieces of paper.

The other interview room had a large square table with a faux-wooden top and two plastic chairs. I much preferred this room to the other one, as none of the windows looked out over the strip searches. I did not, however, ever request this room. While only a few COs went out of their way to make it clear that I was an annoying burden, enough of them did so that I put effort into remaining low maintenance and invisible. My interviews at NCI were usually 1 to 1.25 hours long; toward the end of my time in the field, I got better at getting in and out of the prison, and so my interview times were consistently 1.5 hours. I then started interviewing men twice rather than three times. I interviewed two men four times because I had questions that I did not get answered in my first three interviews. My average interview time for the thirty-five interviews I conducted at NCI was 2 hours and 56 minutes.

At the youth facility (SY), much like at NCI, the process to enter the visiting room was the same as the one to enter the main prison (and occurred in the same place). Visitors and volunteers provided the COs on duty with ID, signed in, and then went through the metal detector. The trap leading to the visiting room was roughly ten by ten feet, with a slider on either side. Inside the visiting area, there was a large room set in the upper corner. This was where noncontact visits took place; there were about a dozen phones separated by small partitions to give at least a modicum of privacy. The rest of the room was open, with twenty sets of two chairs that were linked together. Prisoners entered from the far side of the room, and there was a CO desk next to that door, overlooking the entire visiting area. In one corner of the room, there was a tall black metal cabinet that contained toys. This was opened during some of the special visits for the SY fatherhood program. The one-on-one rooms where I conducted interviews were on the left-hand side of the room.

Unlike at NCI, my interviews were scheduled during the afternoon and well before the official visiting hours. As a result, the visiting room was often quiet and empty when I conducted my interviews. Every once in a while, lawyers, police officers, or social workers were meeting with a prisoner. On rare occasions, Jasper (black, midfifties, group facilitator at SY) was there, overseeing a visit between a father from his program, the man's child, and the child's mother.[18] I conducted one interview during visiting hours. That time, the visiting room was full, as both the noncontact and contact were run at the same time. The room was very loud, with families positioned close to one another in the connected two-seat furniture. It was also very warm in the visiting room.

The largest one-on-one room was about 135 square feet and was usually used for videoconferencing for parole hearings; I did not conduct any interviews in that room. The other two interview rooms were awkwardly shaped, neither triangular nor square, and both about 64 square feet. Both rooms where I conducted interviews were set some distance from the desk where the CO overseeing the visiting room was located. I rarely interacted with the CO on duty inside the visiting room. I did, however, have fairly long conversations with some of the COs as I entered and exited the prison facility. The pace of the afternoons was often quite slow, and some COs were inclined to chat as they waited for the rush of early evening visits to begin. These interactions also provided a comparison for the ways COs interacted with me as I entered the main prison facility where the fatherhood program took place.

My interviews at SY were often quite long, ranging between 1.5 and 2 hours. This meant that I conducted two interviews with each father (rather than the three I usually conducted at NCI). The average length for the fourteen interviews I conducted at SY was 3 hours and 5 minutes. Being able to spend more time with each interviewee was interesting. It often allowed for a more relaxed pace and longer, more intricate storytelling. That said, there was a subset of interviewees who limited their answers to two or three words. In the end, though, I think the longer time frame resulted in better interviews, as most of these men eventually warmed up to me and began to talk more.

About halfway through my interviews, as I exited an interview at SY, the CO at the front booth asked me to wait in the seating area for Justine (white, midthirties, the volunteer coordinator at SY). I did so, wondering what she wanted. After we exchanged greetings, she asked me if I was recording my interviews. I replied that I was. She shook her head and said, "You're not supposed to. I thought you were taking notes." I blinked a couple of times, my mind frozen, and found I could not look at her. I looked to her left, to her right, and at the floor. Finally, I managed to squeeze out, "I'm sorry. I'm envisioning my project grinding to a halt in the middle." Justine shrugged: "Perhaps it's a misunderstanding?" The rise in her voice gave me the impression she did not believe what she was saying. I told her that as far as I knew, I had permission to record my interviews. I told her that I would email and fax her my documentation.

Though I had paperwork giving me permission to bring my computer in, my research proposal clearly stated that I wanted to use my computer to record interviews, and I had written permission to bring in a microphone, an administrator from the DOC central administrative office (whose rank I never quite understood, as she was not part of the research unit and her title was "director of organization"[19]) decided that it was necessary for me to resubmit my research proposal. The staff person who had given me permission to bring in a microphone was no longer working for the DOC, and there were concerns about the legal ramifications of my recording the interviews. I could not get anyone to tell me what the exact concerns were (e.g., was it a concern that prisoners might protest being recorded and sue the DOC, or was it that the DOC administration was concerned I would end up with a recording of something damning?).

I was stunned and frustrated but had no choice but to resubmit my paperwork. While I was waiting for my paperwork to be reprocessed, I got permission to bring in a keyboard to my interviews. This allowed me to tuck the keyboard under the table and leave the computer off to one side, ensuring I would be able to make eye contact with the men I was interviewing and try to make the interview process more comfortable for the interviewees. I finished the interviews with the men I was in the process of interviewing and then took a four-month hiatus from interviewing while my paperwork was reprocessed. Consequently, 20 of the 118 interviews (or 16.9 percent) were typed up rather than recorded. However, having my computer and a separate keyboard with me (which I could keep in my lap) meant that I was able to capture nearly all of what the interviewees said, their turns of phrases, and the overall flow of the interview. After I got home, I filled in everything I could remember and set the text up in an interview format. All told, it took approximately six months for my resubmitted proposal to go through the necessary bureaucratic channels, including a perusal by the DOC legal department. In the end, the DOC gave me permission to, again, record the interviews. That second time around, I made sure I had paperwork that specified, in several locations, that I was allowed to use my computer to record interviews.

I understood that the DOC administration was primarily interested in protecting their interests and that allowing me into the facility was a favor and a privilege. What I could not get over was the constant feeling that I was doing the "wrong" thing, though I went to great lengths to do as I was asked. I did not want to cause problems, and I appreciated the time and energy any number of COs and staff invested in my project. In the beginning, I was more than happy to follow the rules. I found as I progressed, however, that the rules were often inconsistent and no matter what I did, I was doing it "wrong." I hated regularly feeling like an incompetent fool. The issue over whether I was allowed to record my interviews was the most extreme example of the constantly shifting requirements for accessing the prison, but it was far from the only one.

At some point, as I dealt with managing the intensity of my frustrations, I realized that my feelings must pale in comparison to the emotional reactions of the prisoners who could not leave the prison facility and had little or no access to private or safe emotional outlets, as their phone calls to family were recorded and letters were read by correctional staff. The realization changed the way I reacted to and interpreted expressions of anger or frustration from the men I interacted with, particularly since people inside and outside of the prison facility regularly suggested that the prisoners lacked self-control. Instead, I began to see the myriad techniques prisoners used to control their emotions, many of which were linked to their understanding of enacting successful masculinity.

Weaknesses of the Study

Throughout my research project, I tried to pay attention to the ways my social position—white, female, young, and upper-middle class—affected my data collection. Over time, I came to see the ways people responded to me based on my identity as valuable sources of data, responses that helped to shape my analysis of masculinity and fatherhood in prison. If another researcher conducted a similar project, the findings would be different, and I assert that this is one of the strengths of qualitative research, not one of its weaknesses.

That said, any qualitative study must consider how "honest" their interviewees are in course of its research. Prisoners, in particular, are part of a stigmatized group, and the belief that prisoners are manipulative liars is a powerful one. During my security orientation, for example, the booklet provided to me by the DOC outlined the ways prisoners manipulate others, and the training that accompanied the booklet emphasized that prisoners are "sly." There is some truth to this assessment of prisoners, though I would argue that the institutional setting produces this behavior, as does the innate human inclination to use lies to smooth social interactions.[20]

In the end, I addressed the question of honesty in three ways: First, I used the multiple opportunities I interacted with men (groups, interviews, and special visits), to identify both consistencies and inconsistencies in how men talked about manhood and fatherhood. Second, I did not assume that inconsistencies meant that men were actively lying. Few of us are perfectly consistent about how we approach, think, and talk about our lives; these fissures reveal where competing ideas, morals, and expectations exist. Put another way, inconsistencies are as valuable to a qualitative researcher as consistencies. Finally, lies tell a researcher what their subjects believe the researcher wants to know. I did identify some overt lies when men talked to me. When this happened, I asked myself, "Why did he lie? What did he want me to think? What did he get out of the lie?" When approached this way, a lie can also be a valuable data point.

There is one other major potential weakness that I must address: How representative are the men in this study? Unfortunately, the answer is unsatisfying: I do not know. More importantly, the research on fathers in prison is sufficiently limited that there are few answers to the question of whether being an incarcerated father makes a prisoner significantly different from his non-parental counterparts; this book seeks to contribute to our expanding knowledge about incarcerated fathers. However, other existing studies on fathers in prisons suggest that there are parallels in the ways that the incarcerated fathers in this study experience their roles as men and fathers. For example, a number of authors have found that many incarcerated fathers work to overcome extensive barriers in order to remain connected with their children.[21] I cannot provide my readers with a comparison between the men I spoke with and the other prisoners at the same facility.[22] The individuals I spoke with as I began putting together my research proposal for the DOC and Healthy Connections strongly discouraged me from extending my study to include interviews with men not involved in the program.

Even if I could have interviewed men outside of the program, I would have ameliorated some weaknesses of my study only to open up new flaws. Interacting with men in the fatherhood program accomplished two important tasks. First, the group provided a safe environment for me to form a rapport with the interviewees. Even if I had been allowed to interview men who were not in the program, interviews with men who did not know me would have been fundamentally different. Given that many of the men in the fatherhood groups initially responded to me as if I were a social worker, the opportunity to develop a rapport as a researcher improved the quality of responses in my interviews. The differences in the interviews would have been significant. Second, I had the opportunity to interact with men in a group setting and in one-on-one interviews, and for many of my participants, I also observed them interacting with their children. The different ways men presented themselves in these settings contributed to my understanding of how they understood themselves as men and fathers, as well as providing glimpses into the ways the institution of prison shaped their behavior. I formed strong rapports with a fairly sizable group of incarcerated men who were invested in their roles of fathers. Despite this investment, these men faced extensive challenges and difficulties navigating prison, fatherhood, and masculinity. My study tells us that the barriers for men who could not access the program must be greater still.

The research on fathers in prison, while not providing an easy set of comparisons, at least makes it clear that the men in this study are not remarkable. I did not interview all the men who participated in the program, and the wait-lists for the fatherhood programs at both facilities suggest that I did not even have a chance to meet all the men interested in being connected with their children at the facilities where I conducted my research. I extend work on masculinity in prison, arguing that dangerous masculinity serves local needs by creating legitimacy for security protocols, as well as larger societal needs in that prison reinforces the racial and class-based logic that legitimates mass incarceration and the use of the prison system as a tool of social control.

ACKNOWLEDGMENTS

MOST OBVIOUSLY, I OWE a debt to the staff, COs, and prisoners. This is especially true because sociologists are the "Debbie Downers" of the social sciences. More often than not, we point out the flaws and the weaknesses of institutions and cultural patterns of behavior. Inevitably, this means that individuals in any given situation enact and reinforce these cultural and structural flaws. During one fatherhood group, one of the young men asked me what I was going to write about. I shrugged and replied, "I'm not sure yet." The young man frowned at me, unhappy with my answer, and continued, "I mean, is it positive or negative? Some people, they want to trash us." I nodded to show that I understood what he was asking and told him that I wasn't intending to trash anyone but that I was also going to be honest about what I observed. I hope I have kept this promise.

I also couldn't have done my research project without the social work agency Healthy Connections. Not only did they give me access to the programs they ran, but they also offered extensive training, helping me navigate the bureaucracy of the prison system. This is also true of the men and women who worked in the DOC research unit and ultimately decided to approve my research project. Several of the COs went out of their way to help me acclimate to the rules of the prison facility, and I'm grateful for their efforts; these officers helped me connect with the day-to-day challenges of working inside a prison. Even the COs with whom I didn't get along were still trying to do their jobs to the best of their abilities, a dedication that I respect. Finally, I have to thank the men in the fatherhood program who allowed me to observe them as they struggled to talk about their concerns about their children or interacted with their families during the special visits. For many of the men, allowing me to see this aspect of themselves required a certain amount of emotional vulnerability. It is not an easy thing to be vulnerable, either in prison or out of it.

I received small professional development grants from the University of Massachusetts and the State University of New York at Cortland that helped me with transcription, editing, and indexing costs for this manuscript. I deeply appreciate every little bit of financial assistance, and while I likely would have finished without it, there have been moments where just a little bit of help made a huge psychological difference. This process certainly would have been more grueling without the occasional bit of money to ease the way.

There are also so many people who have helped me complete this book that I cannot possibly name them all. To start, my dissertation committee— Dr. Joya Misra, Dr. Andrew Papachristos, Dr. Timothy Black, and Dr. Kristin Bumiller—were central figures in the development of the core ideas of this project, and I am grateful for the amount of time and energy they devoted. At UMass, Dr. Mike Lewis, Dr. Michelle Budig, Dr. Jennifer Lundquist, Dr. Jill McCorkel, Dr. Enoch Page, Dr. Robert Zussman, Dr. Naomi Gerstel, Dr. Doug Anderton, and Dr. Don Tomaskovic-Devey all played important roles in my development as a scholar. During my time at the Center for Social Research in Hartford, Connecticut, Dr. Mary Erdmans offered me insights into ethnographic research that shaped my approach to data collection. And finally, several of my colleagues on SUNY Cortland, particularly Dr. Herbert Haines and Dr. Sharon Steadman, have been steadfast in their support. I have no doubt that I have missed people who helped me by letting me bounce ideas off of them, answering questions, or by suggesting that is was time to stop thinking about prison and go get a drink. Thanks to everyone, even if I didn't name you directly.

Finally, my husband has been there for every step of this process and has been my most reliable and consistent editor and confidant. He witnessed every moment of doubt, uncertainty, jubilation, and annoyance. He helped me work through ideas when I got stuck and was unendingly patient. He was sure I would finish this book even in moments when I couldn't stand to look at another line of it. I'm thanking him in the acknowledgments because that's what you do, but this is one of those times when words are insufficient. If you've got a partner who supports you, go home and kiss them.

Notes

Introduction   Masculinity, Fatherhood,
and Race inside America's Prisons

1. See Sabo, Kupers, and London (2001a, 12).
2. Britton's work on correctional officers and the prison as a workplace documents the ways that the institution of prison assumes that correctional officers are male, as well as the work female COs do in order to be taken seriously. See, in particular, Britton's book *At Work in the Iron Cage: The Prison as Gendered Organization* (2003).
3. See Visher, Bakken, and Gunter (2013) for further discussion of the importance of familial ties and positive postincarceration outcomes. Arditti (2012) also provides an extensive analysis of the impact of parental incarceration on children, parents, and extended families.
4. Much of the research on father involvement focuses on middle- or upper-middle-class intact families. In some ways, this reflects the challenge of studying families that may be more unstable due to precarious employment or keeping tabs on fathers who access their children only with permission of their ex-partners. In the case of a failed romantic relationship, leftover tensions and anger may make it more difficult for men to participate in raising or nurturing their children.
5. Both Hairston (1995) and Nurse (2002) point out the difficulties incarcerated men have remaining in contact with their families.
6. For example, prison offers some men the opportunity to desist from drug use, and doing so may make a good impression on their children's mothers (Roy and Dyson 2005).
7. The names and locations of the prison facilities and the name of the agency that ran the fatherhood programs have been changed (or left out) to protect confidentiality. All of the names of staff, volunteers, and prisoners have been changed to protect anonymity. The prisoners chose their pseudonyms, and I chose the pseudonyms for the staff and COs.
8. About halfway through my time conducting interviews, the DOC administration decided that I had not actually been approved to record interviews. I was allowed to bring my computer into the facility and so, while I resubmitted my paperwork, I completed the interviews that were already in progress by typing notes as near verbatim as I could. I then cleaned and expanded these typed interviews shortly after finishing them. Additionally, one prisoner declined to be recorded.
9. See Jacobs (1979), National Gang Threat Assessment Report (2005), Black (2009), Trammell (2012).
10. See Hemmens and Marquart (2000).
11. See Britton (2000).
12. See Deitz and Orr (2006).

13. Cowell (2015) discusses the impact of manufacturing loss on eight Midwestern cities. Cowell's focus is on the resilience and recovery some cities managed to accomplish, while others did not.

14. See Deitz and Orr (2006).

15. See Autor and Dorn (2013).

16. My understanding of neoliberalism relies on David Harvey's *A Brief History of Neoliberalism* (2005) and I strongly recommend the book to anyone interested in this school of political and economic thought.

17. See Harvey (2005), Cowell (2015), and Temin (2016) for further discussion.

18. Harrison (1997) dismantles the myth that most job growth in the United States comes from small businesses and instead focuses on the ways that large corporations have benefitted the most from a decentralized and globalized capitalist system. While he barely mentions neoliberalism, his discussion of flexible production and contingent labor is, nonetheless, a critique of neoliberal economic practices.

19. See Soss, Fording, and Schram (2011).

20. See Wacquant (2009) for a broad discussion of the impact of neoliberalism on the criminal justice system. Gustafson (2009) explicitly examines the tightening ties between social welfare programs and the criminal justice system. Coco (2012) examines the growing number of laws that punish debt and therefore the poor.

21. See Garland (2001, 3).

22. See Tonry (2009) for a discussion of these historical patterns in the United States. He is arguing that neoliberalism is a poor explanation for mass incarceration on the international level. While I agree that it is not the only explanation and Tonry does a compelling job explaining why, I argue that neoliberalism worked with these unique features of American culture in a way that made mass incarceration seem, to the white majority, like an "obvious" and "commonsense" solution.

23. See Mauer (2001) for a brief but clear description of these changes.

24. David Musto's book *The American Disease: Origins of Narcotic Control* (1999) provides a thorough (if somewhat dry) analysis of the earliest cultural and legal responses to narcotics. Ken Burns and Lynn Novak's documentary *Prohibition* (2011) offers a compelling look into the broader cultural influences and consequences of how Americans outlawed and then legalized alcohol consumption. And for those of you interested in exploring the ties between racism and opium, Hickman (2000) has an interesting take on Orientalism, addiction, and the law.

25. The racial disparities at every level of the criminal justice system have been extensively analyzed. For example, see Miller (1996), Flavin (2001), Beckett and Sasson (2004), Clear (2007), Black (2009), Pager (2007), Alexander (2010), Rios (2011), or Tonry (2011).

26. See Garland (2001) and Alexander (2010).

27. See Garland (2001, 10–12).

28. See Alexander (2010).

29. See U.S.S.C. (2013).

30. See Alexander (2010, 78–84) for a more detailed description of civil forfeiture. On February 20, 2019, the Supreme Court handed down a decision in *Timbs v. Indiana* that will impact civil forfeiture practices going forward. The majority opinion described the seizure of a drug dealer's vehicle "grossly disproportionate to the gravity of Timbs' offense" and that the Eighth and Fourteenth Amendments protect against "excessive punitive economic sanctions." The ruling does not eliminate civil asset forfeiture, and it is likely that it will take a series of lawsuits to establish what constitutes "grossly disproportionate" in other cases.

31. See Guerino, Harrison, and Sabol (2012) and Minton (2011).

32. The Bureau of Justice calculates the county and local jail incarceration rate (242 in 2010, according to Minton 2011) and the state and federal prison rate (502, according to West, Sabol, and Greenman 2010) separately. I have combined these numbers for clarity.

33. The U.S. state prison population declined 1–2 percent each year between 2010 and 2012. Carson and Golinelli (2013) point out that California's rapid and court-mandated decarceration is driving much of the overall declination in the U.S. state prison population. The federal prison population, on the other hand, continues to inch upward.

34. See Glaze (2010).

35. See Minton (2011).

36. Garfield (2010) focuses on the cultural and historical context specific to black men's experiences of the relationship between masculinity and violence. As part of her analysis, she discusses the effect of the "criminal black man" theme as a set of ideas that many black men must navigate as they move through their day to day lives. The belief that black men are dangerous criminals has links to both "the street" and "prison culture." In his analysis of the origins of the prison system after the American Revolution, Kann (2005) points out that black men, female criminals, and "foreigners" were treated as beyond redemption. Kann's work points to an early overlap between "black" and "outsider" status. Oboler (2009), in her edited volume, explores the experiences of Latino prisoners in the United States.

37. Bruce Western explores the demographics of incarceration in a number of works, most notably in his book *Punishment and Inequality in America* (2006). Alexander (2010) specifically addresses the race and class background of America's prison population in her discussion of prison as an institution of social control.

38. See Tonry (1995, 2011) for a more extended discussion of the shift in racial demographics over the second half of the twentieth century.

39. See Harrison and Beck (2006).

40. See Harlow (2003). This number includes those on probation in 1997.

41. See Western (2006, 73).

42. See Pettit and Western (2010).

43. See Alexander (2010, 192).

44. See Saperstein and Penner (2010, 109).

45. Kimmel's book *Guyland* (2008) does a particularly good job of laying out how certain kinds of violence are normalized through links to masculinity.

46. Judith Butler's (1993) analysis on gender performativity remains a compelling and nuanced analytic approach to the (re)creation of gendered subjectivities.

47. There is a whole field of academic study aimed at examining the practices of masculinity. Michael Kimmel (2008), Kimmel and Matthew Mahler (2003), Douglas Shrock and Michael Schwalbe (2009), R. W. Connell (1998, 2000, 2005), Michael Messner (2002), Derek Kreager (2007), and Peggy Reeves Sanday (2007) are just a few scholars who have adeptly examined violence and sexual aggression as central practices of manhood in America.

48. See Stoudt (2006) or Kimmel and Mahler (2003) for a more extended discussion of how the public responds to violent behavior in "normal" boys.

49. The research on the links between the legitimation of institutional racism and cultural representations of minorities as deviant is extensive. Angela Davis, Patricia Hill Collins (2005), Matthew Guttman, bell hooks (2004), and Michelle Alexander (2010) have all examined such links. Collins (2005), for example, points out that representations of black men and women in the media emphasize their deviance and offer support for laws and policies that disproportionately punish minorities.

50. For Latino men in the United States, the terms "macho" and "machismo" are major components of the popular imagining of Latino masculinity. These terms have a "rather explicitly racist history" (Gutmann 1996, 227), which paints Latino men as little more than violent and oversexed brutes. Mirande (2004) found that Latino men have contradictory definitions of macho—on the one hand, it can mean violence and selfish behavior, and on the other hand, it can mean selflessness and honor. Furthermore, a number of studies on masculinity in South America, Central America, and Mexico have found that being a father "emerged as the highest form of male responsibility" (Vigoya 2001, 245). Despite this, or perhaps because of it, masculinity for Latin American men often hinges on their performance as workers or authority-bearers, their sexual prowess, or their physical strength.

51. Several authors have explored the relationship between "street culture" and "prison culture," including Anderson (1999), Bourgois (1995), Black (2009), and Trammell (2012). While Bourgois (1995) was primarily focused on considering the illegal drug market and the cultural milieu of a poor urban neighborhood, going to and returning from prison was one of the major life events of many men in Bourgois's study. Trammell (2012), on the other hand, is primarily focused on the way male and female prisoners manage violence within prison. However, the raced and gendered ways incarcerated men and women approach managing violence within prison draws on patterns of interactions from the outside world. This is particularly true of the way gangs form and maintain order within the prison system.

52. See Maher and Daly (1996) or Black (2009) for a more extended discussion of masculinity and the illicit drug market in the United States.

53. Strader (2007–2008) points out that American "society is deeply conflicted about white collar crime and punishment" (45). This conflict results in contradictory and inconsistent prosecutions and punishments for white-collar crime.

54. This is particularly easy to see in the welfare system (Gustafson 2009) and in the laws and policies geared toward addressing the homeless population (National Law Center on Homelessness and Poverty and the National Coalition for the Homeless 2009). Furthermore, law enforcement agencies and politicians have shown a remarkable lack of interest in punishing middle-, upper-middle, and upper-class drug users and dealers. See Mohamed and Fritsvold (2010).

55. See the Human Rights Watch (2001) report on rape in men's prisons for further discussion of this point.

56. The role of homophobia in the construction of masculinity inside prison presents some interesting questions that I only tangentially address in this book. See Trammell (2012).

57. See Mohamed and Fritsvold (2010) for a discussion of drug dealing on campus. Sanday (2007) provides an unblinking look at the impact of fraternities on college campus sexual assaults.

58. See Britton (2011).

59. See Britton (1999).

60. See Dilulio (1995) for the introduction of the term "superpredator."

61. I would argue that violence is also a component of the feminine gender performances, though in entirely different ways profoundly affected by social location.

CHAPTER 1   NEOLIBERAL RESPONSIBILITY
AND "BEING THERE" AS A FATHER

1. See Sabol and Couture (2008) or Glaze and Maruschak (2009) for further discussion.

2. See Glaze and Maruschak (2009). See also Wildeman (2009).

3. According to Wildeman (2009), "by age 14, 50.5% of black children born in 1990 to high school dropouts had a father imprisoned" (365) as compared to 7.2 percent of white children born in 1990 (273).
4. See Wildeman (2009).
5. Creasie Finney Hairston (2001b) points to the structural limits on male prisoners' ability to call or write their families. Dyer (2005) focuses on how incarceration disrupts men's identity formation as fathers.
6. See Brown (2014).
7. See Hairston (2001b).
8. Roetigger and Swisher (2013) offer a concise summary of the research on both the positive and the negative impact of paternal incarceration on children. Arditti does the same in chapters 4 and 5 of her book *Parental Incarceration and the Family: Psychological and Social Effects of Imprisonment on Children, Parents, and Caregivers* (2012).
9. See Bahr et al. (2005) for more discussion of the factors correlated with low rates of recidivism. Visher and Travis (2003) also discuss the impact of family ties on successful reintegration into the community.
10. See Castillo, Welch, and Sarver (2013) for further discussion.
11. Of the 999 wardens contacted, 397 responded, for a response rate of 39 percent (Hoffman, Byrd, and Kightlinger 2010, 403).
12. See Hoffman, Byrd, and Kightlinger (2010) for further discussion of parenting programs in prison. The authors also discuss the limited research on the efficacy of such programs and call for more to establish which programs have a positive impact on parents or children and, therefore, are worth the investment.
13. See Arditti, Smock, and Parkman (2005) for a further discussion of men struggling to believe in their ability to be fathers while incarcerated.
14. See Tripp (2001), Nurse (2002), Arditti, Smock, and Parkman (2005), and Roy (2005).
15. See Dyer (2005).
16. In its earliest incarnations, prison reformers and staff assumed that only white men could be rehabilitated. For a nuanced discussion of race, masculinity, and punishment, see Kann (2005).
17. See Dyer (2005).
18. See Edin, Nelson, and Paranal (2004), as well as Arditti, Smock, and Parkman (2005).
19. For a more policy-oriented analysis of prisoners returning home, see Travis (2005). Alternatively, Clear (2007) conducted an ethnographic analysis of how communities with high numbers of returning prisoners react and understand incarceration and its consequences for their neighborhoods and families. Carlson and Cervera (1991) and La Vigne et al. (2005) both consider how contact with families influences recidivism. La Vigne et al., for example, argue that prisoners who maintained positive connections with families while incarcerated are less likely to recidivate. On the other hand, contact during incarceration with intimate partners where the relationship was negative *before* serving time actually had a negative impact on family support postrelease.
20. See Tripp (2001).
21. Devah Pager's extensive work on the effects of incarceration on employment prospects shows not only that a criminal record had a negative impact on the chances of employment but also that the close association between minority status and criminality affects noncriminal minority men in search of work. In her 2003 article, she states, "This evidence is suggestive of the way in which associations between race and crime affect interpersonal evaluations. Employers, already reluctant to hire blacks, appear even more wary of blacks with proven criminal involvement. Despite

the fact that these testers were bright articulate college students with effective styles of self-presentation, the cursory review of entry-level applicants leaves little room for these qualities to be noticed. Instead, the employment barriers of minority status and criminal record are compounded, intensifying the stigma toward this group" (959).

22. See Jeffries, Menghraj, and Hairston (2001) and Dyer, Pleck, and McBride (2012) for further discussion or the limited programs aimed at incarcerated fathers.

23. See Roy and Dyson (2005) and Arditti, Smock, and Parkman (2005).

24. Prisoners were assigned a security rating between one and five (five being the most dangerous) based on the nature of their crime, the length of their incarceration, the staff's best guess about their gang affiliation, and their prior history of violence (or lack thereof) in previous prison sentences. As men moved toward release or accrued time without disciplinary infractions, their level dropped. This qualified them to move to lower-security prison facilities in the state.

25. See Ilcan (2009, 221).

26. In her book *Offending Women* (2010), Lynne Haney outlines how the decentralization and devolution of the state impacted the programs and underlying logic in women's prisons in California. While Haney doesn't specifically refer to neoliberalism, the emphasis on individual responsibility in one of the programs she analyzes is nonetheless a neoliberal project. Her discussion of the struggle for funding that these programs experienced is also consistent with the widespread changes in the social safety net.

27. See Nurse (2002).

28. For a good discussion of the impact of incarceration in families, both during and after imprisonment, see chapter 5 in Joyce Arditti's *Parental Incarceration and the Family: Psychological and Social Effects of Imprisonment on Children, Parents, and Caregivers* (2012).

29. Drawing on data from the Fragile Families survey, Woldoff and Washington (2008) found that contact with the criminal justice system—being booked or incarcerated—has a negative impact on men's engagement with their children. As the authors state, "For many fathers, incarceration severs relationships with children and loved ones" (200). What contact men may have had with children before incarceration is likely to be diminished well before they return home.

30. I can't provide specific information on the cost of calls, as this might reveal the state where my research took place. However, a fifteen-minute collect call cost more than fifteen dollars after fees and per-minute costs are included. The high cost of calls from prison is a nationwide issue. See the U.S. FCC (2013) report and Williams (2015) for further information.

31. Each cycle received an average of thirty-three handouts, so there was variety in terms of the material. The focus on communication, however, was a central aspect of all five cycles.

32. Additionally, eleven (11.96 percent) of the ninety-two handouts were icebreakers or brain teasers. Seven were inspirational quotes (7.61 percent). Three (3.26 percent) were materials for Healthy Connections including an outline of the resources available to them through the agency. There were also two handouts (5.43 percent) that prompted discussions solely about men's relationships with their parents. Because these handouts did not discuss children's perspectives, they are not included in the 59 documents discussed in this paragraph.

33. Malik's wife had a much older child that was technically his stepson, and though Malik didn't claim to be the young man's father, he was interested in helping guide the younger man.

34. The extended family visit was the unicorn of NCI. There was a single trailer on the prison grounds where men could receive overnight visits with their children and their children's guardian. The guardian could be a spouse or the prisoner's parent (but not the prisoner's unmarried coparent). I only knew one man of the fifty-three I interacted with who successfully organized an extended family visit. The bureaucratic red tape was extensive, as was the wait-list.

35. In his interview, Malik felt that spankings were an important part of parenting and that he loved his father in part because he had been a firm disciplinarian. When it came to his own children, he said, "I give them spankings. My wife don't give them spankings, and my kids, they love me more than they love my wife. She yells at 'em, and they don't listen until you spank 'em. So pop them on the hand or . . . I know, something like that, and they'll listen more."

36. Jasper did not give in to these requests. He showed only one other movie during my two and a half years of fieldwork: *The Pursuit of Happyness*.

37. The author of this quote has written several books aimed at teaching men to be men according to Christian principles.

38. See Sum et al. (2011) and Pedulla (2012) for more detail on the decline in employment for teenagers and young adults.

39. See Manning and Smock (1995).

40. See Castillo, Welch, and Sarver (2013).

41. When I began my fieldwork at NCI, snacks were part of the special visits. A shift in the policy of the central administration, however, made is progressively more difficult for the facility to supply snacks. At the last special visit I attended, there were no snacks.

42. It's likely that either these five men were transferred or their families couldn't come up, but I don't know for sure.

43. His youngest daughter was six years old and conceived while Brown was out on an appeal for two months. However, in his mind, he'd been incarcerated for seven years despite the short break.

44. I'm not sure how they managed to bring his niece into the visit. I assume, given the rules of the facility, that his wife had either temporary or permanent custody of the little girl.

45. Clayton got in a car accident while driving with a suspended license. He was charged with reckless endangerment and offered a plea deal for three and a half years. He qualified for parole twenty-one months into his sentence.

46. In the last four to six weeks of my fieldwork, Jasper brought in eight new members. Technically, this means I interacted with forty-five fathers. However, I didn't really get to know the eight men who joined at the end of my fieldwork, there was no opportunity to interview them, I don't know when and how they left the facility, and there wasn't a special visit in that last stretch. As a result, I'm not including these young men in my total numbers.

47. One young man, Achilles, is counted twice in these statistics, as he went home, violated his parole, earned a new six-month sentence, returned to SY, and then was transferred to an adult facility.

48. See Haney (2010, 224).

Chapter 2 Little Me versus My Princess

1. See Messner (2002).

2. The differences in the expectations, roles, and obligations between mothers and fathers have been extensively documented. In her now classic text *The Cultural*

Contradictions of Motherhood, Sharon Hays states, "In sum, the methods of appropriate child rearing [for mothers] are construed as *child-centered, expert-guided, emotionally absorbing, labor-intensive,* and *financially expensive*" (1996, 8; italics in original). Hays goes on to point out that all mothers are held up to these impossible—and often contradictory—expectations and that some women (namely, white, middle- and upper-class women) can achieve more of the ideal qualities of a "good" mother. Scott Coltrane, in his book *The Family Man*, explores the equivalent pressures on men that demand that men operate as financial providers and nurturers while leaving little space for them to engage in care work.

3. The academic work on the impact of children's gender on parenting is also extensive and often considers how parents explicitly or implicitly teach their children what behaviors are "normal" for their gender (Paechter 2007).

4. A number of scholars discuss the impact of popular parenting books and the naturalization of gender differences as they discuss gender and parenting more broadly, including Hays (1996), Kane (2012), and Kaufman (2013). Krafchik et al. (2005) specifically examine the gendered content of six best-selling self-help books on parenting.

5. In their review on gender and family process, Raley and Bianchi (2006) point out, "Fathers more often marry and stay married and mothers report more marital happiness in families with sons—although associations are weakening and differentials are not large. Divorced fathers more often have custody of sons than of daughters" (401).

6. See Sharp and Ispa (2009).

7. Using the 1997 Child Development Supplement to the Panel Study of Income Dynamics, Sandra Hofferth (2003) examined the effect of economic circumstance, the neighborhood context, and cultural differences on the patterns of paternal engagement by race. She found that "Black children's fathers exhibit less warmth but monitor their children more, Hispanic fathers monitor their children less, and both minority groups exhibit more responsibility for child rearing than White fathers" (185). The families in Hofferth's study were all two-parent households and included biological and stepfathers.

8. See Williams (2009).

9. Hill (2002) interviewed thirty-five African American parents and divided them into three groups: stable middle class, first-generation middle class, and less educated. The parental expectations for "normal" masculine and feminine behavior shifted among these three class positions, becoming less traditional with more education and class stability.

10. It may be that expressing concerns that their sons might end up incarcerated and their daughters manipulated and used by men served as a proxy for an overt discussion of racism, though none of my interviewees suggest that this was the case.

11. See Shade et al. (2012).

12. See Shade et al. (2012, 443).

13. The DOC staff who approved my research project requested that I not ask prisoners about illegal activities. As a result, I opted not to ask men directly about their sentences and why they were incarcerated. I could access a certain amount of information publicly (though sentences were often presented in ranges and gave very basic information about the charges), and a number of men volunteered information. For the purposes of providing readers with a general impression of the men I quote, I've divided sentences into three categories: (1) *short* for those serving fewer than ten years, (2) *long* for men serving more than ten years but eventually going home, and (3) *life* sentences. If men specifically shared their sentence lengths with me and indicated they felt comfortable with that being public, I have included that information.

14. Tyler was unwilling to provide me with a more specific definition for the slang term *chickenhead* because I was, in his words, a "good girl." The term refers to women who perform fellatio on multiple partners, often for drugs or other favors.

15. For example, Snyder and Sickmund (2006) report that the nonfatal violent victimization rate for boys was 50 percent higher than for girls and that the most common setting for violent altercations was school. Female juvenile offenders represent a higher percentage of the juvenile detention population (15 percent) as compared to their adult counterparts (7 percent). However, girls remain the minority in the juvenile detention population (Snyder and Sickmund 2006, 206). Similarly, research on disciplinary action in schools suggests that boys are more likely to be violent and that minority boys are more likely to get expelled as compared to their white peers (Ferguson 2000; Welch and Payne 2010).

16. For differences in mother-father communication about sexual issues, see DiIorio, Kelley, and Hockenberry-Eaton (1999) and Wilson and Koo (2010). For a discussion on parental discomfort discussing sexual topics, see Elliott (2010). For a discussion of fathers' emphasizing the need to protect their daughters from other men and the consequences of sex, see Wilson, Dalberth, and Koo (2010).

17. Even though I interviewed Derek, he isn't counted as one of the fourteen fathers I interviewed at SY because something went wrong with the recording about twenty minutes into his second interview. He was then transferred to an adult facility before I could reinterview him. Because his interview was incomplete compared to the others, I opted not to count him in the overall statistics. Nonetheless, I have more data on him than some of the other fathers in the group.

18. Alex was twenty-eight, Puerto Rican, and had long curly black hair. He was just shy of six feet and very thin. The skin on his face was pockmarked from acne, and he spoke with a fairly heavy Spanish accent though he'd spent most of his life in the United States. He had a nine-year-old son that he rarely got to see. He and his child's mother did not get along, and she believed that Alex was a bad influence on their child. During his interview, Alex spoke at length about how painful it was to be unable to communicate with his son.

19. See Townsend (2002, 186).

20. See Townsend (2002).

CHAPTER 3   UNRULY BOYS AND DANGEROUS MEN

1. Chapter 4 of Howard Snyder and Melissa Sickmund's (2006) national report on juvenile offenders and victims provides a concise summary of the history and philosophical roots of the juvenile justice system.

2. See Roberts (1997), Lyons and Rittner (1998), and Cox (2015).

3. See Dilulio (1995) for the original article. Haberman (2014) discusses the consequences of this widespread anxiety even though, ultimately, the dreaded wave of superpredators did not appear.

4. See Howell (2009, 7).

5. See Mears, Hay, Gertz, and Mancini (2007) and Applegate, Davis, and Cullen (2009) for a discussion on the emphasis in the juvenile justice system on saving children.

6. For example, Abrams, Anderson-Nathe, and Aguilar (2008) study the construction of masculinity in two different juvenile facilities, pointing out that "the [penal] institutions helped young men to develop new resources for expressing their identities, while . . . the staff and the institutions [also] reinforced ways of being 'a man' that are strongly linked to crime" (39).

7. See Giroux (2003), Simon (2006), Hirschfield (2008), Public Agenda Media (2004), and DeVoe et al. (2005) for further discussion of schools managing unruly boys.

8. See Foucault (1978).

9. See Foucault (1978, 2).

10. See Garland (2001).

11. Institutions play a central role in the reproduction of gendered norms, and the research on the institutional production of masculinity is extensive. A number of authors have examined the reproduction of masculinity in schools, looking at race (Ferguson 2000), heterosexuality (Pascoe 2007), and violence (Hasbrook and Harris 1999; Klein 2006). Analyses of masculinity at work, on the other hand, often emphasize the tensions between the masculinized ideals of the "good" worker and the nurturing components of fatherhood (Cooper 2000; Ranson 2001). Britton and Williams (1995) argue that assumptions of heterosexuality marginalize the contributions of enlisted gay men and lesbians. Johnson (2010) examines the (re)production of masculinity in a military-style school, pointing out that the "warrior hero archetype" valued in the military is understood to both be white and possess a capacity for violence rooted in the protection of those who are weak. Johnson's analysis is particularly interesting because it highlights the sets of expectations that are imported and exported among institutions such as school, the military, and the workplace.

12. See Connell and Messerschmidt (2005).

13. See Mosher (1998).

14. See Rosen, Knudson, and Fancher (2003) and Scharrer (2001).

15. See Toch (1998) and Miller (2006).

16. There is a large and rich field of study focused on masculinity. To name just a few of the more general analyses, see Kimmel (2008), Connell and Messerschmidt (2005), and McCaughey (2008). Additionally, there are a number of researchers who have conducted specific analyses of masculine gender roles and performances in particular social situations. For example, see Simon and Nath (2004) and Kimmel (2008) for effective examinations of men and emotional expression. Similarly, a number of authors have addressed how race informs perceptions of violence among men, including Vigoya (2001), hooks (2004), Collins (2005), and Alcalde (2011). For analyses that focus on the masculinized assumptions about the intrinsic nature of criminality and the consequences of such assumptions, see Foucault (1978), Garland (2001), and Kann (2005).

17. Nancy Fraser, in her book *Unruly Practices: Power, Discourse, and Gender in Contemporary Social Theory* (1989), considers, among a number of other topics, the work done to construct women's "needs" as "wants" the state isn't obligated to meet (e.g., childcare). In both of her books, *The Unruly Woman: Gender and Genres of Laughter* (1995) and *Unruly Girls, Unrepentant Mothers: Redefining Feminism On Screen* (2010), Kathleen Rowe draws on images of unruly women in television and cinema to consider the perception and treatment of women unable to confine themselves to their "proper place."

18. Some scholars discuss the way the disabled student also embodies the "unruly subject" who violates or upsets the even, disciplined routine of the school. See, for example, Erevelles (2000).

19. This is in contrast to the state training school for delinquent youths that houses juvenile offenders under the age of seventeen who are serving shorter sentences (months instead of years); this training school overtly references rehabilitation in their public materials in ways SY does not.

20. Correctional officers work in a deeply masculine workplace (Britton 1997a; Savicki, Cooley, and Gjesvold 2003; Haney 2008) where the ability to deal with dangerous

prisoners allows male COs to engage in taint management. That is, both COs and the larger public believe that doing the hard work of managing rebellious prisoner bodies is a work practice worthy of respect (Tracy and Scott 2006). A desire for respect is one of the reasons most COs prefer to work in men's prisons instead of women's facilities (Britton 1999) and why female COs struggle to gain promotions at the same rate as their male counterparts (Griffin, Armstrong, and Hepburn 2005; Rader 2005).

21. Among other points, Comfort's (2003) analysis of women visiting men in prison demonstrates how the policing of clothing assists COs in maintaining control over outsiders.

22. Hairston has conducted several studies on the structural limits on the ability of incarcerated fathers to remain in contact with their children (2001a, 2001b, 2003).

23. See Goffman (1961, 7–8).

24. See Conover (2000, 223).

25. Indeed, the clothing associated with hip-hop (particularly from the 1990s) is a stylized reflection of the consistently oversized pants and shirts offered prisoners. Similarly, most prison administrations do not allow prisoners to have belts because it is too easy to commit suicide or murder with one. For an interesting discussion of clothing and power, see Baker (2009).

26. The maintenance of the division between COs and prisoners, reinforced by the exertion of power over the day-to-day aspects of prison life, is a central aspect of a total institution. In this regard, the juvenile facility was no different than the adult facility (Goffman 1961).

27. See Kimmel (2008).

28. Morris's (2005) article on schools, clothing, and discipline is an interesting comparison to my fieldwork in the juvenile facility. At the school where Morris conducted his research, the teachers and staff disciplined male students with the refrain "Tuck in that shirt." The ultimate goal of the educators that Morris observed was to train the children under their care to behave "properly."

29. Acker (1990) generated a massive literature on the ways organizations rely on, re-create, and naturalize gender divisions.

30. See Sexton, Jenness, and Sumner (2010), Jenness and Fenstermaker (2014), and Rosenberg and Oswin (2015).

31. See Britton (1999).

32. See McCorkel (2004) and McCorkel (2013).

33. Over my two and a half years entering prison, I had a couple of heartfelt conversations with COs about prisoners and their families. These COs acknowledged the challenges many of the prisoners had faced and believed that it was important for prisoners to stay connected to their children. I thank these COs for being willing to discuss their understanding of prison and prisoners with an outsider.

34. Estimates for the number of incarcerated men with children are difficult to come by and the reliability of such estimates vary widely from state to state. That is even truer for juveniles. The Bureau of Justice Statistics produced a report in 2009 that estimated that roughly half of men in prison are also fathers. This report, however, doesn't address juveniles. Nurse (2001) conducted her research on juvenile fathers in California and the California Youth Authority estimated that as of 1995, a quarter of the male juvenile population had children.

35. Unruh, Bullis, and Yovanoff (2003)

36. See Nurse (2001).

CHAPTER 4   GAME FACE AND GOING UP THE WAY

1. For a discussion of the historical origins of felony-murder laws in the United States, see Binder (2004).
2. Levan, Polzer, and Downing (2011) analyze comedic and dramatic representations of sexual assault among prisoners. Britton (2000) discusses images of the "sadistic guard" in her introduction to her analysis of COs and prison as a gendered organization.
3. See Curtis (2014) for further discussion of this point.
4. See Miller (2006).
5. Human Rights Watch (2001, 5).
6. See Man and Cronan (2001).
7. The Prison Rape Elimination Act may eventually have a significant impact. Change, however, is quite slow. The two major successes emerging from PREA are the increased attention to collecting data on sexual assault rates in prison, particularly by the Bureau of Justice Statistics, and the creation of national guidelines for the prevention and reduction of prison rape by the Department of Justice. Additionally, there is slow progress taking place as individual prisons and jails attempt to initiate programs to reduce sexual assault and violence in prison (see La Vigne et al. 2011 for such an example).
8. Wolff, Shi, and Bachman (2008) attempt to redress this lack by making suggestions on how to improve the survey questions researchers often use when trying to examine both sexual and physical assault. In 2009, Wolff and Shi collected data from a random sample of 6,964 prisoners. Using 2,400 cases of both physical (n = 2200) and sexual (n = 200) assault, the authors examined inmate-on-inmate as well as staff-on-prisoner sexual and physical assault. They suggest the importance of interventions both before and after assaults, as the physical and emotional aftermath increases feelings of anger and depression. Interestingly, a third of their sample for physical assault and half of the sample for sexual assault reported that they believed their race or ethnic identity was at least part of the motivation behind their assault.
9. See Sabo, Kupers, and London (2001b) as well as Phillips (2001).
10. See Connell (2005).
11. For more on the subject, see R. W. Connell's (1998, 2000, 2005) compelling body of work. Michael Kimmel has also written extensively on the formation of masculinity in concert with (and in opposition to) femininity. In particular, I recommend Kimmel's book *Guyland: The Perilous World Where Boys Become Men* (2008).
12. Telling me, of course, would have made him a snitch.
13. Because I didn't interview COs, I cannot speak to how the female COs in this study internally experienced their work environment. Roughly 20 percent of the COs in my study were women, and in many ways, they behaved similarly to their male counterparts. That said, no female CO ever attempted to persuade me that she was a better man than the prisoners she oversaw. On occasion, female COs did try to remind or teach me that prisoners were the worst of the worst. They were also more likely than male COs to be verbally direct in their assessment of my clothing. Female COs remain an underresearched group in prisons, particularly for the strategies they use to manage their gender performances in order to do their jobs. For some exceptions, see Dana Britton's work (1997a, 1997b, 1999, and 2003). Additionally, Rader (2005) interviewed twelve female COs and analyzes the strategies they used for managing the "ultramasculine" environment of prison.
14. During his interview, he told me that his grandmother had been a member of the Blackfoot tribe but that he identified as black.
15. See Connell and Messerschmidt (2005).

16. Chris was not married to his daughter's mother, but the two had been together off and on for several years, and Chris had a relationship with her young son (who was not his biological child). Chris often referred to the boy as his son, and during the special visit, he spent as much time playing with the little boy as he did holding his infant daughter.

17. It was also thanks to a little bit of luck that he wasn't transferred to another facility while he waited, something that happened to a number of fathers at NCI.

18. The work on how prison functions as a total institution to shape both prisoner and CO behavior is quite extensive. Goffman's (1961) outline of a classic total institution and the Stanford Prison Experiment (Haney, Banks, and Zimbardo 1973; Zimbardo, Maslach, and Haney 2000) often form the building blocks for this analytic approach. Carroll (1974) is primarily focused on the ways prisoners, staff, and the structure of the prison both create and rely on divisions drawn along racial lines. More recently, Trammell (2012) attempts to examine the differences in the strategies prisoners use to manage violence at male and female penal institutions.

19. See Wacquant (2000, 2001, 2009) for well-developed analyses of the race and class management embedded in a number of major institutional and structural practices in the United States. Having a solid grasp of neoliberalism can help in reading Wacquant's work effectively, and I recommend David Harvey's *A Brief History of Neoliberalism* as a prerequisite. Finally, while Kaaryn Gustafson (2009) analyzes the ties between the criminal justice system and welfare administration, her approach demonstrates that law enforcement is increasingly intertwined with welfare practices (e.g., capturing people with outstanding warrants via welfare participation and paperwork). She argues that these connections criminalize poverty and increased the likelihood that poor people will be punished for crimes unrelated to welfare fraud.

20. Britton's (2003) analysis of prison as a gendered workplace touches on a number of issues that COs face. Among these concerns is minimizing violence, which sometimes requires COs to bend the rules slightly. For a perspective on how prisoners seek to minimize violence, Trammell's (2012) comparison between a men's prison and a women's facility suggests that many of those incarcerated perceive that some kinds of violence (e.g., getting in a fight with someone harassing you) can prevent other, more dangerous kinds (e.g., sexual assault).

21. For exceptions, see Bandyopadhyay (2006) or Miller (2006).

CONCLUSION   THE CONDITIONS OF POSSIBILITY

1. The DOC staff have far more power in this negotiation, though clearly prisoners are not without agency.
2. See Britton (1999, 464).
3. See Britton (1999, 469).
4. See Hannah-Moffat (2000), McCorkel (2004), and Haney (2010).
5. Foucault (1978, 2).
6. See Woodruff (2014), *Wall Street Journal* (2015), and Hurst (2014).
7. See Clear (2007), Wildeman (2009), and Arditti (2012).
8. See Curran and Abrams (2000) and Roy and Dyson (2010).
9. See Roy (1999).
10. See Roy and Dyson (2010).
11. See Bronte-Tinkew et al. (2007).
12. See Jeffries, Menghraj, and Hairston (2001, 48).
13. See Jeffries, Menghraj, and Hairston (2001).
14. See Block et al. (2014).

15. See Arditti (2012, 103).
16. See Travis and Waul (2003).
17. See Raphael (2011).
18. See Jeffries, Menghraj, and Hairston (2001, 51).
19. For example, Vuolo and Kruttschnitt (2008) focus their analysis on ways corrections officers can improve prisoners' adjustments to incarceration in two women's facilities.
20. The best urban ethnographies that sociology has to offer capture the ways some individuals make the choice to become involved in the illegal drug market. Here are a selection, to name just a few such texts: Philippe Bourgois's *In Search of Respect: Selling Crack in El Barrio* (1995), Victor Rios's *Punished: Policing the Lives of Black and Latino Boys* (2001), Tim Black's *When a Heart Turns Rock Solid: The Lives of Three Puerto Rican Brothers On and Off the Streets* (2009), Jay Macleod's *Ain't No Makin' It: Leveled Aspirations in a Low-Income Neighborhood* (1987), Carol Stacks's *All Our Kin: Strategies for Survival in a Black Community* (1997), Kathy Edin and Maria Kefalas's *Promises I Can Keep: Why Poor Women Put Motherhood before Marriage* (2005), and Mary Pattillo-McCoy's *Black Picket Fences: Privilege and Peril among the Black Middle Class* (2000).
21. Too often, those who imagine undoing the damage of the War on Drugs make claims that legalization will solve all of our problems. This can never be true, as every solution brings with it new sets of problems. However, we have choices about how we go about dismantling the War on Drugs, and many authors have put together nuanced examinations of our options, including Hughes and Steven (2010), Nadelmann (2008), Shaw and Lavan (2011), and Caulkins et al. (2012).
22. See the ACLU's (n.d.) summary of the Fair Sentencing Act of 2010.
23. See Mosher and Akins (2007, 212–215) and Inciardi, Surratt, and Kurtz (2008).
24. For a good example of a global analysis of workplace family policies for fathers, see Hobson (2002).
25. See Sanday (2007) for a compelling discussion of sexual assault—and what we can do about it—on college campuses.
26. While this book is focused on minority men, such work also needs to be done for women of color and poor folks of all colors. See Collins (2005), Harvey Wingfield (2008), and Garfield (2010) for analyses focused on race and work. Adia Harvey Wingfield, in particular, offers compelling insight into the intersection of race, class, and gender in the workplace.
27. I focus on men in this book, but the work addressing the impact of racial stereotypes on women is well developed and compelling. Patricia Hill Collins's book *Black Sexual Politics: African Americans, Gender, and the New Racism* (2005) analyzes the impact of American masculine and feminine ideals on African Americans. Julie Bettie's book *Women without Class: Girls, Race, and Identity* (2003) explores some of the raced and classed assumptions that impact girls' beliefs and opportunities.
28. I draw on this phrase from Foucault's analysis of the birth of the clinic. In his analysis, Foucault (1973) states that he is addressing "the silent configuration in which language finds support: the relation of situation and attitude to what is speaking and what is spoken about" (xi). In other words, he is examining that which systemizes what people say and do not say, the "common structure" that opens up some possibilities and closes down others, the "conditions of possibility" (xxi–xxii).
29. See Alexander (2010, 199).
30. See Garland (2001, 12; italics in original).
31. Alexander (2010) points out that the erosion of civil liberties has greatly impacted poorer, predominantly minority neighborhoods. Alexander's analysis focuses on the structure of the legal system. Tom Clear (2009) focuses on the impact of

incarceration and the reintegration of prisoners on the people in predominantly poor, minority communities.

32. See Morín (2009) for a brief discussion of the links between incarceration rates and immigration patterns in the United States. Cole and Dempsey (2002) provide an extensive discussion of civil liberties, risk management, and terrorism in their book *Terrorism and the Constitution: Sacrificing Civil Liberties in the Name of National Security.*

33. Alexander (2010, 176).

34. See Frieden (2012).

35. See the *National Defense Authorization Act (NDAA) for Fiscal Year 2012* (U.S. Congress 2011) and the *Foreign Intelligence Surveillance Act (FISA) of 1978 Amendments Act of 2008* (U.S. Congress 2008).

36. For example, the report *Out of the Shadows: Getting Ahead of Prison Radicalization* (2006) focuses on the possibilities of Islamic radicals recruiting domestic terrorists in American prisons. Useem (2012) highlights the myths and misinformation on the links between incarceration and terrorism.

37. For a discussion of the debate on religious texts in prison, see Associated Press (2007) or Moore (2009).

38. See Alexander (2010, 176–180) for a discussion of how many people see but do not see the impact of racial inequality and incarceration in the United States.

APPENDIX   METHODS AND RESEARCH SETTING

1. The director of Healthy Connections was the first "gatekeeper," a person with the ability to provide or deny me access to the field site, who I encountered. Prison research, as I would later learn, requires negotiating with numerous gatekeepers, sometimes more than once, and every negotiation affected how, when, and where I could conduct my data collection.

2. See Gertz (1973) for a discussion of the importance of detailed descriptions.

3. See Emerson, Fretz, and Shaw (1995) for an excellent discussion of how to approach analytic memos and coding schemes.

4. See Edin, Nelson, and Paranal (2004, 52).

5. See Polletta et al. (2011, 114).

6. See Polletta et al. (2011, 110).

7. See Ewick and Silbey (1998) for an interesting analysis of the impact of storytelling about institutional structures on perceptions of rights and access.

8. For a good discussion of narrative inquiry practices, see Bochner and Riggs (2014).

9. Any scholar owes a debt to the people who trained her. For me, my time as a research assistant for Dr. Timothy Black and Dr. Mary Erdmans profoundly shaped how I thought about the interview process and the value of multiple interviews with your research participants. In my graduate program, both Dr. Robert Zussman and Dr. Michael Lewis influenced my understanding of narrative inquiry.

10. See Arendell (1997, 348).

11. See McCorkel and Myers (2003) for an analysis of the risks of ignoring privilege as a researcher.

12. See Smith (2006, 2).

13. See Smith (2005).

14. See also West and Fenstermaker (1995).

15. See West and Zimmerman (1987, 136).

16. See Deutsch (2007).

17. See Harvey Wingfield (2007) or Markus and Moya (2010) for examinations of learning to "do" race.

18. Jasper scheduled individual contact visits between fathers and their children as often as he could. For some men, this meant regular visits. As long as there was an adult (who was, to my observation, always a woman) willing to bring the child to the facility, Jasper was willing to fill the paperwork out. I wanted to attend some of these visits, but the scheduling was inconsistent and often conflicted with my work/ school schedule. As a result, I did not observe any visit outside of catching the occasional glimpse during interviews.

19. This title is a pseudonym, though one I chose that is as equally vague as her real title.

20. I drew on Erving Goffman's work for this assertion, particularly *The Presentation of Everyday Life* (1959).

21. For research on incarcerated men interested in remaining connected with their children, see Tripp (2001), Nurse (2002), Lanier (2003), Arditti, Smock, and Parkman (2005), Roy and Dyson (2005), and Clarke (2005).

22. The men in this study undoubtedly differed from other fathers in the two prison facilities where I conducted my research. They had managed to navigate and overcome significant bureaucratic barriers posed by the DOC in order to access the program. This was not true for many men in prison, and it is likely that this skill set differentiated the fathers in this study from other incarcerated men with children. Even at the youth facility, there was limited space, support, and resources focused on fatherhood. The adult facility had even fewer resources. Many of these men were employed within the prison and had desirable jobs in the kitchen, in the gym, in the library, and doing industrial work. For example, working in the gym was considered one of the better jobs at NCI because prisoners could work out during their shifts; this was also one of the more common jobs held by men in the fatherhood groups at NCI. Similarly, the young men at SY considered working in the kitchens to be one of the better jobs because the shifts were short and the pay was good (as compared to a job cleaning the facility); this was also a common job among the young men in the group at SY. In other words, my interviewees were good at getting what they needed from a bureaucracy designed to limit their resources. Despite their skills at navigating the prison bureaucracy, these men faced extensive difficulties in having any kind of relationship with their children, balancing their expectations as men and fathers, and keeping their personal lives and families private from both COs and other prisoners. If these men had such difficulties, it is likely that other men less experienced or successful would have significantly more challenges with remaining connected to their children on the outside.

WORKS CITED

Abrams, Laura, Ben Anderson-Nathe, and Jemel Aguilar. 2008. "Constructing Masculinities in Juvenile Corrections." *Men and Masculinities* 11 (1): 22–41.

Acker, Joan. 1990. "Hierarchies, Jobs, Bodies: A Theory of Gendered Organizations." *Gender & Society* 4 (2): 139–158.

Alcalde, M. Cristina. 2011. "Masculinities in Motion: Latino Men and Violence in Kentucky." *Men and Masculinities* 14 (4): 450–469.

Alexander, Michelle. 2010. *The New Jim Crow: Mass Incarceration in the Age of Colorblindness.* New York: New Press.

American Civil Liberties Union (ACLU). n.d. "Fair Sentencing Act." Accessed June 14, 2018. https://www.aclu.org/issues/criminal-law-reform/drug-law-reform/fair-sentencing-act.

Anderson, Elijah. 1999. *Code of the Street: Decency, Violence, and the Moral Life of the Inner City.* New York: W. W. Norton.

Applegate, Brandon, Robin King Davis, and Francis T. Cullen. 2009. "Reconsidering Child Saving." *Crime & Delinquency* 55 (1): 51–77.

Arditti, Joyce. 2012. *Parental Incarceration and the Family: Psychological and Social Effects of Imprisonment on Children, Parents, and Caregivers.* New York: New York University Press.

Arditti, Joyce A., Sara A. Smock, and Tiffaney S. Parkman. 2005. "'It's Been Hard to Be a Father': A Qualitative Exploration of Incarcerated Fatherhood." *Fathering: A Journal of Theory, Research, and Practice about Men as Fathers* 3 (3): 267–288.

Arendell, Terry. 1997. "After Divorce: Investigations into Father Absence." *Gender & Society* 6 (4): 562–586.

Associated Press. 2007. "Inmates Sue over Clearing of Religious Books from Libraries." *USA Today*, June 10, 2007. Accessed May 15, 2012. https://usatoday30.usatoday.com/news/nation/2007-06-10-prison-book-ban_N.htm.

Autor, David, and David Dorn. 2013. "The Growth of Low-Skill Service Jobs and the Polarization of the US Labor Market." *American Economic Review* 103 (5): 1553–1597.

Bahr, Stephen, Anita Armstrong, Benjamin Gibbs, Paul Harris, and James Fisher. 2005. "The Reentry Process: How Parolees Adjust to Release from Prison." *Fathering: A Journal of Theory, Research, and Practice about Men as Fathers* 3 (3): 243–265.

Baker, Lee. 2009. "Saggin' and Braggin.'" In *Anthropology off the Shelf: Anthropologists On Writing*, edited by Alisse Waterston and Maria Vesperi. Hoboken, N.J.: Wiley-Blackwell.

Bandyopadhyay, Mahuya. 2006. "Competing Masculinities in a Prison." *Men and Masculinities* 9 (2): 186–203.

Beckett, Katherine, and Theodore Sasson. 2004. *The Politics of Injustice: Crime and Punishment in America.* Thousand Oaks, Calif.: Sage.

Bettie, Julie. 2003. *Women without Class: Girls, Race, and Identity*. Berkeley: University of California Press.

Bhattacharyya, Gargi. 2008. *Dangerous Brown Men: Exploiting Sex, Violence and Feminism in the "War on the Terror."* London: Zed Books.

Binder, Guyora. 2004. "The Origins of American Felony Murder Rules." *Stanford Law Review* 57 (1): 59–208.

Black, Timothy. 2009. *When a Heart Turns Rock Solid: The Lives of Three Puerto Rican Brothers on and off the Streets*. 1st ed. New York: Pantheon Books.

Block, Steven, Christopher Brown, Louis Barretti, Erin Walker, Michael Yudt, and Ralph Fretz. 2014. "A Mixed-Method Assessment of a Parenting Program for Incarcerated Fathers." *Journal of Correctional Education* 65 (1): 50–67.

Block v. Rutherford. 1984. 468 U.S. Case Law. Docket Number 83-317. Supreme Court of the United States. July 3, 1984.

Bochner, Arthur, and Nicholas Riggs. 2014. "Practicing Narrative Inquiry." In *The Oxford Handbook of Qualitative Research*, edited by Patricia Leavey, 195–222. Oxford: Oxford University Press.

Bourgois, Philippe. 1995. *In Search of Respect: Selling Crack in El Barrio. Structural Analysis in the Social Sciences*. Cambridge: Cambridge University Press.

Britton, Dana. 1997a. "Gendered Organizational Logic: Policy and Practice in Women's Prisons." *Gender & Society* 11:796–818.

———. 1997b. "Perceptions of the Work Environment among Correctional Officers: Do Race and Sex Matter?" *Criminology* 35:85–105.

———. 1999. "Cat Fights and Gang Fights: Preference for Work in a Male-Dominated Organization." *Sociological Quarterly* 40 (3): 455–474.

———. 2000. "The Epistemology of the Gendered Organization." *Gender & Society* 14 (3): 418–434.

———. 2003. *At Work in the Iron Cage: The Prison as Gendered Organization*. New York: New York University Press.

———. 2011. *The Gender of Crime*. Boulder, Colo.: Rowman & Littlefield.

Britton, Dana, and Christine Williams. 1995. "Don't Ask, Don't Tell, Don't Pursue: Military Policy and the Construction of Heterosexual Masculinity." *Journal of Homosexuality* 30 (1): 1–21.

Bronte-Tinkew, Jacinta, Jennifer Carrano, Tiffany Allen, Lillian Bowie, Kassim Mbawa, and Gregory Matthews. 2007. "Exhibit G." In *Elements of Promising Practice for Fatherhood Programs: Evidence-Based Research Findings on Programs for Fathers*. U.S. Department of Health and Human Services. Office of Family Assistance. Administration for Children and Families.

Brown, Alex. 2014. "Despite New Rules, Prisoners Still Paying Big to Call Home." *National Journal*, July 9, 2014. Accessed March 16, 2019. https://www.theatlantic.com/politics/archive/2014/07/despite-new-rules-prisoners-still-paying-big-to-call-home/442170/.

Burns, Ken, and Lynn Novak, dir. 2011. *Prohibition*. Walpole, N.H.: Florentine Films.

Butler, Judith. 1993. *Bodies That Matter: On the Discursive Limits of "Sex."* New York: Routledge.

Carlson, Bonnie, and Neil Cervera. 1991. "Inmates and Their Families: Conjugal Visits, Family Contact, and Family Functioning." *Criminal Justice and Behavior* 18 (3): 318–331.

Carroll, Leo. 1974. *Hacks, Blacks, and Cons: Race Relations in a Maximum Security Prison*. Lexington, Mass.: Lexington Books.

Carson, E. Ann, and Daniela Golinelli. 2013. *Prisoners in 2012—Advance Report*. Bureau of Justice Statistics Bulletin. U.S. Department of Justice. Office of Justice Programs. Bureau of Justice Statistics.

Castillo, Jason, Greg Welch, and Christian Sarver. 2013. "The Relationship between Disadvantaged Fathers' Employment Stability, Workplace Flexibility, and Involvement with Their Infant Children." *Journal of Social Service Research* 39:380–396.

Caulkins, Jonathan, Angela Hawken, Beau Kilmer, and Mark Kleiman. 2012. *Marijuana Legalization: What Everyone Needs to Know*. New York: Oxford University Press.

Clarke, Lynda. 2005. "Fathering behind Bars in English Prisons: Imprisoned Fathers' Identity and Contact with Their Children." *Fathering: A Journal of Theory, Research, and Practice about Men as Fathers* 3 (3): 221–241.

Clear, Todd R. 2007. *Imprisoning Communities: How Mass Incarceration Makes Disadvantaged Neighborhoods Worse*. Studies in Crime and Public Policy. Oxford: Oxford University Press.

Coco, Linda. 2012. "Debtor's Prison in the Neoliberal State: 'Debtfare' and the Cultural Logics of the Bankruptcy Abuse and Prevention and Consumer Protection Act of 2005." *California Western Law Review* 49 (1): 1–49.

Cole, David, and James Dempsey. 2002. *Terrorism and the Constitution: Sacrificing Civil Liberties in the Name of National Security*. New York: The New Press.

Collins, Patricia Hill. 2005. *Black Sexual Politics: African Americans, Gender, and the New Racism*. New York: Routledge.

Coltrane, Scott. 1996. *Family Man: Fatherhood, Housework, and Gender Equity*. New York: Oxford University Press.

Comfort, Megan. 2003. "In the Tube at San Quentin: The 'Secondary Prisonization' of Women Visiting Inmates." *Journal of Contemporary Ethnography* 32 (1): 77–107.

Connell, R. W. 1998. "Masculinities and Globalization." *Men and Masculinities* 1 (1): 3–23.

———. 2000. *The Men and the Boys*. Berkeley: University of California Press.

———. 2005. *Masculinities*. 2nd ed. Berkeley: University of California Press.

Connell, R. W., and James W. Messerschmidt. 2005. "Hegemonic Masculinity: Rethinking the Concept." *Gender & Society* 19 (6): 829–859.

Conover, Ted. 2001. *Newjack: Guarding Sing Sing*. New York: Vintage Books.

Cooper, Marianne. 2000. "Being the 'Go-To Guy': Fatherhood, Masculinity, and the Organization of Work in Silicon Valley." *Qualitative Sociology* 23 (4): 379–405.

Cowell, Margaret. 2015. *Dealing with Deindustrialization: Adaptive Reliance in American Midwestern Cities*. London: Routledge.

Cox, Alexandra. 2015. "Responsible Submission: The Radicalized Consequences of Neoliberal Juvenile Justice Practices." *Social Justice* 41 (4): 23–39.

Curran, Laura, and Laura Abrams. 2000. "Making Men into Dads: Fatherhood, the State, and Welfare." *Gender & Society* 14 (5): 662–678.

Curtis, Anna. 2014. "'You Have to Cut It off at the Knee': Dangerous Masculinity and Security inside a Men's Prison." *Men and Masculinities* 17 (2): 120–146.

Day, Randall D., Alan C. Acock, Stephen J. Bahr, and Joyce A. Arditti. 2005. "Incarcerated Fathers Returning Home to Children and Families: Introduction to the Special Issue and a Primer on Doing Research with Men in Prison." *Fathering: A Journal of Theory, Research, and Practice about Men as Fathers* 3 (3): 183–200.

Deitz, Richard, and James Orr. 2006. "A Leaner, More Skilled US Manufacturing Workforce." *Current Issues in Economics and Finance* 12 (2): 1–7.

Deutsch, Francine. 2007. "Undoing Gender." *Gender & Society* 21 (1): 106–127.

DeVoe, Jill, Katharin Peter, Margaret Noonan, Thomas Snyder, and Katrina Baum. 2005. *Indicators of School Crime and Safety 2005.* Washington, D.C.: U.S. Departments of Education and Justice.

DiIorio, Collene, Maureen Kelley, and Marilyn Hockenberry-Eaton. 1999. "Communication about Sexual Issues: Mothers, Fathers, and Friends." *Journal of Adolescent Health* 24:181–189.

Dilulio, John. 1995. "The Coming of the Superpredators." *Weekly Standard*, November 27, 1995, section 1.

Dowd, Nancy E. 2000. *Redefining Fatherhood.* New York: New York University Press.

Dyer, W. M. Justin. 2005. "Prison, Fathers, and Identity: A Theory of How Incarceration Affects Men's Paternal Identity." *Fathering: A Journal of Theory, Research, and Practice about Men as Fathers* 3 (3): 201–219.

Dyer, Justin, Joseph Pleck, and Brent McBride. 2012. "Imprisoned Fathers and Their Family Relationships: A 40 Year Review from a Multi-theory View." *Journal of Family Theory & Review* 4:20–47.

Edin, Kathryn, and Maria Kefalas. 2005. *Promises I Can Keep: Why Poor Women Put Motherhood before Marriage.* Berkeley: University of California Press.

Edin, Kathryn, Timothy J. Nelson, and Rechelle Paranal. 2004. "Returning to Strangers: Newly Paroled Young Fathers and Their Children." In *Imprisoning America: The Social Effects of Mass Incarceration*, edited by Mary E. Pattillo, David F. Weiman, and Bruce Western, 45–75. New York: Russell Sage Foundation.

Elliott, Sinikka. 2010. "'If I Could Really Say That and Get Away with It!' Accountability and Ambivalence in American Parents' Sexuality Lessons in the Age of Abstinence." *Sex Education: Sexuality, Society and Learning* 10 (3): 239–250.

Emerson, Robert, Rachel Fretz, and Linda Shaw. 1995. *Writing Ethnographic Field Notes.* Chicago: University of Chicago Press.

Erevelles, Nirmala. 2000. "Educating Unruly Bodies: Critical Pedagogy, Disability Studies, and the Politics of Schooling." *Educational Theory* 50 (1): 25–47.

Ewick, Patricia, and Susan Silbey. 1998. *The Common Place of Law: Stories from Everyday Life.* Chicago: University of Chicago Press.

Ferguson, Ann. 2000. *Bad Boys: Public Schools in the Making of Black Masculinity.* Ann Arbor: University of Michigan Press.

Fisher, Christy, Nicholas Bakken, and Whitney Gunter. 2013. "Fatherhood, Community Reintegration, and Successful Outcomes." *Journal of Offender Rehabilitation* 52:451–469.

Flavin, Jeanne. 2001. "Of Punishment and Parenthood: Family-Based Social Control and the Sentencing of Black Drug Offenders." *Gender & Society* 15 (4): 611–633.

Florence v. Board of Chosen Freeholders of County of Burlington et al. 2012. 566 U.S. Case Law. Docket Number 10-945. Supreme Court of the United States. April 2, 2012.

Foucault, Michel. 1973. *The Birth of the Clinic: An Archaeology of Medical Perception.* New York: Vintage Books.

———. 1978. "About the Concept of the 'Dangerous Individual' in 19th-Century Legal Psychiatry." *International Journal of Law and Psychiatry* 1 (1): 1–18.

Fraser, Nancy. 1989. *Unruly Practices: Power, Discourse, and Gender in Contemporary Social Theory.* Minneapolis: University of Minnesota Press.

Frieden, Terry. 2012. "Holder: Not 'Assassination' to Target Americans in Terror Hunt." *CNN*, March 5, 2012. Accessed March 16, 2019. http://security.blogs.cnn.com/2012/03/05/holder-targeting-american-terrorists-not-assasination/.

Garfield, Gail. 2010. *Through Our Eyes: African American Men's Experiences of Race, Gender, and Violence*. New Brunswick, N.J.: Rutgers University Press.

Garland, David. 2001. *The Culture of Control: Crime and Social Order in Contemporary Society*. Chicago: University of Chicago Press.

Gertz, Clifford. 1973. *The Interpretation of Culture*. New York: Basic Books.

Giroux, Henry. 2003. "Racial Injustice and Disposable Youth in the Age of Zero Tolerance." *International Journal of Qualitative Studies in Education* 16 (4): 553–565.

Glaze, Lauren. 2010. *Correctional Populations in the United States, 2009*. Bureau of Justice Statistics Bulletin. U.S. Department of Justice. Office of Justice Programs. Bureau of Justice Statistics.

Glaze, Lauren, and Laura Maruschak. 2009. *Parents in Prison and Their Minor Children*. Bureau of Justice Statistics Special Report. U.S. Department of Justice. Office of Justice Programs. Bureau of Justice Statistics.

Goffman, Erving. 1959. *The Presentation of Self in Everyday Life*. Garden City, N.Y.: Doubleday.

———. 1961. *Asylums: Essays on the Social Institution of Mental Inmates and Other Patients*. New York: Anchor Books.

Griffin, Marie, Armstrong, Gaylene, and John Hepburn. 2005. "Correctional Officers' Perceptions of Equitable Treatment in the Masculinized Prison Environment." *Criminal Justice Review* 30 (2): 189–206.

Guerino, Paul, Paige Harrison, and William Sabol. 2012. *Prisoners in 2010*. Bureau of Justice Statistics Bulletin. U.S. Department of Justice. Office of Justice Programs. Bureau of Justice Statistics.

Gustafson, Kaaryn. 2009. "Criminal Law: The Criminalization of Poverty." *Journal of Criminal Law and Criminology* 99 (3): 643–716.

Gutmann, Matthew C. 1996. *The Meanings of Macho: Being a Man in México City*. Men and Masculinity. Berkeley: University of California Press.

Haberman, Clyde. 2014. "When Youth Violence Spurred 'Superpredator' Fear." *New York Times*. Accessed March 16, 2019. https://www.nytimes.com/2014/04/07/us/politics/killing-on-bus-recalls-superpredator-threat-of-90s.html.

Hairston, Creasie Finney. 1995. "Fathers in Prison." In *Children of Incarcerated Parents*, edited by D. Johnston and K. Gables, 31–40. New York: Lexington Books.

———. 2001a. "Fathers in Prison: Responsible Fatherhood and Responsible Public Policies." *Marriage & Family Review* 32 (3–4): 111–135.

———. 2001b. "The Forgotten Parent: Understanding the Forces That Influence Incarcerated Fathers' Relationships with Their Children." In *Children with Parents in Prison*, edited by Cynthia Seymour and Creasie Finney Hairston, 149–171. New Brunswick, N.J.: Transaction.

———. 2003. "Prisoners and Their Families: Parenting Issues during Incarceration." In *Prisoners Once Removed: The Impact of Incarceration on Children, Families, and Communities*, edited by Jeremy Travis and Michelle Waul, 259–282. Washington, D.C.: Urban Institute Press.

Haney, Craig. 2008. "A Culture of Harm: Taming the Dynamics of Cruelty in Supermax Prisons." *Criminal Justice and Behavior* 35 (8): 956–985.

Haney, Craig, Curtis Banks, and Phillip Zimbardo. 1973. "Interpersonal Dynamics in a Simulated Prison." *International Journal of Criminology and Penology* 1 (1): 69–97.

Haney, Lynne A. 2010. *Offending Women: Power, Punishment, and the Regulation of Desire*. Berkeley: University of California Press.

Haney, Lynne, and Miranda March. 2003. "Married Fathers and Caring Daddies: Welfare Reform and the Discursive Politics of Paternity." *Social Problems* 50 (4): 461–481.

Hannah-Moffat, Kelly. 2000. "Prisons That Empower: Neo-liberal Governance in Canadian Women's Prisons." *British Journal of Criminology* 40:510–531.

Harlow, Caroline. 2003. *Education and Correctional Populations.* Bureau of Justice Statistics Special Report. U.S. Department of Justice. Office of Justice Programs. Bureau of Justice Statistics.

Harrison, Bennett. 1997. *Lean and Mean: Why Large Corporations Will Continue to Dominate the Global Economy.* New York: Guilford Press.

Harrison, Paige, and Allen Beck. 2006. *Prisoners in 2005.* Bureau of Justice Statistics Bulletin. U.S. Department of Justice. Office of Justice Programs. Bureau of Justice Statistics.

Harvey, David. 2005. *A Brief History of Neoliberalism.* Oxford: Oxford University Press.

Harvey Wingfield, Adia M. 2007. "The Modern Mammy and the Angry Black Man: African American Professionals' Experiences with Gendered Racism in the Workplace." *Race, Gender & Class* 14 (2): 196–212.

———. 2008. "Bringing Minority Men Back In: Comment on Andersen." *Gender & Society* 22 (1): 88–92.

Hasbrook, Cynthia, and Othello Harris. 1999. "Wrestling with Gender: Physicality and Masculinities among Inner-City First and Second Graders." *Men and Masculinities* 1 (3): 302–318.

Hays, Sharon. 1996. *The Cultural Contradictions of Motherhood.* New Haven, Conn.: Yale University Press.

Hemmens, C., and J. W. Marquart. 2000. "Friend or Foe? Race, Age, and Inmate Perceptions of Inmate-Staff Relations." *Journal of Criminal Justice* 28:297–312.

Hickman, Timothy. 2000. "Drugs and Race in American Culture: Orientalism in the Turn-of-the-Century Discourse of Narcotic Addiction." *American Studies* 41 (1): 71–91.

Hill, Shirley A. 2002. "Teaching and Doing Gender in African American Families." *Sex Roles* 47 (11/12): 493–506.

Hirschfield, Paul. 2008. "Preparing for Prison? The Criminalization of School Discipline in the USA." *Theoretical Criminology* 12 (1): 79–101.

Hobson, Barbara. 2002. *Making Men into Fathers: Men, Masculinities, and the Social Politics of Fatherhood.* Cambridge: Cambridge University Press.

Hofferth, Sandra. 2003. "Race/Ethnic Differences in Father Involvement in Two-Parent Families: Culture, Context, or Economy?" *Journal of Family Issues* 24 (2): 185–216.

Hoffman, Heath, Amy Byrd, and Alex Kightlinger. 2010. "Prison Programs and Services for Incarcerated Parents and Their Underage Children: Results from a National Survey of Correctional Facilities." *Prison Journal* 90 (4): 397–416.

hooks, bell. 2004. *We Real Cool: Black Men and Masculinity.* New York: Routledge.

Howell, James. 2009. *Preventing and Reducing Juvenile Delinquency: A Comprehensive Framework.* 2nd ed. Thousand Oaks, Calif.: Sage.

Hughes, Caitlin Elizabeth, and Alex Stevens. 2010. "What Can We Learn from the Portuguese Decriminalization of Illicit Drugs?" *British Journal of Criminology* 50:999–1022.

Human Rights Watch. 2001. *No Escape: Male Rape in U.S. Prisons.* Accessed March 16, 2019. https://www.hrw.org/report/2001/04/01/no-escape-male-rape-us-prisons#.

Hurst, E. J., II. 2014. "Federal Sentencing and Prison Reform Now Bipartisan Issues." *The Hill*, August 13, 2014. Accessed March 16, 2019. https://thehill.com/blogs/pundits-blog/crime/214998-federal-sentencing-and-prison-reform-now-bipartisan-issues.

Ilcan, Suzan. 2009. "Privatizing Responsibility: Public Sector Reform under Neoliberal Government." *Canadian Review of Sociology* 46 (3): 207–234.

Inciardi, James, Hilary Surratt, and Steven Kurtz. 2008. "African Americans, Crack, and the Federal Sentencing Guidelines." In *The American Drug Scene*, edited by James Inciardi and Karen McElrath, 5th ed., 214–224. Oxford: Oxford University Press.

Jacobs, J. B. 1979. "Race Relations and the Prison Subculture." In *Crime and Justice: An Annual Review of Research*, vol. 1, edited by N. Morris and M. Tonry, 1–28. Chicago: University of Chicago Press.

Jeffries, John, Suzanne Menghraj, and Creasie Finney Hairston. 2001. *Serving Incarcerated and Ex-offender Fathers and Their Families: A Review of the Field*. New York: Vera Institute of Justice.

Jenness, Valerie, and Sarah Fenstermaker. 2014. "Agnes Goes to Prison: Gender Authenticity, Transgender Inmates in Prisons for Men, and the Pursuit of 'the Real Deal.'" *Gender & Society* 28 (1): 5–31.

Johnson, Brooke. 2010. "A Few Good Boys: Masculinity at a Military-Style Charter School." *Men and Masculinities* 12 (5): 575–596.

Kane, Emily. 2012. *The Gender Trap: Parents and the Pitfalls of Raising Boys and Girls*. New York: New York University Press.

Kann, Mark E. 2005. *Punishment, Prisons, and Patriarchy: Liberty and Power in the Early American Republic*. New York: New York University Press.

Kaufman, Gayle. 2013. *Superdads: How Fathers Balance Work and Family in the 21st Century*. New York: New York University Press.

Kimmel, Michael S. 2008. *Guyland: The Perilous World Where Boys Become Men*. New York: Harper.

Kimmel, Michael S., and Matthew Mahler. 2003. "Adolescent Masculinity, Homophobia, and Violence: Random School Shootings, 1982–2001." *American Behavioral Scientist* 46 (10): 1439–1458.

Klein, Jessie. 2006. "Cultural Capital and High School Bullies." *Men and Masculinities* 9 (1): 53–75.

Krafchik, Jennifer, Toni Zimmerman, Shelley Haddock, and James Banning. 2005. "Best-Selling Books Advising Parents about Gender: A Feminist Analysis." *Family Relations* 54 (1): 84–100.

Kreager, Derek A. 2007. "Unnecessary Roughness? School Sports, Peer Networks, and Male Adolescent Violence." *American Sociological Review* 72 (5): 705–724.

Lanier, Charles. 2003. "Who's Doing the Time Here, Me or My Children? Addressing the Issues Implicated by Mounting Numbers of Fathers in Prison." In *Convict Criminology*, edited by J. Ross and S. Richards, 170–190. Belmont, Calif.: Wadsworth.

La Vigne, Nancy G., Rebecca L. Naser, Lisa E. Brooks, and Jennifer L. Castro. 2005. "Examining the Effect of Incarceration and In-Prison Family Contact on Prisoners' Family Relationships." *Journal of Contemporary Criminal Justice* 21 (4): 314–335.

La Vigne, Nancy, Sara Debus-Sherrill, Diana Brazzell, and P. Mitchell Downey. 2011. *Preventing Violence and Sexual Assault in Jail: A Situational Crime Prevention Approach*. Urban Institute, Justice Policy Center. Accessed March 16, 2019. https://www.urban.org/research/publication/preventing-violence-and-sexual-assault-jail-situational-crime-prevention-approach.

Levan, Kristine, Katherine Polzer, and Steven Downing. 2011. "Media and Prison Sexual Assault: How We Got to the 'Don't Drop the Soap' Culture." *International Journal of Criminology and Sociological Theory* 4 (2): 674–682.

Lyons, Peter, and Barbara Rittner. 1998. "The Construction of the Crack Babies Phenomenon as a Social Problem." *American Journal of Orthopsychiatry* 68 (2): 313–320.

Macleod, Jay. 1987. *Ain't No Makin' It: Leveled Aspirations in a Low-Income Neighborhood*. London: Routledge.

Maher, Lisa, and Kathleen Daly. 1996. "Women in the Street-Level Drug Economy: Continuity or Change?" *Criminology* 34 (4): 465–491.

Man, Christopher D., and John P. Cronan. 2001. "Forecasting Sexual Abuse in Prison: The Prison Subculture of Masculinity as a Backdrop for 'Deliberate Indifference.'" *Journal of Criminal Law and Criminology* 92 (1/2): 127–186.

Manning, Wendy D., and Pamela J. Smock. 1995. "Why Marry? Race and the Transition to Marriage among Cohabitors." *Demography* 32 (4): 509–520.

Markus, Hazel, and Paula Moya, eds. 2010. *Doing Race: 21 Essays for the 21st Century*. New York: W. W. Norton.

Mauer, Marc. 2001. "The Causes and Consequences of Prison Growth in the United States." *Punishment & Society* 3 (1): 9–20.

McCaughey, Martha. 2008. *The Caveman Mystique: Pop-Darwinism and the Debates over Sex, Violence, and Science*. New York: Routledge.

McCorkel, Jill. 2004. "Criminally Dependent? Gender, Punishment, and the Rhetoric of Welfare Reform." *Social Politics: International Studies in Gender, State & Society* 11 (3): 386–410.

———. 2013. *Breaking Women: Gender, Race, and the New Politics of Imprisonment*. New York: New York University Press.

McCorkel, Jill A., and Kristen Myers. 2003. "What Difference Does Difference Make? Position and Privilege in the Field." *Qualitative Sociology* 26 (2): 199–231.

Mears, Daniel, Carter Hay, Marc Gertz, and Christina Mancini. 2007. "Public Opinion and the Foundation of the Juvenile Court." *Criminology* 45 (1): 223–257.

Messner, Michael A. 2002. *Taking the Field: Women, Men, and Sports*. Minneapolis: University of Minnesota Press.

Miller, Jerome. 1996. *Search and Destroy: African-American Males in the Criminal Justice System*. Cambridge: Cambridge University Press.

Miller, Teresa. 2006. "Incarcerated Masculinities." In *Progressive Black Masculinities*, edited by Athena Mutua, 155–174. New York: Routledge.

Minton, Todd. 2011. *Jail Inmates at Midyear 2010—Statistical Tables*. Bureau of Justice Statistics Statistical Tables. U.S. Department of Justice. Office of Justice Programs. Bureau of Justice Statistics.

Mirande, Alfredo. 2004. "Macho: Contemporary Conceptions." In *Men's Lives*, edited by Michael Kimmel and Michael Messner. 6th ed. Boston: Allyn & Bacon.

Mohamed, A. Rafik, and Erik Fritsvold. 2010. *Dorm Room Drug Dealers: Drugs and Privileges of Race and Class*. Boulder, Colo.: Lynne Rienner.

Moore, Solomon. 2009. "Plan Would Limit Prison Chapel Books." *New York Times*, March 17, 2009. Accessed March 16, 2019. https://www.nytimes.com/2009/03/18/us/18prison.html.

Morín, Jose Luis. 2009. "Latino/as and U.S. Prisons: Trends and Challenges." In *Behind Bars: Latino/as and Prison in the United States*, edited by Suzanne Oboler, 17–38. New York: Palgrave Macmillan.

Morris, Edward. 2005. "'Tuck in That Shirt': Race, Class, Gender, and Discipline in an Urban School." *Sociological Perspectives* 48 (1): 25–48.

Mosher, Clayton, and Scott Akins. 2007. *Drugs and Drug Policy: The Control of Conscious Alternation*. Thousand Oaks, Calif.: Sage.

Mosher, Donald. 1998. "Hypermasculinity Inventory." In *Handbook of Sexuality-Related Measures*, edited by Clive Davis, William Yarber, Robert Bauserman, George Schreer, and Sandra Davis, 472–474. Thousand Oaks, Calif.: Sage.

Musto, David. 1999. *The American Disease: Origins of Narcotic Control*. Oxford: Oxford University Press.

Nadelmann, Ethan. 2008. "Commonsense Drug Policy." In *The American Drug Scene*, edited by James Inciardi and Karen McElrath, 5th ed., 464–472. Oxford: Oxford University Press.

National Gang Threat Assessment. 2005. Bureau of Justice Assistance. National Alliance of Gang Investigations Associations. Federal Bureau of Investigations. National Drug Intelligence Center. Bureau of Alcohol, Tobacco, Firearms, and Explosives.

National Law Center on Homelessness and Poverty and the National Coalition for the Homeless. 2009. "Homes Not Handcuffs: The Criminalization of Homelessness in U.S. Cities." Accessed March 16, 2019. https://timefolds.com/nch/wp-content/uploads/2013/11/CrimzReport_2009.pdf.

Nurse, Anne. 2001. "The Structure of the Juvenile Prison: Constructing the Inmate Father." *Youth & Society* 32:360–394.

———. 2002. *Fatherhood Arrested*. Nashville: Vanderbilt University Press.

———. 2010. *Locked Up, Locked Out: Young Men in the Juvenile Justice System*. Nashville: Vanderbilt University Press.

Oboler, Suzanne. 2009. *Behind Bars: Latino/as and Prison in the United States*. New York: Palgrave Macmillan.

Out of the Shadows: Getting Ahead of Prison Radicalization. 2006. Special report. The George Washington University Homeland Security Policy Institute and the University of Virginia Critical Incident Analysis Group. Accessed March 16, 2019. https://cchs.gwu.edu/sites/g/files/zaxdzs2371/f/downloads/HSPI_Report_8.pdf.

Paechter, Carrie. 2007. *Being Boys, Being Girls: Learning Masculinities and Femininities*. Maidenhead, Berkshire: Open University Press.

Pager, Devah. 2003. "The Mark of a Criminal Record." *American Journal of Sociology* 108 (5): 937–975.

———. 2007. *Marked: Race, Crime, and Finding Work in an Era of Mass Incarceration*. Chicago: University of Chicago Press.

Pascoe, C. J. 2007. *Dude, You're a Fag: Masculinity and Sexuality in High School*. Berkeley: University of California Press.

Patillo-McCoy, Mary. 2000. *Black Picket Fences: Privilege and Peril among the Black Middle Class*. Chicago: University of Chicago Press.

Pedulla, David. 2012. "To Be Young and Unemployed." *New Labor Forum* 21 (3): 26–36.

Pettit, Becky, and Bruce Western. 2010. "Incarceration and Social Inequality." *Dædalus* 139 (3): 8–19.

Phillips, Jenny. 2001. "Cultural Construction of Manhood in Prison." *Psychology of Men & Masculinity* 2 (1): 13–23.

Polletta, Francesca, P. C. Bobby Chen, Beth Gharrity Gardner, and Alice Motes. 2011. "The Sociology of Storytelling." *Annual Review of Sociology* 37:109–130.

Public Agenda Media. 2004. *Teaching Interrupted: Do Discipline Policies in Today's Public Schools Foster the Common Good?* Public Agenda, May 2004. Accessed on February 4, 2019. https://www.publicagenda.org/media/teaching-interrupted.

Rader, Nicole. 2005. "Surrendering Solidarity: Considering the Relationships among Female Correctional Officers." *Women & Criminal Justice* 16:27–42.

Raley, Sara, and Suzanne Bianchi. 2006. "Sons, Daughters, and Family Processes: Does Gender of Children Matter?" *Annual Review of Sociology* 32:401–421.

Ranson, Gillian. 2001. "Men at Work: Change—or No Change?—in the Era of the 'New Father.'" *Men and Masculinities* 4 (1): 3–26.

Raphael, Steven. 2011. "Incarceration and Prison Reentry in the United States." *Annals of the American Academy of Political and Social Science* 625:192–215.

Rios, Victor M. 2011. *Punished: Policing the Lives of Black and Latino Boys*. New York: New York University Press.

Roberts, Dorothy. 1997. *Killing the Black Body: Race, Reproduction, and the Meaning of Liberty*. New York: Vintage Books.

Roetigger, Michael, and Raymond Swisher. 2013. "Incarcerated Fathers." In *Father Involvement in Children's Lives: A Global Analysis*, edited by Jyotsna Pattnaik, 107–122. New York: Springer.

Rosen, Leora, Kathryn Knudson, and Peggy Fancher. 2003. "Cohesion and the Culture of Hypermasculinity in U.S. Army Units." *Armed Forces & Society* 29 (3): 325–351.

Rosenberg, Rae, and Natalie Oswin. 2015. "Trans Embodiment in Carceral Space: Hypermasculinity and the US Prison Industrial Complex." *Gender, Place and Culture* 22 (9): 1269–1286. First published October 22, 2014, https://doi.org/10.1080/0966369X.2014.969685.

Rowe, Kathleen. 1995. *The Unruly Woman: Gender and Genres of Laughter*. Austin: University of Texas Press.

———. 2010. *Unruly Girls, Unrepentant Mothers: Redefining Feminism On Screen*. Austin: University of Texas Press.

Roy, Kevin. 1999. "Low-Income Fathers in an African-American Community and the Requirements of Welfare Reform." *Journal of Family Issues* 20 (4): 432–457.

———. 2005. "Nobody Can Be a Father in Here: Identity Construction and Institutional Constraints on Incarcerated Fatherhood." In *Situated Fathering: A Focus on Physical and Social Spaces*, edited by William Marsiglio, Kevin Roy and Greer Litton Fox, 163–186. Boulder, Colo.: Rowman & Littlefield.

Roy, Kevin M., and Omari L. Dyson. 2005. "Gatekeeping in Context: Babymama Drama and the Involvement of Incarcerated Fathers." *Fathering: A Journal of Theory, Research, and Practice about Men as Fathers* 3 (3): 289–310.

———. 2010. "Making Daddies into Fathers: Community-Based Fatherhood Programs and the Construction of Masculinities for Low-Income African-American Men." *American Journal of Community Psychology* 45:139–154.

Sabo, Don, Terry Kupers, and Willie London. 2001a. "Gender and the Politics of Punishment." In *Prison Masculinities*, edited by Don Sabo, Terry Kupers, and Willie London, 3–18. Philadelphia: Temple University Press.

———. 2001b. *Prison Masculinities*. Philadelphia: Temple University Press.

Sabol, William J., and Heather Couture. 2008. *Prison Inmates at Midyear 2007*. Bureau of Justice Statistics Bulletin. U.S. Department of Justice. Office of Justice Programs. Bureau of Justice Statistics.

Sanday, Peggy Reeves. 2007. *Fraternity Gang Rape: Sex, Brotherhood, and Privilege on Campus*. New York: New York University Press.

Saperstein, Aliya, and Andrew Penner. 2010. "The Race of a Criminal Record: How Incarceration Colors Racial Perceptions." *Social Problems* 57 (1): 92–113.

Savicki, Victor, Eric Cooley, and Jennifer Gjesvold. 2003. "Harassment as a Predictor of Job Burnout in Correctional Officers." *Criminal Justice and Behavior* 30 (5): 602–619.

Scharrer, Erica. 2001. "Tough Guys: The Portrayal of Hypermasculinity and Aggression in Televised Police Dramas." *Journal of Broadcasting & Electronic Media* 45 (4): 615–634.

Sexton, Lori, Valerie Jenness, and Jennifer Macy Sumner. 2010. "Where the Margins Meet: A Demographic Assessment of Transgender Inmates in Men's Prisons." *Justice Quarterly* 27 (6): 835–866.

Shade, Kate, Susan Kools, Howard Pinderhughes, and Sandra Weiss. 2012. "Adolescent Fathers in the Justice System: Hoping for a Boy and Making Him a Man." *Qualitative Health Research* 23 (4): 435–449.

Sharp, Elizabeth, and Jean Ispa. 2009. "Inner-City Single Black Mothers' Gender-Related Childrearing Expectations and Goals." *Sex Roles* 60 (9–10): 656–668.

Shaw, Charles, and Cara Lavan. 2011. "After the War on Drugs: Envisioning a Post-prohibition World." *Drugs and Alcohol Today* 12 (1).

Shrock, Douglas, and Michael Schwalbe. 2009. "Men, Masculinity, and Manhood Acts." *Annual Review of Sociology* 35:277–295.

Simon, Jonathan. 2006. *Governing through Crime: How the War on Crime Transformed American Democracy and Created a Culture of Fear*. New York: Oxford University Press.

Simon, Robin, and Leda Nath. 2004. "Gender and Emotion in the United States: Do Men and Women Differ in Self-reports of Feelings and Expressive Behavior?" *American Journal of Sociology* 109 (5): 1137–1176.

Smith, Dorothy. 2005. *Institutional Ethnography: A Sociology for People*. Lanham, Md.: AltaMira Press.

———. 2006. *Institutional Ethnography as Practice*. Lanham, Md.: Rowman & Littlefield.

Snyder, Howard, and Heather Sickmund. 2006. *Juvenile Offenders and Victims: 2006 National Report*. U.S. Department of Justice: Office of Justice Programs and the Office of Juvenile Justice and Delinquency Prevention.

Soss, Joe, Richard Fording, and Sanford Schram. 2011. *Disciplining the Poor: Neoliberal Paternalism and the Persistent Power of Race*. Chicago: University of Chicago Press.

Sourcebook of Criminal Justice Statistics. 2008. "Estimated Number and Percent Distribution of Prisoners under Jurisdiction of State Correctional Authorities." Accessed April 15, 2011. http://www.albany.edu/sourcebook/pdf/t600012008.pdf.

Stack, Carol. 1997. *All Our Kin: Strategies for Survival in a Black Community*. New York: Basic Books.

Stoudt, Brett. 2006. "'You're Either In or You're Out': School Violence, Peer Discipline, and the (Re)Production of Hegemonic Masculinity." *Men and Masculinities* 8 (3): 273–287.

Strader, J. Kelly. 2007–2008. "White Collar Crime and Punishment: Reflections on Michael, Martha, and Milberg Weiss." *George Mason Law Review* 15:45–108.

Sum, Andrew, Ishwar Khatiwada, Joseph McLaughlin, and Sheila Palma. 2011. "No Country for Young Men: Deteriorating Labor Markets for Low-Skilled Men in the United States." *Annals of the American Academy of Political and Social Science* 635:24–55.

Swisher, Raymond, and Maureen Waller. 2008. "Confining Fatherhood: Incarceration and Paternal Involvement of Nonresident White, African American and Latino Fathers." *Journal of Family Issues* 29 (8): 1067–1088.

Temin, Peter. 2016. "The American Dual Economy: Race, Globalization, and the Politics of Exclusion." *International Journal of Political Economy* 45:85–123.

Timbs v. Indiana. 2019. 586 U.S. Case Law. Docket Number 17-1091. Supreme Court of the United States. February 20, 2019.

Toch, Hans. 1998. "Hypermasculinity and Prison Violence." In *Masculinities and Violence*, edited by Lee H. Bowker, 168–178. Thousand Oaks, Calif.: Sage.

Tonry, Michael H. 1995. *Malign Neglect*. New York: Oxford University Press.

———. 2009. "Explanations of American Punishment Policies: A National History." *Punishment & Society* 11 (3): 377–394.

———. 2011. *Punishing Race: A Continuing American Dilemma*. New York: Oxford University Press.

Townsend, Nicholas W. 2002. *The Package Deal: Marriage, Work, and Fatherhood in Men's Lives*. Philadelphia: Temple University Press.

Tracy, Sarah, and Clifton Scott. 2006. "Sexuality, Masculinity, and Taint Management among Firefighters and Correctional Officers: Getting Down and Dirty with 'America's Heroes' and the 'Scum of Law Enforcement.'" *Management Communication Quarterly* 20 (1): 6–38.

Trammell, Rebecca. 2012. *Enforcing the Convict Code: Violence and Prison Culture*. Boulder, Colo.: Lynne Rienner.

Travis, Jeremy. 2005. *But They All Come Back: Facing the Challenges of Prisoner Reentry*. Washington, D.C.: Urban Institute Press.

Travis, Jeremy, and Michelle Waul. 2003. *Prisoners Once Removed: The Impact of Incarceration and Reentry on Children, Families, and Communities*. Washington, D.C.: Urban Institute Press.

Tripp, Brad. 2001. "Incarcerated African American Fathers: Exploring Changes in Family Relationships and the Father Identity." *Journal of African American Men* 6 (1): 13.

Unruh, Deanne, Michael Bullis, and Paul Yovanoff. 2003. "Community Reintegration Outcomes for Formerly Incarcerated Adolescent Fathers and Nonfathers." *Journal of Emotional and Behavioral Disorders* 11 (3): 144–156.

U.S. Congress. 2003. *Prison Rape Elimination Act (PREA) of 2003*. Public Law 108-170. 108th Congress.

———. 2008. *Foreign Intelligence Surveillance Act (FISA) of 1978 Amendments Act of 2008*. HR 6304. 110th Congress.

———. 2011. *National Defense Authorization Act (NDAA) for Fiscal Year 2012*. HR 1540. 112th Congress.

Useem, Bert. 2012. "U.S. Prisons and the Myth of Islamic Terrorism." *Contexts* 11 (2): 34–39.

U.S. Federal Communications Commission. 2013. *In the Matter of Rates for Interstate Inmate Calling Services*. Washington, D.C. Accessed March 16, 2019. https://www.federalregister.gov/documents/2013/11/13/2013-26378/rates-for-interstate-inmate-calling-services.

U.S. Sentencing Commission (U.S.S.C.). 2013. "Table 10: Guilty Pleas and Trials in Each Circuit and District (Fiscal Year 2013)." Sourcebook of Federal Sentencing Statistics. Accessed February 28, 2019. https://www.ussc.gov/sites/default/files/pdf/research-and-publications/annual-reports-and-sourcebooks/2013/Table10.pdf.

Vigoya, Mara Viveros. 2001. "Contemporary Latin American Perspectives on Masculinity." *Men and Masculinities* 3 (3): 237–260.

Visher, Christy, Nicholas Bakken, and Whitney Gunter. 2013. "Fatherhood, Community Reintegration and Successful Outcomes." *Journal of Offender Reintegration* 52 (7): 451–469.

Visher, Christy, and Jeremy Travis. 2003. "Transitions from Prison to Community: Understanding Individual Pathways." *Annual Review of Sociology* 29:89–113.

Vuolo, Mike, and Candace Kruttschnitt. 2008. "Prisoners' Adjustment, Correctional Officers, and Context: The Foreground and Background of Punishment in Late Modernity." *Law & Society Review* 42 (2): 307–336.

Wacquant, Loic. 2000. "The New 'Peculiar Institution': On the Prison as Surrogate Ghetto." *Theoretical Criminology* 4 (3): 377–389.

———. 2001. "Deadly Symbiosis: When Ghetto and Prison Meet and Mesh." *Punishment & Society* 3 (1): 95–133.

———. 2009. *Punishing the Poor: The Neoliberal Government of Social Insecurity*. Durham, N.C.: Duke University Press.

Wall Street Journal. 2015. "Bipartisan Prison Reform: Jail Isn't Meant to Be a Country Club but It Shouldn't Be a Jungle." Opinion. *Wall Street Journal*, July 6, 2015. Accessed March 16, 2019. https://www.wsj.com/articles/SB12104187675579354294504581043790644676376.

Welch, Kelly, and Allison Payne. 2010. "Racial Threat and Punitive School Discipline." *Social Problems* 57 (1): 25–48.

West, Candace, and Sarah Fenstermaker. 1995. "Doing Difference." *Gender & Society* 9 (1): 8–37.

West, Candace, and Don H. Zimmerman. 1987. "Doing Gender." *Gender & Society* 1 (2): 125–151.

West, Heather C., William J. Sabol, and Sarah J. Greenman. 2010. *Prisoners in 2009*. Bureau of Justice Statistics Bulletin. U.S. Department of Justice. Office of Justice Programs. Bureau of Justice Statistics.

Western, Bruce. 2006. *Punishment and Inequality in America*. New York: Russell Sage Foundation.

Wildeman, Christopher. 2009. "Parental Imprisonment, the Prison Boom, and the Concentration of Childhood Disadvantage." *Demography* 46 (2): 265–280.

Williams, Robert. 2009. "Masculinities and Vulnerability." *Men and Masculinities* 11 (4): 441–461.

Williams, Timothy. 2015. "The High Cost of Calling the Imprisoned." *New York Times* (New York edition), March 31, 2015, A12.

Wilson, Ellen, Barbara Dalberth, and Helen Koo. 2010. "'We're the Heroes!': Fathers' Perspectives on Their Role in Protecting Their Preteenage Children from Sexual Risk." *Perspectives on Sexual and Reproductive Health* 42 (2): 117–124.

Wilson, Ellen, and Helen Koo. 2010. "Mothers, Fathers, Sons, and Daughters: Gender Differences in Factors Associated with Parent-Child Communication about Sexual Topics." *Reproductive Health* 7 (31): 1–9.

Woldoff, Rachael, and Michael Cina. 2007. "Regular Work, Underground Jobs, and Hustling: An Examination of Paternal Work and Father Involvement." *Fathering: A Journal of Theory, Research, and Practice about Men as Fathers* 5 (3): 153–173.

Woldoff, Rachael, and Heather Washington. 2008. "Arrested Contact: The Criminal Justice System, Race, and Father Engagement." *Prison Journal* 88 (2): 179–206.

Wolff, Nancy, and Jing Shi. 2009. "Contextualization of Physical and Sexual Assault in Male Prisons: Incidents and Their Aftermath." *Journal of Correctional Health Care* 15 (1): 58–82.

Wolff, Nancy, Jing Shi, and Ronet Bachman. 2008. "Measuring Victimization inside Prisons: Questioning the Questions." *Journal of Interpersonal Violence* 23 (10): 1343–1362.

Woodruff, Betsy. 2014. "Bipartisan Prison Reform: Many Conservatives and Liberals Agree: We're Putting Too Many People in Jail." *National Review*, January 20, 2014. Accessed March 16, 2019. https://www.nationalreview.com/2014/01/bipartisan-prison-reform-betsy-woodruff/.

Zimbardo, Phillip, Christina Maslach, and Craig Haney, eds. 2000. "Reflections on the Stanford Prison Experiment: Genesis, Transformations, Consequences." In *Obedience to Authority: Current Perspectives on the Milgram Paradigm*, edited by Thomas Blass, 193–238. Mahwah, N.J.: Erlbaum.

INDEX

African Caribbean fathers, 45
Alexander, Michelle, 107, 110
American Correctional Association, 109
American workforce, 9–10
anti-immigration sentiments, 110
Arditti, Joyce, 104–105
At Work in the Iron Cage (Britton), 105

basketball games, 92–93
Bhattacharyya, Gargi, 110
black men: criminality connected to, 14; education levels, 15; as hyperhetero-sexual, 72
Block v. Rutherford, 109
body alarms, 17
bogeyman prisoners, 67, 99
boys. *See* sons
breadwinner role, 23–24
Britton, Dana, 78, 100, 105

child protective services (CPS), 51
children: disenfranchised grief, 104–105; impact of incarceration on, 21–22, 104–105; negative outcomes of, 22; parenting programs that include, 22; parents' gendered expectations for, 44; showing affection to, 49; special visits and, 38; teaching to navigate racism, 45. *See also* daughters; sons
children of color, 21
cigarettes/cigarette smoking, 84
civil liberties, elimination or reduction of, 108, 110

clothing monitoring, 69–72
communication: embedded in program materials, 101; fathers writing their children, 28; focus on, 26–31; honesty in, 27; maintaining phone contact, 28–29; phone calls, 26
Comprehensive Crime Control Act of 1984, 13
Connell, Raewyn, 63
Conover, Ted, 75–76
constitutional rights of citizens, 108
contact visits. *See* noncontact visits; normal visits
corrections officers (COs): avoiding violence, 96; controlling movement of prisoners, 77–78; deviant masculinity, effects of, 100; divisions between prisoners and, 75–79; female, 18, 105; goodwill of, 42–43; insulting, 89–91; maintaining control over prisoners, 85–86; managing visits, 72–73; power by technology and blackmail, 85–86; prefer male prisons, 18; on prisoners as sexual predators, 69; prisoners dismissing power of, 89–91; regulating visitors' clothing, 68–70; rule enforcement of, 62; safety desires of, 100; on security/safety, 4; at special visits, 74–75; training and behavior, 105; treating masculinity as static identity, 66; violence toward, 90–91; visitors interacting with, 75; workplace culture shaping, 18

About the Author

Anna Curtis is an assistant professor at the State University of New York at Cortland. Her current research examines masculinity, fatherhood, and security practices within prison. Her research interests include mass incarceration, law and society, and gender and family, as well as an occasional flirtation with methodology.

Mariana Valverde, *Law and Order: Images, Meanings, Myths*

Michael Welch, *Crimes of Power and States of Impunity: The U.S. Response to Terror*

Michael Welch, *Scapegoats of September 11th: Hate Crimes and State Crimes in the War on Terror*

Saundra D. Westervelt and Kimberly J. Cook, *Life after Death Row: Exonerees' Search for Community and Identity*